Claire Ellis is a writer, editor and animal lover. From an early age, she found comfort and joy in creative writing, letting her imagination run wild through stories and poetry. She pursued a career in financial journalism, and as the pressures and demands of life and work took their toll, the creative writing hit a wall. Falling into and emerging from a dark place enabled Claire to reconnect with her inner purpose, and discover how her life could be truly fulfilling by doing what she loves. She reconnected with poetry and writing. This switched on the light that went out inside.

For my mum who is the humblest person I will ever know, my beautiful sisters Bethan and Erica, Simon who I will never forget and my soulmate, John. I love you with all of my heart.

Claire S. Ellis

—————————————

WORDS FOR THE RESTLESS

AUSTIN MACAULEY PUBLISHERS™

LONDON • CAMBRIDGE • NEW YORK • SHARJAH

A CIP catalogue record for this title is available from the British Library.

ISBN 9781528986922 (Paperback)
ISBN 9781528986939 (ePub e-book)

www.austinmacauley.com

First Published (2021)
Austin Macauley Publishers Ltd
25 Canada Square
Canary Wharf
London
E14 5LQ

ON ANXIETY (VOLUME I)

Words to Move You

Words for the Restless is a collection of words for living. Born from a dream to reconnect to the healing power of words and passion to help others, the words are for every single beautiful one of you. Dive in and share – for we all need some love today.

SOME WORDS ON ANXIETY

Anxiety is all too often a silent battle and epidemic. It's a journey...with an end. If you're reading this as an anxiety sufferer, you will get there. The feelings can be a melting pot of despair, panic, paranoia, exhaustion, confusion, anger, failure and loneliness. But the best thing you will ever do is ask for help. Many, many people have the same thoughts and feelings, so you are definitely not alone.

This volume of words stems from my own journey with anxiety, on which I found writing to be a wonderful distraction and source of comfort. One of the core antidotes is to always do something you love and writing this collection gave me that outlet. Having the courage to share these words with the outside world has been a challenge, but knowing they can touch and move others, fills me with purpose and joy. This is for you and me, but please spread far and wide. Remember, you really are amazing. Much love.

If only we held onto hope
as hard as we cling on to
the battles in our mind.

Someone somewhere
is thanking you
for being you.

This will not be forever
or a road to a place
out of the darkness
that I cannot see.
For anxiety is
everything that isn't me.

This will pass
and you will shine
even brighter.

It's not real.
It's not true.
And when you feel
they steal your light
drain your worth.
Remember
they will never be you.

When all the rooms are dark
the doors are closed.
Remember
I will believe in you
more than you will ever know.

Allow yourself
to fall through the layers of fear.
For we all know
what lies beneath.

You're much more than
a photograph
a to-do list
a to-be list.
You are much more
than all of this.

She said to herself
Love will change you.
It won't make you sick.

Step inside my world
if only just to see
the shattered remnants
of fears, hopes, dreams
eating away the heart and soul of me.
Step inside for a while
for there's a vast world
underneath my skin.
And I will give you permission
to touch, to tell me
that real beauty still lies within.

Losing yourself is
finding the drops of Jupiter
sparkling deep inside.
It's finding peace
out of it all.
Falling to feel truly alive.

Healing is dropping the guard
silencing the voices
watching the tears flow free.
It's breaking down walls
letting go of all the things
I choose to see.
Everything that isn't me.

You just can't see it
All that you have
all that you give.
There you go.

"Be mine!"
The love letter I wrote to myself.
A note to not fall into
the images, dreams, desires
of anyone else.

Remember, the number of times
you go against all odds
is nothing short of phenomenal.

Trust in your stunning bravery.

For all of the attacks
out of nowhere
I will be your light.
For all of the loneliness
the awkward silences
the trapped tears
I will be your light.
For all of the insecurities
burning like a furnace inside
the unfounded fears
the floods of tears
I will be your light.
For every step you take
through this journey of hell
trust that you are more
than the nothing you feel
Trust that I am your light.

When you sit down beside me
the grip of the angst loosens
the volume of the voice lowers
and for once
I can touch the gold dust
deep inside of me.

Happiness lives deep inside.
Have the courage
to touch its deep roots.

Have faith that many
are walking these footsteps
with you on the undulating path to home.
You are never ever alone.

You don't have to say anything.
or do anything
to be someone, to go somewhere.
Everything you need is inside of you
right there.

No matter how small
we can always take something
from all of those fragments
that are just too sharp to touch.

I will take you back
to this beautiful place
lost inside of you.
I will take you there.

The light you lost.
It's right here.
Inside of you.

Let me love you
and I will love you.
Until you learn
to love yourself.

It's amazing how we can lose ourselves
but not love ourselves.

The only flicker of light
left on inside of me
is shining on the part of you
that's lost in a dark place.

You didn't just watch my journey.
You walked right beside me
You became part of it.

They are not the setbacks that you conquer.
They are not the differences that you make.
They are not your energy.
They are not you.

There is life after dark.

You are worth more
than the failings
only you choose to believe.

When you need to turn down the volume
or slow down the dance
shaking up your insides.
Stop the last beat of the mix
by closing your eyes.

When they try to drown you out with their voice
shatter you with their imagery.
Remember we're all scared of the same things
scared of ending up alone
scared our best isn't good enough
scared of getting old.

The passing sunset splashes autumn's
promise to let go all over you.

What's that you hear?
It's the sound of the sea.
I travelled to see you
as you rise and spray
showering the deepest blue diamonds
you were ready to hit me
I was fearful.
Until I stopped moving
I breathed with you
breathed you in.
With every crash
it was then
you caressed me
for when you trust the sea
it trusts and loves you.
For the sea
can break you
or embrace you.
But that day
the sea brought stillness.
Showing me how to
just love me.

I returned to this special place
where the deepest blue sea
was as far as my eyes could see.
When I heard the gentle voice of the waves
I felt the promise I made
the last time to the sea.
A promise to just love me.

When you feel like you want to give up or feel utterly
worthless
think of what you're made of.
A billion cells renewing with the turn of each day
a unique voice that doesn't have to carry noise
the most beautiful dazzling glow
which in time you'll touch, you'll know.
Amazingly unique deep eyes
through which you live a story that only you know.
For you were put on this earth to thrive, to grow
and someone, somewhere is not giving up on you
so take the courage to love your insides
just let it go.

Like the full moon
sometimes I radiate and project
all of my light
for the world to see.
Other times
I hide behind
the darkest cloud
searching for solitude
gently casting my light
over those who love me.

There is nothing greater
than feeling safe.

The day is done.
Forgive yourself.

The best love songs
are lost inside of us.
Silent notes that come alive
when we choose to live
not just survive.

Above all else
set yourself free.
Free from following
from thoughts
from fear.

This stone is beautiful and like its rough edges
its fragile cracks exuding soft energy
you should not be afraid.
You should not be afraid of imperfection
and to show just how beautiful
you really are.

I love you for every single failure you feel.

I wish you could see what I see in you.

One day the walls will come tumbling down.

You may give up on you
but I'm not giving up on you.

If you simply don't have the words
accept your vulnerability
celebrate your humility
and connect with the blindingly
beautiful world that is
the one, the only you.
Celebrate you.

You can be in the darkest places
but growing and learning in ways
only others can imagine.

Note to self:
Always enough.
Now, forever, always.

It was so hard to be her friend
to touch her and make her sparkle.

I long to see
you love your insides
as much
as I love you.

Your energy is like water.
All of the drops make hope the only choice.

Hold onto your beautiful self.

You don't need the eyes of the crowd
to prove your worth today.

Your life is a journey
not a masterpiece.

No one can do a better job of
being the beautiful
human that you are.

Nobody knows
how your inner energy
moves you in ways,
only you have the power over.
Just one reason why you're amazing.

Hold on, have faith
do the best that only you can do.
In time, what feels impossible
will come true.

One day you'll make friends with her
dance with her, touch her
feel every breath she takes.
Reinvention and intuition
it's never too late.

Every day I'm getting closer to
touching her
knowing her
feeling her
loving her.
Who is she?
This is me.

Sometimes, the only way
to end our suffering
is to go home.
A place rooted
deep inside of us all.
We just have to stop to go there.
There's so much colour and happiness within.
Grant yourself permission to dive in.

If the ebb and flow of the ocean's crashing waves
carries my anguish and wasted dreams
hope is always my anchor.

The cyclone of fear was unbearable.
But something inside of me was so strong.

And until you believe
I will believe in you
for you.

There was a time
when the world didn't tell you
to be faster, prettier, stronger, better.
A time when you looked up to the sky for hope
listened to the birdsong for solitude
believed in something inside of you so strong.
Only by drowning in all you have lost
can you save yourself from
the failure you feel every day...the true cost.

Mercy was the water
that put out the fire.

I will give you my voice to make
you feel like you belong here.

You always had
and always will have a place here.

Broken is the label.
Sensational is what you will always be.
You always were.

Let those tears roll
and look inside.
For sometimes
there is nowhere more lonely
than the outside.

And out of the darkness
I will come
and find you.

You are the one piece of hope
that really matters to someone today.

You are
just as beautiful
as the one with more.

I took the time
to see underneath your insecurities
as we're all going the same way.

Look at the stripped back canvas
not the painted picture of life.

I need this place
to hide away from life.
To dream
feel my emotions
raw from the inside.
This is a place
where I could die
yet feel truly alive.

There's a million things
just right about you
right now.
Believe more, doubt less.

Like the pink blossom
you fall.
And then
you bloom.

There's a picture
buried like a pixel
on the horizon
of her broken mind.
A picture of someone
who drowns in her own love
accepts herself
is truly alive.
For this picture
to come into her view
she has to shake out
all the fears that are not true.

The joy of life
is not in
trying so hard
to live it
beyond your beautiful self.

You will never know
how much better
you make me feel.

Feed me with your fear
to make me survive.
For I am the fuel
that keeps you alive.
Try to run away from me
every single waking hour.
To no avail
for I have the power.
But when you feel
the numb or sharp edge of my sting
remember, I don't belong here
you can break free
you will win.

With every spin of the earth
every cell, every day
that renews so fast.
You are brave
you are still enough
you are not your past.

Why am I falling
when I should be flying?
Why am I crying
when I should be smiling?
Why am I losing
when I should be winning?
Why am I sinking
when I should be swimming?
But I can kick back
if I'm strong.

For it's not me
it's the images
the way I think of me
that's wrong.

If all the things
you choose to hear are true.
You will never accept the beauty
the gift that is you.

If only you could be proud
of everything you do.
For like a snowflake
you are unique
there is only one you.

Breathe deeply
for how you see yourself
is not the same
as through the eyes
of someone else.

Safe is
waking up from a dream.
Catching, breathing in
the moment of relief
of it not being true.
The fears, fails, falls
are the scars healing in time.
They are not you.

When I feel lost
like I don't belong.
I remember
the journey, the one
that made me so strong.

Fall into the passing sunset
not the harsh false lights
of the wilderness...the mind.
Dream it in
soak it up.
Don't let go...
until it gently passes
with all the love
in its ruby trail.

Thank yourself
for pulling through.

You have a lot of strength left.

Don't give up.
For you are loved.

I see the light that you cast out.

Only do what makes you happy.

You have more control than you think.

If you can only say one thing
to yourself today
let it be thank you.

The bitterly harsh winters and the long dark days
never stop a tree from blooming.
Begin again, make peace
and above all
do it for you.
You can bloom.

You're not broken anymore.
You're not guilty anymore.
You're not captive anymore.

You are the stardust
in the days
I wrote off as dead.

Strength isn't beauty.
It's breathing through the fire
raging deep inside.

It's showing up
when your insides are shaking.
It's accepting all the love
thrown your way,
it was real, it was alive.

It's seeing light
in the dark depths.
It's knowing that
with every passing day,
you do have a lot of strength left.

One day
you'll wonder
why you listened,
why you cared.
You'll walk away.

Anxiety was then.
It's not today.

Anxiety.
Thoughts not facts.
Discovery not failure.
The past, not the future.
A story, not a destiny.
Intense, not fatal.
Everything that isn't me.

ACKNOWLEDGEMENTS

Since writing this collection of words, the world has suddenly become a different place. Days in lockdown have reminded me to hug with all my heart, to pause and to appreciate every moment with loved ones. I hope this book helps you to hold onto hope. Writing the words switched on the light that went outside for me, and I will always be truly grateful for the healing power of writing feelings down on the page.

Thank you to Austin Macauley for giving me the opportunity to publish my first book. It is one of the best things that has ever happened to me and a childhood dream. The illustrations depict places that are very close to my heart (mainly south-west Ireland) and are simply beautiful.

My beautiful friends Suzanne, Charlotte, Jo, the two Rachels (you know who you are!), Emma, Jenny Stark, Debs, "weightlifting" Claire, Theresa, Christine, Alex Vaughan and Emma Brookes (we will meet in person soon) – you are all amazing humans who have guided, loved, and inspired me. Thank you to Jenny H for being an endless source of strength and Grace Marshall for being chief encourager.

They say family is everything and this is so true. Thank you to my sisters and Mum who are truly beautiful inside and out and the rest of my large and lovely family. I love you with all of my heart.

John – my love and soul mate, thank you for always being there. I am nothing without you.

CAUGHT BENEATH THE LANDSLIDE

MANCHESTER CITY IN THE 1990s

CAUGHT BENEATH THE LANDSLIDE

MANCHESTER CITY IN THE 1990s

TIM RICH

First published as a hardback by deCoubertin Books Ltd in 2018

First Edition

deCoubertin Books, 46B Jamaica Street, Liverpool. L1 0AF

www.decoubertin.co.uk

ISBN: 978-1-909245-80-8

A CIP catalogue record for this book is available from the British Library.

Cover design by Thomas Regan/Milkyone. Typeset by Leslie Priestley.

To Sally,

who entered a football press box

long before I did.

This is the story of a football club.

Contents

Journey's End

'I CAN'T BELIEVE YOU DON'T KNOW WHO ROBBIE FOWLER AND Steve McManaman are.'

A father is holding court, trying to tell his young family a story. 'They played for Liverpool but they also played for us. For City.

'I met them once. They were in a coffee shop in Manchester. I went over to Robbie and told him, "You tried really hard for us, you scored some great goals." He nodded and by then Steve McManaman had come back with the coffees. He looked at me and I said, "Steve, you were shite."'

There is laughter, although the daughter looks quizzical, probably still wondering who Robbie Fowler and Steve McManaman are. The family get on with their pre-match meal.

There is less than an hour until Manchester City's final home game of the 2017/18 season begins. The 93:20 lounge in the Etihad Stadium is not especially busy. The match, against Brighton, has little riding on it. Manchester City won the title with five games to spare. They have been near-certainties to win the championship since they beat Manchester United at Old Trafford in December.

The matchday experience at the Etihad Stadium has a slick, American feel to it. There are table-tennis tables, penalty shootout competitions for the kids. Your ticket is presented to you in a wallet, the stewards smile and say they hope you enjoy the match.

Uwe Rösler and Paul Walsh, one of Manchester City's more formidable strike partnerships of the 1990s, are conducting a talk-in on a stage by the club shop. With his long grey hair, high cheekbones and tortoiseshell glasses,

Walsh has the air of an ageing rock star – think Bill Nighy in *Love Actually*.

The Tunnel Club, with its £7,500 membership fee that allows you to watch the players warming up in the tunnel after a five-course meal, may have been derided as the last word in corporate excess, but a version of it has been included in the specifications for Tottenham's redeveloped stadium.

After the match, in the queue for the tram back to Manchester, you hear foreign languages spoken in a young, racially-mixed crowd. And yet there are hints of a distant past, from even before Robbie Fowler and Steve McManaman played for Manchester City.

There is the old blue-and-white scarf with the dark red stripe, the replica shirt sponsored by Brother, another by Saab. Beneath a jacket a T-shirt peeks out with a picture of the old Kippax Stand bearing the slogan: 'We're Not Really Here'. Someone is carrying an inflatable banana. Behind my padded, premium seat are the words: 'Paul Lake 1987-1992', as if he were a casualty of war, which in a sense he was. The past is here, shimmering just below the surface.

The 93:20 lounge commemorates a final day of the season when everything mattered. It was May 2012. There were shades of the last time Manchester City had won the title, in 1968. Then, as now, City had to match United's result to become champions. Then as now, one of the clubs had finished their season in the North East. In 2012 Manchester United were at Sunderland. In 1968 Manchester City had been at St James' Park.

On the day of the match, Roberto Mancini, the Manchester City manager, had visited the chapel of St Bede's College, an independent Catholic school where the club educates its academy students. He had knelt and prayed. When he arrived at the Hilton Hotel to brief the team there was hardly a word spoken – not one member of the squad asked a question. Usually, there would be a few queries about what Mancini actually meant. There would be some banter.

Once in the dressing room, Mancini said barely a word, or at least nothing that anyone remembers. There was no attempt to make a great speech as Alex Ferguson had done during the interval of the Champions League final against Bayern Munich: 'If you lose, you will pass within six inches of that cup and you won't be able to touch it.' Gary Neville's response when reminded of his manager's oratory is to reply that Manchester United played even worse in the second half.

Both matches were snatched from the brink by two goals in stoppage time and Sergio Aguero's, the one that came after 93 minutes and 20 seconds against Queens Park Rangers, is commemorated along with Martin Tyler's commentary on Sky Sports. It was the making of the modern Manchester City.

You could say the same of the man who is saying goodbye to Manchester on a damp, cool May evening. When Yaya Touré arrived from Barcelona in July 2010, Manchester City had not won a significant trophy in 34 years. At Old Trafford, there was a banner on the Stretford End designed to look like the mileage counter on a car dashboard. It ticked over every year that Manchester City finished without silverware. It did not reappear for the 2011/12 season. Six years later, to quote Touré's own words, Manchester United had been 'put into the shadows'.

Every time Touré comes anywhere near the Brighton goal there are screeches of 'shoot' but though there are some fine touches there is not a repeat of the goal against Manchester United in the FA Cup semi-final that saw him muscle his way past Nemanja Vidić and slide the ball through Edwin van der Sar's legs. With enormous sentimentality, he is announced as man of the match even though the night has belonged to the quick mind and dazzling feet of Leroy Sane.

After the 3-1 win over Brighton saw Manchester City equal the record for the number of top-flight victories in a single season, set by Tottenham in the glory, glory season of 1960/61, Touré gave a long, meandering interview on the pitch. It was self-indulgent, but it was a better way to say goodbye than some of Manchester City's other greats had been given.

Neil Young, the man who, like Touré, had scored the winner in an FA Cup final, was refused a testimonial and shunted off to Preston North End. You think of Francis Lee scoring for Derby on his return to Maine Road, punching the air, yelling at Peter Swales, the man who sold him and then tried to squeeze a bit more out of the deal: 'You can stick that up your fucking jumper.'

There had been times when the relationship between Touré and Manchester City had threatened to snap. In 2014 his agent, Dimitry Seluk, commented that Touré was considering his future at the Etihad Stadium because 'nobody had wished him a happy birthday'.

Seluk commented that Roberto Carlos had been given a Bugatti Veyron by Suleyman Kerimov, the billionaire owner of Anzhi Makhachkala, the club in faraway, strife-torn Dagestan that was then trying to buy its way to the Russian Premier League title. 'Yaya only got a cake'.

There were many who wondered what Touré was doing with Dimitry Seluk, why he seemed to go along with everything his agent said. To understand, you had to realise they met when Touré found himself transferred to Metalurh Donetsk, a little club deep in Ukraine's coal belt, which Seluk ran as his fiefdom.

Seluk took over Touré's business deals. His subsequent transfers were to Olympiakos, Monaco, Barcelona and Manchester City. When the Ukrainian civil war saw Donetsk under artillery fire, Metalurh, like Shakhtar, fled the besieged city for Kiev. Shakhtar survived, little Metalurh went bankrupt. When he was asked for the best birthday present he had ever given Yaya Touré, Seluk replied: 'His career.'

He is royalty now. When Touré, microphone in hand, says his goodbyes, he mentions Sir Alex Ferguson, recovering from a brain haemorrhage at Salford Royal Hospital, which brings applause, a sign of the crowd's generosity towards its bitterest opponent.

When he is asked afterwards to recall his best moment in a sky-blue shirt, Touré mentions the winner in the FA Cup semi-final against Manchester United which is greeted by a vast, rolling cheer. A mention of Sheikh Mansour also brings applause in a way that it would not have done for Swales, Lee or David Bernstein. Above me is a banner that reads: 'Manchester Thanks You, Sheikh Mansour'. Except as a piece of extreme irony, Maine Road could never have sported the slogan: 'Manchester Thanks You, Peter Swales'.

A few weeks after all the applause, after he had been given a season ticket for life, Touré gave an interview to *France Football*. He was pitiless in his assessment of Pep Guardiola, a man he claimed had never understood African footballers, either at Barcelona or Manchester City. It was in the same spirit of Francis Lee's gesture to Swales. Though so much had changed, this was typical City.

The team had taken its leave of the Etihad Stadium to the sound of 'Heroes' by David Bowie. The swaggering rhythm, driven forward by Robert Fripp's guitar, has always attracted those who stage sports events. They have never, presumably, examined the lyrics which in Bowie's words spoke of 'a yearning for a future we all knew would never come to pass'.

From the grandiose opening, 'I will be king and you, you will be queen,' 'Heroes' climaxes with 'Nothing will keep us together. We could steal time, just for one day.' The title is in quotation marks for a reason.

It is a song of deep, doomed, hopeless love and as such it deserved to be the battle hymn of another club that existed in 1977, the year of its release. It was a grittier, earthier club than the one that is parading the league championship now. It lived more dangerously. It was also called Manchester City.

Another Time,
Another Place

THE WOMAN PUSHED OPEN THE DOOR AND SAW HER HUSBAND lying flat out on the bed, a pillow over his head. It was a late September evening, daylight was still filtering through the leaded windows in the couple's mock-Tudor house.

'What's wrong?' said the woman. 'What was the score?'

'We got beaten 5-1,' her husband replied.

'Oh Jesus, I can't believe it.'

Cathy Ferguson always said football took itself too seriously: 'It's such a silly game,' was one of her pet expressions. This was different. This was the end.

A few miles from the house they called Fairfields, after the Clydeside shipyard where Alex Ferguson's father once worked, United had been annihilated in the Manchester derby.

Ferguson thought it the worst performance of his managerial career. It was Manchester City's biggest derby victory since they had beaten United 5-0 at Old Trafford in February 1955, a match remembered as Don Revie's finest in a sky-blue shirt.

That was 34 years before and then the *Manchester Guardian*'s headline had been gentle: 'Manchester City in Form'. The headlines now would be damning.

In the away dressing room at Maine Road, a place of light wood panelling and a blue linoleum floor, Ferguson's players had waited for their manager.

Gary Pallister, then the most expensive footballer in England, braced himself. Ferguson had a habit of picking out only certain players for the invective that came to be called 'The Hairdryer' and Pallister was to become one of the regulars on the receiving end of it. Against a Manchester City side that contained half-a-dozen youth-team products, he had performed dreadfully.

However, when Ferguson tried to speak almost nothing came out of his mouth. Pallister thought he seemed shell shocked. He left without saying anything coherent. Upstairs, in the cramped press room, he gathered his thoughts and became more articulate. Trying to control the game, he said, had been 'like trying to climb a glass mountain'.

As he nursed the Mercedes home towards Wilmslow, towards Fairfields, Ferguson would have known how close he now was to the edge. In six weeks or so, he would celebrate, if celebrate was the word, his third anniversary at Old Trafford.

He had spent plenty of the club's money - £2.3m on Pallister, £1.2m on Paul Ince, another million on Neil Webb – at a time when Manchester United was valued at £10m. He had inherited a stylish, entertaining, if brittle, side from Ron Atkinson and created a galumphing mess.

The men who had hired him, Martin Edwards and Bobby Charlton, were leaving. The man the press referred to as Manchester United's new owner, Michael Knighton, had witnessed the humiliation from the directors' box at Maine Road and had been photographed ostentatiously brandishing his mobile phone. The speculation was that he would use it to call Howard Kendall, who had won two championships with Everton and who was nearing the end of a two-year sojourn in Spain with Athletic Bilbao.

Some seven hours before Cathy Ferguson saw her husband, Paul Lake had been driving towards Maine Road. He was twenty years old, one of the brightest talents Manchester City had known. He pulled up at some traffic lights in Longsight.

'And stood there at the adjacent bus stop is a City fan in his thirties with his arm around his young son, both of them kitted out in replica shirts and the old-style blue, red and white scarves.

'Having clocked me sitting there in my car, this fella nudges his lad and then does something that will stay with me forever,' Lake recalled. 'Pressing his palms together as if in prayer, he looks at me beseechingly and simply mouths, "Please, please."'

Their prayers were soon answered more fully than the pair on the corner of Stockport Road could have dreamed of.

Lake's manager was Mel Machin. He was 44, two years younger than Ferguson, but considerably less charismatic. Because he had been brought in from Norwich, the City fanzine *Blueprint* called him 'Farmer Mel'. Two months later, his chairman, Peter Swales, would sack Machin, essentially for being too dull. In Swales' famous malapropism Machin had 'lacked a repartee with the crowd'. He meant 'rapport', Machin was not an end-of-pier comedian, although in the decade that followed there would be plenty of jokes at Manchester City's expense.

Before the derby, the home dressing room was becoming agitated. The return to Division One had not gone well. The first four games had produced just one point. They had then overcome Queens Park Rangers 1-0, but two matches in London had seen them beaten by Wimbledon and by Brentford in the League Cup. When an apprentice walked into the dressing room wearing a red tie, Lake yelled at him to take it off.

The core of the team was made up of the lads who had won the 1986 FA Youth Cup – Paul Lake, David White, Ian Brightwell, Steve Redmond and Andy Hinchcliffe. On their path to glory they had beaten an Arsenal side containing Paul Merson and Michael Thomas in the semi-final, and had dominated Manchester United in the second leg of the final at Maine Road in front of 18,000.

Lake's bonus for the entire cup run amounted to £56. He spent it on a pair of Arthur Ashe trainers, volume eight of *Now That's What I Call Music* and a Terry's Chocolate Orange for his parents.

Tony Book, the man who had managed them that night, now moved around the dressing room, shaking the hands of his boys and offering them encouragement. Everyone called him 'Skip'.

He had been brought up as a bricklayer in Somerset but the dressing room at Maine Road was his spiritual home. He was thirty and had already been given a carriage clock by Bath City when Malcolm Allison persuaded Joe Mercer to bring him to Manchester on the grounds that Mercer's own playing career at Arsenal had flourished after he left Goodison Park for Highbury at precisely Book's age.

Book had gone on to lift all the heavy silverware of the Mercer-Allison glory years. It was a photograph of Tony Book, sitting on Mike Doyle's shoulders and holding aloft the 1969 FA Cup, that dominated the players' lounge at Maine Road.

He had managed as well as captained Manchester City, taken them to the League Cup, which until the takeover by the men from Abu Dhabi would be the club's last major trophy. The following year, 1977, had seen him take City to second place in the league. Now it was his voice, rather than Machin's, they could hear calling for calm as United began to dominate the game as most expected they would.

There was a disturbance in the North Stand that had been infiltrated by United supporters. It was five months after the slaughter at Hillsborough and yet Maine Road still had steel fences topped with barbed wire. United fans spilled over them and on to the pitch. The referee, Neil Midgley, stopped the game, which upon the restart changed completely.

City's attacking was as ruthless and glorious as United's defending was inept. Pallister slipped for the first and was dispossessed by David Oldfield for the third. In between, Trevor Morley extended his leg to stab home the second. When Oldfield's cross cleared Paul Ince and was headed home by Ian Bishop for his first goal for Manchester City, it was a question of how many? The answer was five.

After Mark Hughes' muscled, tree-trunk legs had swung into a bicycle kick and sent Russell Beardsmore's cross clattering in from the underside of the post to give United the hope that something might be salvaged amid the wreckage, Lake ran through an ocean of space to set up Oldfield for a tap-in.

It is the fifth that everyone who was there recalls. Five goals was incontrovertible evidence of a rout. It might not have been called the 'Maine Road Massacre' if it had been 4-1. It was recalled because the scorer was so unlikely. 'Where did Hinchcliffe come from? He's the left-back remember,' spluttered Clive Tyldesley from the commentary positions as he ran at full pace to head White's cross home.

It is also remembered because it was such a beautifully constructed goal; 'as good as Jim Leighton has ever been beaten by', to quote the commentary once more. White allowed a long, beautifully-measured ball from Bishop to bounce twice before launching it precisely for Hinchcliffe to head in.

In 1989, the AC Milan of Gullit, Maldini, Rijkaard and Van Basten was considered the ultimate in world football, but this was as good anything seen at San Siro; a counter-attack launched and finished off in seconds. It was made and scored by White and Hinchcliffe, from Urmston and Hulme, talents the club had fashioned itself.

Twenty years later, before another Manchester derby, they held a reunion dinner for the men who had fired the bullets in the Maine Road Massacre. 'We were a team of lads who had played together since the age of eleven,' said Hinchcliffe.

'We simply played that day as though it were an under-12 game. Everything just clicked for us. I was just twenty but the goal I scored that day was something I never bettered in my career.

'We were such a young team; we didn't realise the significance of the result. Manchester was becoming a vibrant city at that time with the Madchester scene but I was always low key. I was married at twenty and wasn't the type to go out celebrating. I don't know if we did anything or not.' David White's father did at least buy every Sunday newspaper he could lay his hands on.

The day after the reunion, the two sides of Manchester met again in a September derby. Twenty years on, Ferguson still ruled Old Trafford. In 1989 he had been their manager, clinging on, expecting the end. Now he was emperor. Eighteen days after he had buried his head beneath the pillow, Michael Knighton's accountants had signalled their unease. He did not have the £20m required to take over Manchester United, so the bid faded as quickly as it had appeared. Charlton turned on Edwards, whom he accused of deceiving the board, and proposed himself as chairman.

Gradually, differences were plastered over, the cracks were sealed and, amid it all, Ferguson survived. In July 2009, Ferguson was more concerned with Manchester City than he had been in twenty years.

In a hotel suite in Kuala Lumpur, in the middle of one of the vast Asian tours Manchester United employed to 'promote the brand', Ferguson could not contain himself.

He had seen the 'Welcome to Manchester' poster on Deansgate, the city's main thoroughfare, that showed Carlos Tevez, arms outstretched, in the blue of Manchester City. They had paid £47m to buy out his contract and take the Argentine from Old Trafford. It was a show of new-found strength that the club's owners were prepared to flaunt.

'It's City isn't it?' Ferguson told the half-dozen journalists, sitting in an expensive, if nondescript, room full of brushed beige sofas. 'They are a small club with a small mentality. All they can talk about is Manchester United, they can't get away from it. That arrogance will be rewarded. It's a go at us, that's the one thing it is. They think taking Carlos Tevez away from Manchester United is a triumph. It is poor stuff.'

It was a rule of Ferguson's managerial career that he reserved his invective for those clubs who could jeopardise Manchester United's pre-eminence. When, in his later years at Arsenal, Arsène Wenger was asked why Ferguson was now so supportive of him, he smiled and said, 'Because I am no longer a threat.'

Manchester City were a threat, and a growing one. At Old Trafford, where they had lost just one derby since the April afternoon in 1974 when Denis Law's backheel helped them on their way to relegation, United snatched a 4-3 victory. It was sealed by one of only two interventions Michael Owen would make to justify his transfer from Newcastle, the other was a hat-trick in a Champions League fixture in Wolfsburg.

Ferguson, seeing Manchester City's head of communications in the tunnel, gave Vicky Kloss a mouthful of invective about 'Welcome to Manchester'. However, for Manchester City this 4-3 defeat had more resonance than the 5-1 annihilation twenty Septembers before. It showed that they were gaining on the club that had dominated English football for a generation. Two years later, Roberto Mancini's side would go to Old Trafford and thrash them 6-1. They would win the title that season from United on goal difference.

The Massacre of Maine Road was a cul-de-sac. 'I feel slightly embarrassed about the hype and frenzy that continues to surround the famous 5-1,' wrote David White in his autobiography, *Shades of Blue*. 'For me, this result represented one solitary victory in an era when Manchester United's side was far superior to ours and regularly turned us over.

'They always seemed to have the upper hand, sadly, and never once during my senior career did I visit Old Trafford thinking we'd be able to compete on the same level. Had September 23, 1989 been the catalyst for a reversal of fortunes and an avalanche of derby victories, I, too, would be reminiscing, commemorating and raising a glass to each anniversary.

'But it didn't. It was a false dawn. There was no golden era, no dramatic revival. Ferguson's side of superstars went on to dominate English football while City's trophy cabinet continued to gather dust.'

The young men of Manchester who were behind the rout of United and who might have formed the bedrock of the club for years to come, did not, generally, last long at Maine Road. Within seven years Manchester United had won their second Double in three seasons, while City had been relegated.

The win did not even guarantee Mel Machin's future, even in the short term. There was no reason for Farmer Mel to think himself under threat. September 23 1989 was his lovely day. He had just signed a fresh three-year contract, spent £2m in the summer and been allowed to bring in Colin Hendry from Blackburn for £800,000.

Ruin came from the Midlands. On Armistice Day, November 11, Manchester City capitulated, 6-0 at Derby. A week later Nottingham Forest beat them 3-0 at Maine Road, and they were knocked out of the League Cup at home to Coventry.

Swales demanded Machin's resignation that night. Machin refused. City were held 1-1 at Charlton the following weekend, a creditable enough result given the carnage of the past fortnight, but Swales had seen enough. This time he didn't allow Machin the opportunity to argue his case. He sacked him the next day.

Machin phoned his players individually to tell them he was finished, which David White thought showed a bit of class. Machin was indignant. Through his eyes, he had promoted the club, pushed their young players to the fore, and then orchestrated one of Manchester City's most stunning results since the glory days of Mercer and Allison.

This, then, was his reward. 'I leave with my conscience clear,' he told the press. 'The club is in a far healthier position than when I arrived both financially and from a playing point of view.

'I am surprised, disappointed and saddened. What do they want at Maine Road? If they react like this no wonder they have remained unsuccessful for so many years.'

The man who had lain prostrate on his bed on the evening of September 23 was still clinging on. On the same Saturday that Manchester City's draw at Selhurst Park forced Swales' hand, United had fought out a goalless stalemate with Chelsea at Old Trafford. Between 12 November and 4 March, the Stretford End would not celebrate a single league victory.

On the afternoon of 9 December, as Mark Bright drove Crystal Palace to a

2-1 win at Old Trafford, Pete Molyneux, a 35-year-old supporter from Salford, pulled out a banner he had been carrying in a plastic bag for three matches.

This was the time to show it: 'Three Years of Excuses and It's Still Crap. Ta-ra Fergie'. Molyneux was shaking with emotion and nerves as he held it up. It was an echo of Bet Lynch's habitual parting remark to Mike Baldwin on *Coronation Street,* 'Ta-ra, cock'. Nobody, least of all Pete Molyneux, expected Bet and Baldwin to have left the Street before Ferguson took his leave of Old Trafford.

PJ

'PETER SWALES HAD A SAYING AND IT'S ONE THAT I STILL USE with my dogs,' says Bernard Halford, who as club secretary worked with Swales every day of his twenty-year tenure as chairman. 'He would ring up and ask for the matchday takings or how much we had made in the club shop and, when I told him, there would be a pause and he'd reply, "Not so good, eh."

'I say it to my dogs when I take them out for a walk and the weather's bloody bad I say, "Not so good, eh."'

Much of Peter Swales' tenure was not so good. In the two decades of his rule, Manchester City were relegated twice and won a single trophy, the 1976 League Cup. They were about to be relegated again when he died of a heart attack a few days before Manchester City were to face Liverpool at Maine Road in the final game of the of 1995/96 season. He was 63.

'Before the game the crowd observed a minute's silence for his death,' wrote David Conn, the journalist and author, in his memoir *Richer than God*. 'As everybody hung their heads, there was a sense of shame. We had hounded Swales out in an unforgiving public humiliation for a childhood hero, Francis Lee, who we believed would make us happy again. And here we all were, on the brink of relegation.'

Manchester City were relegated in farcical circumstances, attempting to play out a draw in a match they had to win. It seemed somehow appropriate.

Twenty years after his death, Gary James, the club's foremost historian, made a film called *The Boys in Blue* from footage uncovered in the North-West Film Archive. Among the treasures James discovered was film of Manchester

City's return from the 1934 FA Cup final, when a million lined the streets to greet them.

There was also a home movie by Harry Dowd, the club's goalkeeper, of the team in Vienna during the 1970 Cup Winners' Cup final. However, it was footage of Peter Swales that produced most comment and interest.

Swales was a stopgap appointment who lasted two decades. His survival in the teeth of so much disdain was remarkable given the fact that he never owned more than a third of the club. He was a politician and as Peter Reid, the last of the eleven managers he fired, remarked nobody becomes chairman of the FA's international committee, as Swales did, without being a politician. To most fans he was Nixon.

His main ally was Stephen Boler, who as a young man had worked with Tom Farmer on a cheap tyre and exhaust company that was to become Kwik-Fit. Boler's company, Homeform, created brands such as Moben Kitchens and Dolphin Showers.

In 1983 Boler had bought the Mere Country Club near the plush Cheshire market town of Knutsford. Reid was sent to the Mere for his job interview. Boler's first question was, 'Why should I give you the fucking job?'

Boler suffered a heart attack and died aged 55 in 1998, while travelling to his beloved game reserve in Johannesburg, but the Mere Country Club and Manchester City maintained strong relations for long after – Manuel Pellegrini stayed there when he succeeded Roberto Mancini as manager and habitually set off the fire alarms with his cigars.

Swales had made his money in Altrincham, first selling sheet music and instruments, then across the North West in television rentals, all in partnership with Noel White, who was to join him at the FA and become chairman of Liverpool. He resigned from the Anfield board in 2006 after accusing Rafa Benítez, accurately, of spending money the club did not have.

Peter Swales was born on Christmas Day and had grown up a fishmonger's son in Ardwick, not far from where the Etihad Stadium now stands. One of his first journeys out of Manchester was to Somerset, where he did his national service.

At the barracks in Yeovil, Swales ran a freelance uniform pressing service. He hired out radios at ten shillings apiece and then charged the twenty men in the dorm a shilling each for listening to it. There was something of Sergeant Bilko about it.

As the partnership with White began making serious money, they bought into Altrincham's football club. Then came the Rolls-Royce, then the racehorse, and then a house in the stockbroker belt of Bowdon.

Then came the investments into Manchester City. He was asked to join the board and in October 1973, when it was split between factions who were for or against Malcolm Allison, who had just walked out of Maine Road for the first but not the last time, Swales was asked to become chairman. He was forty years old.

In December he took to penning programme notes. 'I know for sure that he is the right one,' he wrote of his manager, Ron Saunders. 'If he goes down, I go with him. It's as blunt as that.' It wasn't, of course. Peter Swales was a captain who never felt the inclination to go down with his ship.

Bernard Halford called him 'PJ'. Peter John Swales. In 1976, *The Fall and Rise of Reginald Perrin* had started screening, featuring an overbearing boss called CJ who began every sentence with the phrase: 'I didn't get where I am today by . . .' and who was surrounded by fawning sycophants. There was something of CJ in PJ.

Halford's previous chairman at Oldham had been Ken Bates. They were similar men, although Bates and Swales could not abide each other. 'When I was at Oldham, Ken Bates would ring me at seven in the morning to ask what was in the post. I would say, "But Ken, I'm still at home, I haven't got to the office yet."

'PJ used to do similar things. We had to issue a weekly financial statement showing the opening bank balance, the closing bank balance and all the transactions in between and I remember the phone going at midnight and it was PJ. He said, "Have you changed the supplier of black bags to the stadium?"

'I said "Yes."

"Why have you done that?"

"I got a better price."

'He said "Right," and then the phone went dead.

'I had to ring Peter Swales every night at five past five when the ticket office had closed to tell him how much we had taken on each matchday. I have still got the book with all the amounts on.

'When he died I had worked for him for twenty years. It was like losing a second father. It sounds funny to say it but it was true. He didn't come to the games after Francis Lee replaced him as chairman and for much of his last season we couldn't hold the board meetings at Maine Road because the fans would bombard the cars.

'He suffered terribly from the demonstrations against him. I thought he was impregnable but the campaign against him killed him. He was recovering from a heart problem and then had another heart attack on the day his wife, Brenda, went to pick him up from Wythenshawe Hospital. While she was waiting she saw all these medics dashing about and she didn't realise it was her husband they were dashing about for.

'There were one or two odd things he did towards the end. He began asking me about my life. I was very close to my parents and I'd go to their grave every three weeks, and he was fascinated by that. He would start talking about death and dying. It must have been on his mind. There were not a lot of those conversations but we did have them.'

His love for Manchester City was genuine, if obsessive. Inside the house at Bowdon he created a shrine to the club. The walls were painted light blue, the shelves were full of memorabilia and he would retire there to watch videos of Manchester City victories. They were always wins. He could not stomach even heroic defeat.

However, given that Swales could not separate his love of City from a hatred of Manchester United, it was a flawed love.

'My initial ten years in the job were completely overshadowed by wanting to get over Manchester United. I had seen City do well in the 1960s and we still couldn't catch United for support so my life was devoted to doing them,' he said in an interview with Gary James shortly before his death.

'I wanted to see City's name everywhere, in all the newspapers. I think that's fair. The thing I never calculated upon was the impact Munich had on the world at large. There, you had a great club wiped out in a terrible accident and that really made United.

'It cemented their name worldwide and we could never overcome that. Nobody will ever catch them now and that was the thing I tried to do. We came closer than anyone in the 1970s and we were in the same bloody city.'

One of his fellow directors was Chris Muir, a Labour councillor who was to defect to the Social Democratic Party and who ran Caldwell's Stationers in

St Peter's Square. Muir was close to Swales and argued he was killed by the campaign to oust him. However, he also thought Swales' obsession with Manchester United an embarrassment.

'He was fanatical that City should be on a par with United and he would lose all rationality about it,' Muir told the BBC journalists, Andy Buckley and Richard Burgess, in their book *Blue Moon Rising*. 'I think it was one of his great weaknesses.

'There were others on the board who had this obsession as well. Ian Niven wouldn't even refer to United by name. He always called them Stretford Rangers. It was a bizarre way for a professional company to behave.'

By the Jubilee summer of 1977 Swales was at the height of his powers. His first season as chairman had culminated in United going down on the day of the Manchester derby at Old Trafford, ushered off to the Second Division by Denis Law's back-heel.

City had been to Wembley twice for League Cup finals, losing to Wolverhampton Wanderers in 1974 and beating Newcastle two years later. Then they finished second in the First Division, just a point behind Liverpool.

Swales argued that Manchester City had been denied the championship by an own-goal. He reasoned that, had Dave Watson not headed past Joe Corrigan in December 1976, City would have beaten Liverpool at Maine Road and won the title. It was an argument the centre-half seemed to accept. The guilt gnawed at him.

Dennis Tueart, who had played with Watson in the Sunderland side that had won the FA Cup in 1973 and had won the League Cup with him at Manchester City, was rather more sanguine.

Tueart pointed out that Watson's own-goal had come with four months of the season still to run. Liverpool won the return fixture 2-1 at Anfield in April, far closer to the end of the campaign. Then, with their thoughts turning to the European Cup final in Rome, the Reds had eased up at the finish. Bob Paisley's side had not even needed to win the final game of the season to retain their title, and didn't win any of their final four fixtures in total.

Nevertheless, Manchester City now had 23,000 season-ticket holders, more than any other club in England. Swales had dramatically reduced the price of being a supporter. A season ticket for the Kippax would cost £37 (£160 in today's terms). The cheapest season tickets at Maine Road were cut from £16.50 to £11. Under Tony Book, they had improved season upon season; first a cup and now a serious tilt at the title. A push and a rush and the land would be theirs.

Swales had felt confident enough about the future to have invited the cameras of BBC *Nationwide* to follow Manchester City's 1976/77 campaign. The coverage came with a particularly significant photograph taken outside the entrance to Maine Road.

All City's staff were there. The players were in the background in the corner of the shot. Beside them were two women who washed the kit standing behind a basket of washing. There were the coaches, the groundsmen. There was Tony Book in loud check trousers looking as if he were about to present an episode of *The Generation Game*. Bernard Halford stood beside him. In front of them all was the board of directors and in front of them, in front of everyone, was Peter Swales.

Swales' favourite film was *The Cincinnati Kid*, which starred Steve McQueen as a professional gambler. He sometimes referred to himself as 'The Cincinnati Kid'. The irony is that *The Cincinnati Kid* climaxes with McQueen staking everything on his belief that his opponent, Edward G Robinson, does not have the jack of diamonds. Robinson produces the card and McQueen is ruined. You wonder if Swales ever watched the film to the end.

In 1979 came Swales' jack of diamonds moment, the reckless gamble that would ruin Manchester City financially for a generation.

The previous year had seen the return of one of football's great mavericks, who would upset Swales' calculation that the challenge to Liverpool would come from the blue half of Manchester. It came instead from an altogether more unexpected place.

Brian Clough, whose genius appeared to have been crushed by the 44 days at Leeds and allowed to moulder in a backwater like Brighton, had won the championship with Nottingham Forest in 1978. He would follow it with two European Cups.

Manchester City had a messiah of their own, whom a good number of the board at Maine Road wanted back. Malcolm Allison was living in a remote village in Cornwall, about thirty years before that sort of thing became fashionable. It had one row of houses and a single pub. He was managing Plymouth, living with his second wife, Sally, a one-time Playboy bunny girl,

24 years his junior.

Clough and Allison had both walked out of the clubs where they had made their name – Derby and Manchester City – in the same year, 1973. They had both sought temporary refuge in ITV's studios covering the 1974 World Cup in West Germany, but Allison's subsequent career had been even more erratic than Clough's.

The highlight had been taking Crystal Palace, who were then in the Third Division, to the FA Cup semi-finals in 1976. The trouble was that Palace were only in the Third Division because Allison had relegated them twice.

It was at Selhurst Park where Allison wore fedoras, fur coats and brandished a Havana cigar more ostentatiously than anyone since Winston Churchill. It was at Selhurst Park, where the soft-porn actress, Fiona Richmond, would join the players and their manager in the bath. It was at Selhurst Park where Malcolm Allison became Big Mal.

He was appointed City coach in January 1979. The country was in a state of anarchic crisis that midway through the month would see 1.5 million public service workers on strike. The winter was one of the coldest in memory and wiped out much of the Football League programme. Airports and train stations were shut. Reports of panic buying filled tabloid front pages, although the panic buying would be nothing to what would happen at Maine Road over the next eighteen months.

Malcolm Allison's second coming wrecked Manchester City completely. By the time the experiment was over, the club had been hollowed out financially, weakened to the extent that it would not compete for the championship until the Abu Dhabi takeover.

There had been a core of the Manchester City board who had long wanted Allison back. Chris Muir, Simon Cussons, who ran the company that produced brands like Imperial Leather soap, and Ian Niven, who owned the Fletchers Arms pub in Denton on the city's east side, were all 'Malcolm's Men'.

Swales was not a member of the club. One of his first announcements when becoming chairman was that there had been 'too much showbiz at Maine Road'. In terms of not knowing Allison well, he was almost alone in the City boardroom.

And yet Niven, who during the war had been parachuted behind Japanese lines in Burma as part of the Chindit operations, said Swales had been the prime mover behind the recruitment of Allison.

It was Swales, said Niven, who had proposed a change of manager. The vote had been carried, 5-4. It was also Swales who proposed that Allison should be recalled. Again, the vote had been 5-4 in favour.

A month after Allison's return, Manchester City's finance director, John Humphreys, who was also the managing director of the shirt manufacturers Umbro, died at the age of 49. Humphreys was a very astute businessman who had ensured that every team in the 1966 World Cup wore Umbro kits. When he died, Manchester City decided they could do without a finance director. Allison would be driving the club without brakes.

There were some who welcomed the year zero fanaticism that saw Gary Owen, Asa Hartford, Peter Barnes, Mick Channon, Brian Kidd and Willie Donachie leave Maine Road. Hugh McIlvanney, then the most resonant voice in British sports journalism, claimed Swales had embraced the heroic aspect of the game. Before Allison's arrival, McIlvanney wrote: 'Manchester City had appeared incapable of getting a result against eleven cunningly-deployed dustbins.'

By the end, it seemed Swales might have done better buying the dustbins and putting blue shirts on them. It would have been much cheaper. The revolution was unimaginably disastrous.

The cost of Malcolm Allison's transfers, wages and signing-on fees not included, was £4.14m. Put another way, it was more than Manchester City's turnover. The entire club was in 1980 valued at £5.8m. The equivalent would be for City to have authorised Pep Guardiola to spend £392m in a single transfer window.

The players who arrived at Maine Road were nowhere near Guardiola quality. Dragoslav Stepanović was dredged from one of the more obscure parts of the German Second Division. Bobby Shinton arrived from Wrexham, Kevin Reeves from Norwich, Michael Robinson from Preston. Steve MacKenzie became English football's most expensive teenager when Crystal Palace were paid £250,000 for his services.

Most notoriously, Steve Daley was signed from Wolverhampton Wanderers for £1.4m. When he was asked to go The Mere to finalise his transfer, Daley discovered he had no money on him and his car would run out of petrol on the M6.

He went back to Molineux and asked a member of staff for a few notes to tide him over. There would be more than a few notes spent when he arrived. It has been calculated that each one of Steve Daley's appearances cost City £26,000, which was then the average price of a house in Manchester.

Allison was to claim that he had agreed a fee of £550,000 with Wolves for Daley when John Barnwell, travelling back to the Midlands from a charity function, was involved in a car crash that left him with a broken skull and a wing mirror embedded in his head. Richie Barker took over as Wolves caretaker manager and the fee rose to £650,000.

Swales took personal charge of the negotiations. Then just before Manchester City played Southampton at the Dell in April, Swales told Book, who was still nominally manager – a title he would lose during the summer – that he had secured Daley for £1.1m 'plus tax'.

Allison argued that Swales had turned down his attempt to sign Ian Rush, who was then a teenager on Chester City's books. According to Allison, the chairman thought £350,000 was too much for 'a reserve'. Rush would become Liverpool's all-time leading goalscorer.

Alan Oakes, Manchester City's most-capped player, was manager of Chester, and was desperate for Rush to go to Maine Road. He said he had 'offered Ian Rush on a plate' to City, but neither manager nor chairman appeared that interested.

After Allison had departed, his successor John Bond was so keen to sign Trevor Francis from Nottingham Forest that he threatened to resign if the deal was not completed. Swales once more took charge. He agreed a fee with Brian Clough of £1.2m and offered Francis a salary of £100,000. Francis thought both fee and salary were far more than had been necessary to seal the deal.

Swales was to confess that two months after bringing Allison back he began to think he had made a terrible mistake. However, he took another seventeen months to act on those thoughts.

They were months of dreadful humiliations. The crowds that went away from Manchester City's 1-1 draw with Borussia Mönchengladbach in March 1979 could not have imagined this would be the last European fixture Maine Road would stage.

Liverpool had played Mönchengladbach twice in recent seasons, most notably in the European Cup final, and Bob Paisley was keen to give Allison advice. He ignored it all. Mönchengladbach's stadium, the Bokelberg, was known as 'The Gravel Pit' and Manchester City were buried, 3-1 in the return leg. On the final whistle, Brian Kidd threw his shirt at Allison.

They had already been knocked out of the FA Cup at Shrewsbury Town. The following season would bring an even greater humbling in the competition, this time live on television. Halifax employed a hypnotist called Ronald Markham to convince the men of Fourth Division England that they could overcome Manchester City.

Markham's effectiveness can be judged from the fact that he once informed the media he could drive a car blindfolded. The assembled press watched him drive down Ilford High Street and plough straight into the back of a police car. He had worked with Allison on Crystal Palace's run to the 1976 semi-finals but complained he had not been paid and subsequently placed a curse on him. Markham was motivated, so were Halifax and Manchester City were beaten, 1-0, at The Shay. Allison was filmed picking his way through the mud wearing a fur coat.

Swales decided the club could do with even more exposure on television. Paul Doherty, the brilliant if acerbic head of Granada Sport, whose father Peter had played for the extraordinary Manchester City side that had won the championship in 1937 and then been relegated the following season, negotiated astonishing access. The result, when it was released in 1981, was called *City!*

Doherty's cameras were allowed into the dressing room and the boardroom. They documented Allison's last days and his replacement by John Bond. They filmed Allison on the bench in his final game at Elland Road with Tony Book sat beside him, cigarette burning low.

They even filmed Bond's interview for the manager's job, which Swales spent flicking a book of matches on the edge of the boardroom table. He had approached Bond long before. He knew what the outcome would be.

City! ends with Allison's return to Maine Road in the FA Cup with Crystal Palace. Palace are beaten and Allison walks into the away dressing room with its light wood panels and blue linoleum floor unable to say a word, just as Alex Ferguson was to do nine years later.

John Bond proved one of Swales' best appointments. He was born in Dedham, where Essex merges into Suffolk, and the rural burr in his voice meant he was often underestimated. Ron Atkinson thought him so good he would drive from Cambridge, where he was manager, to watch him coach Norwich.

He effected a remarkable transformation. He took Manchester City to the semi-finals of the League Cup, where they were unlucky to lose to Liverpool, and the 1981 FA Cup final against Tottenham.

Once more Swales was denied by an own-goal, this time from Tommy Hutchinson. Ricky Villa's sashay through the Manchester City defence settled the replay, although MacKenzie, still only nineteen, scored a goal that was as good.

Five years before, Swales had confessed not to have taken in Manchester City's League Cup triumph. He thought there would be other finals, other cups. This would be their last major final for thirty years.

By now Manchester City's financial reserves were all but exhausted. Allison had lost £3m on transfers; Bond a further £1m and they lost £500,000 on Trevor Francis when they offloaded him to Sampdoria for £700,000 in the summer of 1982.

Bond had signed his son, Kevin, and put him on wages far in excess of others at Maine Road, which had bred a deep resentment. In January 1983, after Manchester City were humiliated 4-0 in the FA Cup by Brighton, a club director confronted Bond and asked for his resignation. If he did not agree to go, details of the manager's chaotic private life would be leaked to the press.

His deputy, John Benson, was promoted on the grounds he would be cheap. Benson did not think he was the right man to manage Manchester City and proved it by relegating them. He was infuriated by the fact that Bond, who had been given a year's salary of £50,000 by Swales and told he would always be welcome at Maine Road, took the chairman at his word.

There is no good time to be relegated, but 1983 was especially bad. The long boom that had sustained the game since the 1966 World Cup was over. The recession of the mid-1970s had hit the middle classes hardest. Between 1974 and 1976 average house prices fell 37 percent, while a cumulative inflation rate of 55 percent destroyed savings.

However, for workers protected by the compact between the trade unions and the Labour government, wages remained high. Football, the game Stoke's manager Tony Waddington had called 'the working man's ballet', escaped relatively unscathed in the 1970s. Manchester City were still able to sell 23,000 season tickets.

The recession of the early 1980s was very different. The heavy industry of the north that had sustained the game from the Tyne to the Trent collapsed, taking its workers with it. The symptom of this recession was not inflation or falling house prices but mass unemployment. In addition, football was in the grip of hooliganism, which further accelerated the decline.

Judged by attendances, Manchester City were the third-biggest club in England during the 1977/78 season. Old Trafford, with an average attendance of 51,860, was still the biggest stadium in the country but Maine Road, with an average of 41,687, was less than 5,000 behind Anfield, the home of the European champions.

Of the eight biggest clubs, six were in the North-West or the Midlands. By 1984, a year that might be counted one of the most successful in English domestic football with Liverpool winning the European Cup and Tottenham the UEFA Cup, attendances had disintegrated.

Manchester United were the only club with crowds above 40,000. In a season in which they would win a Treble, the average gate at Anfield was 31,974, a drop of 29 percent in six years. London's two biggest clubs, Arsenal and Tottenham, had done well, relatively speaking. Gates at Highbury were down twenty percent, while at White Hart Lane they were down just fourteen percent. Across the North and the Midlands there was carnage.

Manchester City, now in the Second Division, were still the sixth-biggest club in England with an average gate of 25,604; a fall of 38 percent on their 1977/78 figures. There had been a similar drop at Villa Park.

After the six most astonishing seasons in their history, attendances at the City Ground were down 45 percent. In 1984, Nottingham Forest would finish third in the league and reach the semi-finals of the UEFA Cup. The FA Cup would be won by Everton, where average crowds at Goodison Park were below 20,000. In six years, they had fallen by more than half. Then, before Sky Television, the bulk of a football club's revenues came through the turnstiles.

Ken Barnes had played for Manchester City in the FA Cup finals of 1955 and 1956. He became the club's chief scout and, in his autobiography, he recalled meeting City's new manager, Billy McNeill. 'Ken, they are telling me there is nothing in the pot,' said the man who had captained Celtic to the European Cup in Lisbon. 'You've picked the wrong time to come to me for sympathy,'

Barnes told McNeill. 'I've just had my fucking phone cut off.'

There were many casualties of relegation. Plans for a purpose-built training ground in Cheadle that would have cost £400,000 were abandoned. It meant Manchester City would have to train on inadequate, council-owned facilities at Platt Lane where anyone could turn up to watch, support or abuse the players.

The project to turn Maine Road into 'one of the great stadia of Europe', which Swales had outlined to the board in 1982, was also shelved at a time when Manchester City were paying £1,000 a day on interest payments alone. The restaurants, the executive lounges and the 32 corporate boxes would not be commissioned for another thirteen years.

This was a bigger loss than almost any player. Some journalists like to compare a season to a military campaign. In this context, the corporate box was, until the arrival of the billionaires from Russia and the Arabian Gulf, a war-winning weapon.

The first corporate boxes in British sport had been installed in 1961 at Castle Irwell racecourse in Manchester. They did not do much for Castle Irwell – the course closed two years later – but their architect, Ernest Atherden, had shown them to Manchester United's directors.

In 1965 Old Trafford began installing hospitality boxes, where for a bottle of wine, a meal and, later on, a chance to meet a former player who would invariably be described as 'a legend', people were prepared to pay vastly-inflated sums for a ticket.

It was an advantage Manchester United never lost. Liverpool, by contrast, were hopelessly slow to see the implications. They did not start installing them at Anfield until 1992, when 32 were built into the new Centenary Stand. By then, one in every seven who watched Manchester United at Old Trafford paid premium prices.

By 1998 even Rochdale had executive boxes which generated £39,000 a year at Spotland, more than their highest-paid player earned. By then Manchester City, under Francis Lee's chairmanship, had built 80 boxes into the redeveloped Kippax and North Stand, which raised £700,000 and cost between £7,500 to £14,000 to rent for a season. However, by 1998 Manchester City were playing in the third tier of English football.

After his monumental gambles with Malcolm Allison, the Cincinnati Kid had become a disciple of the kind of austerity Margaret Thatcher would have applauded. One of the reasons Billy McNeill left Manchester City in 1986 was that his salary of £25,000 a year was half what John Bond had been paid and half what Aston Villa were prepared to offer.

Its effects were felt everywhere. Paul Lake, the greatest jewel that would come into the club's possession between Colin Bell's retirement and David Silva's arrival, would be asked to fly home from California in economy class after knee surgery that might have saved his career. Manchester City's physio, who had gone out to check on his progress, was flown back business class.

When Lake asked if the club would pay for his girlfriend, Lisa, to fly out to Los Angeles to join him for his rehab, the response was an absolute refusal. Peter Reid and Niall Quinn organised a dressing-room whip-round to pay for her ticket. When it came to replacing Lake's company car, he was presented with a mud-spattered Datsun Sunny that broke down on its first outing.

Niall Quinn had discovered first hand just how few luxuries there would be playing for Manchester City. Compared to what he had been used to at his previous club, Arsenal, the training kit felt cheap and nasty. When you trained with Arsenal, you wouldn't be allowed on the pitches at London Colney if you had a hole in your sock. Tony Book winced when Quinn asked for a new pair of boots. He was put up in a hotel for which Howard Kendall had negotiated a rate of £15 a night. Even so, Bernard Halford queried why the club was being asked to pay 'extras' on Quinn's bill, which amounted to two jugs of orange juice.

In the middle of the cutbacks, the disappointments, the relegation followed by promotion, followed by relegation once more, something wonderful happened. Manchester City, coached by the extraordinary Tony Book, won the FA Youth Cup, completely outplaying United over two legs in the final.

Book had built a team of local boys who might transform the club just as a Manchester United team that would win the FA Youth Cup six years later would transform Old Trafford. The present may have been grim and cheap, but the future might be dazzling.

The Lost Boys

DAVID WHITE WAS IN A SCHOOL IN ECCLES WHEN THE NEWS
came through that Barry Bennell had been found guilty. He was at the same
school he had attended when Bennell had first begun to sexually abuse him,
almost forty years before.

Bennell, the coach whom Manchester City considered their 'star maker',
had been found guilty of 43 separate counts of historic child sexual abuse.
White, part of the fabulous Manchester City side that had won the FA Youth
Cup in 1986 and three years later been the core of the team had destroyed
United in the 'Maine Road Massacre', had been one of his many victims.

When the verdicts were read out at Liverpool Crown Court, David White
was accompanied by Ian Ackley, who as a teenager had been repeatedly raped
by Bennell. They had founded a campaign group, the *Save Association*, with
Paul Stewart and Derek Bell, who as young footballers in Manchester and
Newcastle were abused by their coaches.

Their work is important. In May 1979, David was eleven. His parents were
asked by Bennell if he could take David and a friend to Majorca. Bennell
promised to work on their fitness and give them some one-to-one tuition.

Stewart and Elaine White were not naive parents. Stewart, who had just
celebrated Margaret Thatcher's victory in the general election, was described
by his son as 'a hard-nosed go-getter' and an 'alpha male' who ran the
family business.

Elaine was the staunch socialist daughter of Jack McCann, who was Labour
MP for Rochdale for fourteen years until his death in 1972. The constituency

was won by Cyril Smith, a serial sexual abuser of boys.

'The grooming process is very clever,' says David. 'First of all, it was "I am a dead nice guy." Then, it's "I am a brilliant coach" – and Bennell was a very good coach. Then, when he says, "I want to do some extra work with you," it does make you feel privileged.

'So when my dad was presented with the invitation for me – and I had never been abroad before – to go to Majorca for some one-to-one coaching and I'd be able to take a friend, all he thought was, "What a fantastic opportunity".

'My dad would not have expected me to be night fishing with Bennell on top of a cliff on the edge of the Mediterranean at one in the morning. It happens because you can get to a point with any individual where you trust them completely. That is why the majority of abuse happens in the family.'

To those who argue that this could never happen now, that the past was another country where things were done differently, David White offers this observation: 'The rewards in the Premier League are now so great that it still makes young people and their parents vulnerable.

'If your kid does make it at Manchester City or anywhere else in the Premier League, both he and his family are made for life by the time he is twenty. That knowledge makes you vulnerable and it makes your child more vulnerable because we live with the myth that there is one person who could make the difference. I believed I had to endure what I endured with Bennell if I were to make it with Manchester City.

'The leading clubs put a massive amount of money into safeguarding but getting resources down to the grassroots is much harder. If you are a grassroots football club, you could have a thousand kids fairly easily – fifteen in six age groups plus girls' teams. Predatory people do not care whether their victim is playing for the local team or one in the Premier League. They have not gone away.'

Writing his memoirs, *Shades of Blue*, was hard, especially since, because it had to feature Bennell's abuse, David did not feel he could write it while his father was alive. 'I'd first spoken to my wife about it on the back of the police investigation into Bennell in 1997 (he had been arrested and convicted by the Florida police for abusing a thirteen-year-old British boy on a football tour in the United States. He went to prison for four years).

'I knew I couldn't speak to my dad about it. In 2000, my nan – my mum's

CAUGHT BENEATH THE LANDSLIDE

mum – died and the day we buried her I was sitting with my mother. We had too much to drink and I told her. I wrote the book in one go, 100,000 words. It just came tumbling out of me.

'I went to court in the first week of the trial. I went with my wife. He wasn't there; he was on video link and I didn't recognise the guy from what I remembered of him. I rang Paul Stewart and said we should go and Paul and I went pretty much every day we could. Ian went on other occasions. I went back for the sentencing, which was a massively emotional day. It made me realise that this was being taken seriously.'

His work with the *Save Association* is sometimes painful. The best way of teaching young footballers about the dangers of grooming is to tell his own story. 'I know when I get in the car that I'll be in tears after my talk. Very early on after forming *Save*, we were getting calls and contacts through emails and social media. They were talking to us about emotional abuse, physical abuse, neglect – as well as sexual abuse – and they were contacting us because they were football fans.

'They might be a window cleaner, a barrister, a teacher. The connection was they were football fans and, in particular, City fans. They would first talk to us about football and then the conversation would turn to how they were abused in church, at scouts or in their football team or in the family. They didn't necessarily want to go to a counsellor, they just wanted to chew the fat with us.'

Manchester City, the modern Manchester City, have been very supportive, but there remains a suspicion of how much the old Manchester City knew about Barry Bennell and how much of his activities they tolerated on the grounds that, in the words of the club's chief scout, Ken Barnes, he was the 'star maker'. But, as David White says, 'If I blame Manchester City for not knowing, do I also blame my dad for not knowing?'

An attempt to give Bennell a full-time job as Manchester City's youth development officer was blocked on the insistence of one of the club's youth coaches, Steve Fleet, who as a player had been Bert Trautmann's understudy at Maine Road.

In an interview with *The Guardian*, Fleet said, 'I was an FA coach at the time and whenever the talk got to Barry Bennell, it was never good. People would say he was dodgy and, if his name was brought up, everyone would just shake their heads. It was general knowledge.

30

'He nauseated me. I just knew – instant intuition – that the rumours were sound. When Ken Barnes and other people at the club tried to fetch him in (to work full-time) I didn't want anything to do with it.

'Ken said, "He is the star maker, he finds good lads." That was true because Bennell was a very good scout but I also knew he was a risk. I wouldn't even let him into our coaches' room. I felt so strongly about it, I put my job on the line.'

Bennell left Manchester City for Crewe in 1985. The following year, David White, Paul Lake, Andy Hinchcliffe, Steve Redmond, Paul Moulden and Ian Brightwell won youth football's greatest domestic prize, the FA Youth Cup. They were managed by Tony Book, a man who in every conceivable way was Barry Bennell's polar opposite.

You can sense the power and brilliance of the team in the results that led to the final: Tranmere and Blackburn were each thrashed 7-1, Leicester were beaten 4-2, while Fulham were defeated 3-0 at Craven Cottage in the quarter-final.

The only time it seemed City might stumble was a narrow 1-0 victory on a frozen, snowbound January night at Blackpool, and in the two-legged semi-final against an Arsenal side featuring Paul Merson and Michael Thomas. City eventually won that tie on penalties before beating arch-rivals Manchester United 3-1 in the final, though the victory was actually far more straightforward than the final scoreline suggests.

'It was such an attacking team,' says David White. 'Steve Redmond was a forward, Darren Beckford was already at the club as a centre-forward, Paul Moulden (who had scored 340 goals in a single season for Bolton Lads Under-15s) was probably the best young striker in the country.

'One of the good things Tony Book and his assistant, Glyn Pardoe, did was to change the positions because, if they were going to play in the first team, they couldn't all be forwards. Steve Redmond became a central midfielder, while Andy Hinchcliffe went from being a left winger to a left full-back. Andy Thackery became a right-back and then a central midfielder.

'I think winning the Lancashire League was the better achievement. It was a tough league, full of over-age players featuring in United and Liverpool's reserve teams and older players from the likes of South Liverpool, Formby and Morecambe. We lost the first game, 4-1, and then we won every single match. We didn't drop a single point, home or away, until the Lancashire

League gave us dispensation not to play the last few games because we were already so far ahead.

'Yet in that season, we rarely didn't get a bollocking. Tony Book wanted absolute perfection. If we went off having won 4-0, he would tell us we should have won by nine. If we won 6-1, he would ask why we had conceded. We thrashed Nottingham Forest, who had Franz Carr on the wing, 8-0 and Bookie told us afterwards to go and replace the divots on the pitch.

'That is what he was like; hard as nails. He didn't want to be but he knew he had to be because we had to grow up. The culture then was different. If you won the FA Youth Cup in 1986, you were expected to challenge for a place in the first team. You were expected to make it by the time you were twenty. There was no question of being loaned out.'

In 2017/18 Chelsea, who have won seven of the last nine FA Youth Cups, loaned out 38 young footballers at clubs ranging from Sligo Rovers to Spartak Moscow.

Perhaps nobody summed up the situation better than the Croatian goalkeeper, Matej Delač, who had become the longest-serving player in Antonio Conte's squad. He had come to Stamford Bridge in 2010, been loaned to eight other clubs and, by the time he left for a permanent deal in Denmark, he had not played a game for Chelsea.

Of the eleven who started the 1986 final, seven played first-team football for City – Steve Redmond had already participated in a first-team Manchester derby by the time the Youth Cup final came around. Two more – Steve Crompton and Andy Thackeray – played league football. Only Steve Mills and David Boyd, the team's Glaswegian striker, missed out.

Nothing was sadder than what happened to John Bookbinder, who was City's substitute in the final. Bookbinder's father, David, was leader of Derbyshire County Council and, like Derek Hatton and Ken Livingstone, was one of those local Labour politicians who carried on a guerrilla war against the Thatcher government. Unlike some of the others, he left a legacy by helping to persuade Toyota to build their vast car plant on the outskirts of Derby.

John had been brought up by his father to be a fervent City fan and, when he was released, he found the rejection hard to take. There were trials at Derby and Leicester, but the spark had gone.

He moved to London and became a social worker and a street performer.

By the time he was 38, he was dying from mouth cancer. His sister, Susan, who worked for BBC Radio Five and ITN, wrote: 'I remember meeting him in central London after he was first diagnosed and every street urchin and cardboard box person seemed to know him.'

While visiting her brother at University College Hospital on the Euston Road, Susan ran into Martin O'Neill, who had resigned as manager of Celtic to help his wife, Geraldine, in her battle with cancer. Susan mentioned the plight of her younger brother, who by then had had his tongue and larynx removed. O'Neill made a vague promise to see him, which Susan assumed would not be kept.

On her next visit, she encountered Martin O'Neill and Gordon Strachan sitting by John's bedside talking football. The only way John could reply was by writing on a wipe-clean board. Charlton were playing Manchester City in a televised Sky game and O'Neill and Strachan helped John to the nearby Grafton Hotel to watch the match. City won 5-2. John died the following month.

They may have comfortably beaten a Manchester United side managed by Eric Harrison, but the boys of '86 failed to scale the heights of Harrison's Class of '92, who were to form the bedrock of the club that would dominate English football for a decade.

However, there were those at Maine Road who believed that those players should have become the foundations of the club in the same way that David Beckham, Ryan Giggs, Paul Scholes, Nicky Butt and the Neville brothers were allowed to at Old Trafford. They would never forgive Howard Kendall for breaking up the side to bring in footballers who were referred to as 'Everton Reserves'.

In truth, Kendall did not break the team up. The core members of the FA Youth Cup-winning side - Lake, White, Brightwell and Redmond - were all kept on. Only Andy Hinchliffe was sold and Kendall would manage him in two separate spells at Everton. Paul Moulden had been sold by Mel Machin to Bournemouth in the summer of 1989.

'I went to an event celebrating the 1986 side and somebody stood up and said that "Everybody should stand up and applaud this team because you were every bit as good as the Class of '92,"' says White.

'I sat there and thought, "No, we weren't". I am not David Beckham and in football you can only be judged by what you achieve in the game, although nobody knows what Paul Lake would have achieved had he not suffered those injuries. Andy Hinchcliffe was a great left-back for years at Everton. Of all of us, I think he was probably the most successful. Other than Stuart Pearce, he was the best left-back I played against.'

There were some stunning highlights; the first team's 10-1 evisceration of Huddersfield in November 1987 and the 5-1 destruction of Manchester United two years later. David White says he prefers the 10-1 to the 5-1 as a memorial to City's young footballers.

'I find it very, very difficult to celebrate the 5-1 win because it was a false dawn. That game was the only derby I ever won. It wasn't even at a time when they were supposed to be great, it would be ridiculous to celebrate it. On the day we played brilliantly. It was our day in the sun but it didn't last. The 10-1 was unique. I don't think anybody has done it in the league since.'

It was an astonishing display. First Tony Adcock, then Paul Stewart and, in the final seconds, White completed their hat-tricks against a Yorkshire side wearing black and yellow check shirts.

Eight years later at Old Trafford, when Andy Cole had put Manchester United 9-0 up against Ipswich, Alex Ferguson turned to the club's reserve-team manager, Jim Ryan, and said he did not want United to score again for the sake of the Ipswich manager, George Burley. It was, Ferguson said, 'unthinkable' for any manager to lose by ten. City had no such compunctions about inflicting it on Malcolm Macdonald.

In their report of the game, *The Huddersfield Examiner* wrote: 'Town left Maine Road in utter disgrace after being reduced to a laughing stock in the blackest day in their history as a rampant City revelled in Town's ineptitude. The way in which Malcolm Macdonald's side faltered, buckled and threw in the towel amounted to an obituary for the pride and honour of the club they represent.'

Three weeks after that victory for City came a defeat that has gnawed away at the club ever since. It was Ryan Giggs' fourteenth birthday, the day he could sign professional forms. Alex Ferguson's gold Mercedes was outside Giggs' house in Swinton with apprentice forms in the glove compartment and his chief scout, Joe Brown, in the passenger seat while Manchester City, with dozy Mel Machin at the helm, slumbered.

Giggs had been discovered by a Manchester City scout, a milkman called Dennis Schofield, who ran a club called Deans and first spotted Giggs when he was eight. He trained on the Astroturf at Platt Lane on Thursday nights.

Schofield told Ken Barnes to be at Giggs' house on his fourteenth birthday, 29 November 1987. Barnes was in his office. Ferguson was in his car. Giggs' mother went to see Barnes to ask if he wanted to match Ferguson's offer. Barnes said he was not interested.

Giggs himself would point out that he was a passionate Manchester United fan – his hero was a fellow Welshman, Mickey Thomas – that he had not enjoyed Thursday nights at Platt Lane and that he was never serious about playing for City.

Barnes, who died in 2010, always refuted the story that Lynne Giggs had been to see him to offer Ryan's services. Barnes' association with Maine Road stretched back to 1950 when he joined the club from Stafford Rangers. He had played in the FA Cup finals against Newcastle and Birmingham. His son, Peter, would play for the club. His language was industrial and he was rarely without a cigarette.

Barnes had watched Giggs, whom he knew as Ryan Wilson, for a year before his fourteenth birthday. He was also interested in an attacking midfielder from Larne in Northern Ireland called Michael Hughes. Both, he thought, would go right to the top.

Hughes did play for Manchester City, but Peter Reid was less convinced of his ability and, when he became manager, he left Maine Road. In May 1995, while playing for West Ham at Upton Park, Hughes would score the goal that denied Manchester United the league title.

In conversation with the broadcaster, Jimmy Wagg, Barnes explained the failure to sign Ryan Giggs: 'His father (Danny) used to go to a few games at Maine Road and he used to come up to my office for a drink and a bite to eat. His dad used to play rugby league as I recall.

'Ryan's dad used to bring him down and after a while I'd seen enough. I told his dad that there was a job waiting for Ryan at City when he left school. We shook on it and I believed it was a done deal. I always worked in the belief that my word was my bond and a handshake meant it was definitely settled. Ryan was on his way to City.

'A while later, Eric Mullender, a schoolteacher who did some scouting for me and who'd put me on to Ryan in the first place, told me the laddie had signed for United. I heard his father had gone back to Wales, Ryan had taken his mother's maiden name and was now called Ryan Giggs.

'You didn't have to be Einstein to work out what had happened between his parents and all my dealings had been with his dad. I thought the handshake with his father had been worth something.'

As for the meeting with Lynne Giggs when Ken Barnes, told he still had first refusal, turned down the greatest football talent Manchester would ever produce, he replied, 'It's a lovely story of people behaving honourably. It's also absolute bollocks. Ryan's mother never came near me. In fact, to the best of my knowledge, I have never met her.'

The standard of football in Manchester as the 1980s bled into the new decade can be gauged from the fact that City contributed nobody to the squad for the 1990 World Cup. United may have supplied the captain in the shape of the 33-year-old Bryan Robson but injury meant he completed just one match, the dreadful 1-1 draw with Ireland in Cagliari. Neil Webb made no meaningful contribution at all. Bobby Robson's squad was drawn primarily from clubs in the Midlands and London.

The greatest Mancunian involvement in Italia '90 was from New Order, who recorded the FA's World Cup song, 'World in Motion' with a sparse group of England footballers.

Peter Hook, New Order's bassist, recalls the recording session at a studio at a converted watermill by the Thames in Berkshire, owned by the Led Zeppelin guitarist, Jimmy Page. Tony Wilson, the head of Factory Records, arrived with cocaine for the musicians, while the footballers were offered copious amounts of alcohol.

Hook was shocked at how much they drank – Paul Gascoigne polished off three bottles of champagne without feeling the need to use a glass. Factory Records were surprised they were required to give the players envelopes with £2,000 in cash to record a song that was to promote their own World Cup campaign.

Hook thought John Barnes the only footballer genuinely interested in 'World in Motion', which was to have been called 'E for England' until the FA objected to the implied drug reference.

Although he initially liked the song, Paul Lake came to loathe the song, because it was played everywhere in the summer of 1990 and was a reminder of his own non-participation. He had been part of the original thirty-man squad but had not made the final cut, though he was featured as a Panini sticker, the album having gone to press before Bobby Robson's announcement of his final squad.

Paul Lake was everything a club could want in a footballer. He was young, intelligent, technically gifted and could play in a number of different positions. He was captain of Manchester City at the age of 22, with a promise from Howard Kendall that he would become the highest-paid player at Maine Road. He was a prince. He was the future.

The story of how that future faded is told in Lake's autobiography, *I'm Not Really Here*, which like David White's *Shades of Blue* was co-written with his wife, Jo. If *Shades of Blue* is haunted by the presence of Barry Bennell, *I'm Not Really Here* is dominated by the pain of Paul Lake's disintegrating knee.

Before the injury against Aston Villa in September 1990 that wrecked his career, *I'm not Really Here* beautifully displays the optimism of was like to be young, talented and good looking in Manchester, whether it was queueing up for Jamaican patties at Alvino's on Great Western Street or gathering at the Fletchers Arms in Denton that was owned by Ian Niven, a Manchester City director, to take on the night in Joe Bloggs jeans and a white, smiley-face T-shirt.

Although Shaun Ryder, the lead singer of The Happy Mondays, remarked that 'nobody in Manchester used the term unless they were a prick', 1988 was the summer of Madchester, a term that combined fashion, music and, unless you were a professional footballer, ecstasy.

Although he initially preferred Fridays, a club in Didsbury that offered three different dance rooms, Lake and his mates would increasingly journey to the swirling centre of it all, The Haçienda. Unlike most, he did not have to queue. He also noticed that what was worn in the clubs was increasingly worn at Maine Road by City's younger, cooler fans.

The Haçienda was opened in 1982. Its opening act was, of all people, Bernard Manning, who went down so leadenly he returned his fee. By 1991 when another Manchester City player, Richard Edghill, started going, he found it 'shabby and menacing'. It was also losing £480,000 a year. Between those times, The Haçienda was the centre of an Ibiza dance-flecked universe.

By 1991, Paul Lake's universe was centred around hospitals, surgeons and gyms as he struggled to recover from a wrecked cruciate ligament, sustained in his third game as captain of Manchester City.

The first had been a 3-1 defeat at Tottenham engineered by the heroes of Italia '90, Gary Lineker and Paul Gascoigne. City had equalised as Niall Quinn's diving header finished off a beautifully-placed cross from David White. Another cross from White and another header from Quinn should have given them the lead, but the referee had spotted a mysterious foul on the Tottenham keeper, Erik Thorstvedt.

The next match, at home to Everton, was won, 1-0. Then came Aston Villa in front of the new England manager, Graham Taylor. The first qualifier for Euro '92, against Poland at Wembley, was a month away. Then, in the 65th minute, when attempting to intercept a pass from Tony Cascarino, Lake's studs jammed in the Maine Road turf and he ruptured his anterior cruciate ligament.

The European Championships in Sweden had come and, humiliatingly, gone for England when Paul Lake played once more for Manchester City, at home to Queens Park Rangers in August 1992.

It says something about Lake's versatility that he was now deployed as an attacking midfielder, behind Niall Quinn. His last game, nearly two years before, had seen him at centre-half. A block tackle saw his knee almost give way again. At Middlesbrough, three days later in a game he felt he should not have played, the ligaments went completely.

Lake has been compared to Colin Bell not just for his naked ability, but for the knee injury that ended his career. The two shared an aborted comeback and the story has it that the stadium never matched the roar that greeted Bell's return to Maine Road.

However, there are differences. Bell was 29 when his knee was ruined in a tackle with the Manchester United captain, Martin Buchan, in November 1975. Barring the European Cup, he had won every trophy he had gone for with City. He had played 48 times for England and competed in the 1970 World Cup. Lake was 22 and would never play a full international.

Bell complained that Buchan had never thought to visit him in hospital. Lake felt abandoned by his own club. In a confrontation with Peter Swales on the steps inside Maine Road's reception, Lake demanded to know why the chairman of Manchester City had failed to telephone, much less visit him over the two years of his rehabilitation.

Bell was at least treated to the latest technology available in 1975. He was one of the first to undergo keyhole surgery. Lake had to wait until his cruciate ligaments had given way three times – twice on the pitch, once in training – before he was sent to Los Angeles to meet with one of the world's leading specialists in the field.

Even then, Swales only sanctioned the trip after an intervention from Peter Reid, a man who knew what it felt like to suffer a serious knee injury.

On New Year's Day 1979, Reid was playing for Bolton against Everton. Burnden Park was so snowbound that Bolton had to wear red instead of their traditional white home kit. The game should not have started and was abandoned at half-time, but not before Reid had collided with the Everton keeper, George Wood, snapping his medial ligaments and rupturing his cruciate. In 1979 that injury was a death sentence to a footballer, but Reid recovered. He was 22, the same age Paul Lake had been when he first broke down.

Reid, now manager of Manchester City, insisted that Lake be flown to California to see Dr Domenick Sisto, who had salvaged the Crystal Palace winger John Salako's career. 'If I had seen you straight away,' Dr Sisto remarked, 'you'd have been back playing soccer by now.' After the operation, City flew their most precious and most fragile asset, who was over six feet tall, back to Manchester economy class. Lake's leg was so contorted by the lack of space from eight hours in a plane, he was forced to go through customs in a wheelchair.

For David White, the years when Howard Kendall and Peter Reid ran Maine Road were among his happiest in football.

'Howard transformed everything almost overnight,' he says. 'He made things simple and bought better players. People may have complained about the 'Everton Reserves' he brought to Maine Road but they were players who had won championships, won FA Cups, won a European final.

'The fans loved Ian Bishop but he was not Howard's type of player (at Everton he had sold him to Carlisle in 1984). Howard wanted two midfielders to protect the back four, much as almost every manager does now. That was either going to be Peter Reid and Gary Megson or Reidy and Alan Harper.'

Although Kendall's regimes at Everton and Manchester City seemed to specialise in alcoholic blow-outs, White argues they were fewer than is popularly supposed. The day-to-day level of drinking in pre-season was, he said, higher under Mel Machin.

What White admired about Kendall was the sense of responsibility he gave his footballers. They were treated like adults. 'When he arrived, I was playing up front as part of a three,' he says.

'Then, Niall Quinn was signed from Arsenal and we went 4-4-2. Howard said he needed Mark Ward and myself to play wide. I said, "Gaffer, we are both right-wingers; it's impossible."

'We went into the boot room and he told us to sort it out amongst ourselves. Wardy said, "I'll play left," and we took responsibility for our own decisions. Wardy would cut inside and Neil Pointon, bombing down from left-back, would overlap. It worked.

'He would take us out for a Chinese meal, which is what he did at Everton, and the mantra was that you work hard for this football club and you are coming with us into this restaurant. They were sessions that bonded us together, absolutely.

'We would go out never later than a Wednesday if we had a game on the Saturday. We would have a meal with a couple of glasses of wine and Howard would turn to someone and say, "Stand up and sing a song."

'After they'd sung a song, he would point the finger at me and say, "Whitey, sing a song." I was always Johnny Cash. I'd sing 'A Boy Named Sue' and 'Don't Take Your Guns to Town'. I did a bit of Kenny Rogers too. That's how you, as a young player, became a part of the first team.'

A month after Paul Lake had been carried from the field against Aston Villa, came the Manchester derby. On the morning of the match, George Best had been quoted claiming that Kendall was the finest manager in England and after 80 minutes at Maine Road, the Ulsterman's analysis seemed well-judged.

White had scored twice, City were 3-1 up and Reid, at the age of 34, had given a masterclass in midfield play. Had White's header not clanged against Les Sealey's bar, he would have become the first player since Francis Lee destroyed United at Old Trafford twenty years before to have scored a hat-trick in the Manchester derby.

Then Kendall substituted Reid for Ian Brightwell, while Alex Ferguson moved Brian McClair from the right flank to centre-forward in support of Mark Hughes. Tony Coton rolled the ball out to Brightwell, who dawdled and was fatally dispossessed by the boy from Bellshill, who then scored United's third.

Kendall blamed Coton for rolling the ball to Brightwell – rather than the young midfielder for losing possession – for the surrender of two points. Reid rounded on Kendall for taking him off, to be told he was being saved for the League Cup tie with Arsenal on the Tuesday. It was in the aftermath of that match, which was lost, 1-0, that the idea was first planted in Kendall's mind that he could go back to Everton.

'Peter just carried on what Howard had been doing,' says White. 'He brought in Sam Ellis to be his assistant, who was a much deeper thinker than he looked. We were a great counter-attacking side. With me and Terry Phelan down the right we were rapid, but losing Mark Ward to Everton was as damaging as losing Howard. That is how highly I rated Wardy.'

It was Kendall's return to Maine Road in the final match of the 1992/93 season that saw the beginning of the anarchy that was to sweep over the club. Six days before, Manchester United had broken their 26-year-hoodoo by winning the championship. Kendall directed Everton to a 5-2 victory that saw City's keeper, Martyn Margetson, substituted at the interval. Manchester City slid from sixth to ninth place.

'The level of vitriol around the place was horrendous,' says White. 'I genuinely believe the chairman, Peter Swales, knew he did not have the resources to carry on and was looking for a way out. It got so bad that we lost all focus.

'It was all about the protests against the chairman; nobody seemed to be bothered we were playing Leicester or whoever. The chairman wanted to put somebody between himself and the manager and he chose a journalist, John Maddock [whom he appointed General Manager]. We could not stand the bloke. He knew nothing about football and we knew he knew nothing about football.

'In the summer we had a pre-season tour to Holland. You would never go on a summer tour in which nothing happened and there were a couple of incidents which were blown up out of all proportion.

'Reidy dealt with the first one quite well – we had broken a curfew to go to a beer festival. Then one or two of the lads nearly missed the plane, and Reidy went mad. As incidents they were nothing special, but they were leaked to the press and I firmly believe John Maddock leaked them to undermine Peter Reid.

'When Brian Horton came to the club, he said after his first speech that his door was always open. So, no sooner had he given the speech, I went and knocked on it and told him I wanted to leave the club.

'I had nothing against Brian Horton, but he wasn't Howard Kendall and he wasn't Peter Reid. I will say that he was a lot better than the men who followed him – Alan Ball, Steve Coppell, Frank Clark. Until Joe Royle arrived, every Manchester City manager of that era was worse than the man who preceded him.

'At the same time, you had the movement to bring in Francis Lee. I thought this club was going to hell in a handcart. The club was completely toxic. If you had stopped me in August 1993, when I was about to knock on Brian Horton's door, and asked me to predict what might happen to Manchester City, I wouldn't have been far wrong.

'The one regret I do have is that I left City having scored 96 goals. I've often wondered what I thought I was doing. Why didn't I, as a Manchester City fan, stay and score four more and get my century?

'Ten years later, just after they'd played their last game at Maine Road, the club invited me and other former City players back to the ground to play a match. I made sure I scored four.'

A Marriage of Convenience

OF ALL THE MEN WHO HAVE MANAGED MANCHESTER CITY, ONLY Pep Guardiola was more qualified than Howard Kendall. When he took his first coaching session at Manchester City amid rain that was turning to sleet, he could claim to be one of Europe's finest managers.

In the five years before coming to Maine Road, Kendall had taken Everton to two league titles, the European Cup Winners' Cup and the FA Cup. He had gone to Spain and guided Athletic Bilbao to fourth in La Liga. He was spoken of as the next England manager. He was still only 43.

Everything that happened to Kendall happened to him young. He had grown up in the mining belt of the North East, a grammar-school classmate of Bryan Ferry's. Both their parents had been miners. Fred Ferry had looked after the pit ponies at the Washington Main colliery, while Jack Kendall had been forced from the coalface with pneumoconiosis.

Kendall achieved stardom far more quickly. By 1964, when Ferry was preparing to go to Newcastle University to study under Richard Hamilton, the father of the British pop art movement, Kendall had become the youngest footballer to play in an FA Cup final. Six years later, when Ferry had still not put Roxy Music together, he had won the championship with Everton. As a manager, he won the league before he was 40 years old.

At his best there were elements of Brian Clough, another son of English football's far corner, in Kendall's management style. Peter Reid, his lieutenant on the pitch at Goodison Park and Maine Road, recalls the moment when his managerial career took flight.

It was January 1984, Liverpool were league champions and on their way to a fourth European Cup. Everton were in crisis and Kendall's tenure was said to be measured in days. They were drawn away to Stoke in the third round of the FA Cup.

'It was past Christmas when we changed it round,' Reid says. 'We got beat 3-0 at Wolves; we were useless. Then the Coventry game came up and we were hopeless. There were cushions on the pitch, leaflets being handed round.

'In the dressing room at the Victoria Ground we could hear the Everton fans and all Howard did was to open the dressing-room window and say, "Do it for them." It galvanised us. We reached the Milk Cup final and the FA Cup final.'

Kendall's moment of crisis at Manchester City came a little over two months after his appointment. Mel Machin had been sacked after a 1-1 draw away to Charlton. Kendall actually lost the return fixture, 2-1, at Maine Road. Charlton would be relegated, thirteen points from safety.

Kendall was attempting to stiffen the side by bringing in players he had managed at Everton – Reid, Wayne Clarke, Alan Harper and Neil Pointon.

In midweek he had paid £300,000 for another, Adrian Heath. The joke, laced with some withering, midwinter bitterness, was that a young team, made in Manchester, had been swept away to create Everton Reserves. Only Pointon had actually been playing for Everton when he was signed – Heath was at Aston Villa when the call came – but the name stuck.

When Steve Redmond, who had led the side in the Maine Road Massacre, was replaced by Heath after a dreadful hour against a team bottom of the First Division, it was met by anger from the stands. The cracks in the team seemed starkly obvious.

'They booed us off,' Reid recalls. 'We came in on the Monday and we had to build everyone up but it was icy and we only had Platt Lane as a training ground, which wasn't the greatest. There was an indoor place called Bowlers.

'Howard said to me, "What should we do today?" I said, "Five a side, short and sharp, Bowlers." He said, "Nah, get Layachi Bouskouchi (a Mr Fixit at the club) and tell him to get five crates of Budweiser. We'll set up in the players' lounge, get the table-tennis table out and that's that."

'So we go down, half the team behind me, half the team behind him. You had to get the bat, hit the ball and do a little run. Little Wardy knocks one into the net. Howard says to him, "Go over there, get a bottle of Bud and get it down you."

'Now it's half-ten in the morning. Half-ten in the morning. God's honest truth. Five crates of Bud later and we are in Mulligan's (a bar near Manchester Airport) on the piss. What happens? We go on a run and get beat in just two of the next twelve.

'I look back on things like that and you see it changed the whole spirit of the dressing room. The young lads, like Lake and Redmond, had never seen anything like that but from then on, having been seen as Everton Reserves, we were Manchester City. That is great man management.'

Alcohol had always been a part of Kendall's management style but as he grew older it took more of a hold. Tony Coton, one of his finer signings, remembers the meal with the manager shortly after he agreed to join Manchester City from Watford.

Kendall asked Coton and Neil Pointon to join him at Harper's, a restaurant in the city centre. So much wine was poured that through the haze of cigar smoke, Coton thought he might be sick.

'Even by the *laissez-faire* attitudes of the early 1990s, Howard's capacity for drink was unquenchable,' Coton recalled in his autobiography, *There to Be Shot At.* 'On a pre-season tour of Sweden, when the players were granted a night out on the town, those of us who didn't know Howard too well raised our eyebrows when he turned up at the nightclub we were in.

'He made it clear that he wanted to be treated like one of the lads. I was stood with Gary Megson in a prime position close to the bar when the gaffer came in clutching a wad of krona that the club had given him to cover everyday expenses.

'He tapped Meggy on the shoulder and told him to order the drinks. Meggy asked Kendall what his poison was and was told: "Surprise me". With that Gary told the barman to fill a tall glass with shots of whisky, brandy, vodka, port and a couple of other liqueurs before topping it off with a dash of lemonade.

'It was a lethal cocktail and Meggy was biting his fist to prevent Howard hearing his giggles as he asked me to pass the beverage to the boss. Ten minutes later, Kendall was back: "What the hell was that? Get me another."'

Coton disliked Kendall, in particular, for the way he belittled his players with 'a sarcastic or abusive comment that was designed to get a laugh out of his backroom staff and nothing more'. You might say the same of the way

Kenny Dalglish ran his dressing room at Anfield.

David White thought him an exceptional man-manager and Reid argued there was more to Kendall than alcoholic bonding games. 'You know all this modern training, pre-season,' he says. 'Howard was doing that in the 1980s. I'd been used to running up hills. Howard introduces all this technical stuff, all short and sharp. I'll always remember one pre-season at Everton. We were having long runs and Rats [Kevin Ratcliffe] was tailing off. Howard gets us in and we are all thinking, "He might get a bollocking here".

'Howard says, "Well done lads. Kevin Ratcliffe's not the quickest thing ever, but on the pitch he only needs to run fifty yards at the most and we'll work on his fitness and his speed." He treated us like individuals. Some people haven't got the capacity to run, but they are footballers. I took that from him.

'Howard was very good tactically. I remember him playing a 4-4-1-1 in Munich (in the Cup Winners' Cup semi-final against Bayern). Andy Gray was injured but he played Graeme Sharp up front, Trevor Steven in behind and four of us across the middle of the park. Everybody in 1985 played 4-4-2, or three at the back. Let's just say that in today's jargon that the Everton team I played in had two defensive midfielders, just like every team has now.'

White thought he beauty of Kendall's management was its lack of complication. His instructions were clear, simple and precise. To Paul Lake he was 'the best manager I ever had'.

And yet Kendall's achievements at Maine Road seem pamphlet thin. George Graham once remarked that salvaging a club is one of a manager's more straightforward tasks. What is wrong is usually obvious. Taking a club into the top four required an altogether different level of skill.

Kendall would have been in Graham's camp. He told his players on the first day of training that rescuing Manchester City required only 'tweaks'. Six months on, Manchester City finished in fourteenth position, on the same number of points as Manchester United who were to win the FA Cup, the first turn of the great red wheel that was to crush everything in its path.

As a salvage job it was good, if not quite as good as Don Howe's at Queens Park Rangers. At Loftus Road, Trevor Francis was fired on the same day as Mel Machin was sacked by Swales. Rangers, a club with considerably fewer resources, finished eleventh.

However, it confirmed Swales' belief that in Kendall he had found the man for the long term. By November 1990, Manchester City, having signed Coton and Niall Quinn during the summer, were fifth in the First Division.

It was then that Swales rang Freddie Pye, a scrap metal dealer who was now vice-chairman of Manchester City: 'I want you down at the ground now.'

'Why, has the stand burned down?'

'No, it's more serious than that,' said Swales. 'Howard's leaving.'

Swales had always thought Kendall might leave. As head of the FA's International Committee, he would have known for months that Bobby Robson's contract would not be renewed after the Italian World Cup. He knew, too, there was a clause in Kendall's contract, put there against Swales' will, that would have allowed him to leave Maine Road if the England job were offered to him.

Kendall, as the last Englishman to win the title, would have been an obvious candidate, much more so than the man who was the FA's choice to replace Robson, Joe Royle. In one of those sliding-doors moments, Royle, who had transformed Oldham into one of the most surprising forces in the English game, did not turn up to his interview, believing he had little chance of the job.

Graham Taylor, who had taken Aston Villa to second place in the championship and who, rather more importantly, was believed to be able to handle the out-of-control press pack who had wrecked Robson's tenure, did make his way to Lancaster Gate for the interview. He got the job.

In his memoirs, *Love Affairs and Marriage*, Kendall remarked that of the three he was the only who had actually won anything. He also recounts Swales sidling up to him and saying conspiratorially, 'You didn't want the job, did you Howard?'

He did actually, and it might have suited him better than the one he did go for. England's results could only have been better than the ones Taylor achieved, although you wonder how Kendall would have coped when the press turned, as inevitably they would.

He appeared far more concerned about a fall out with the *Manchester Evening News* than someone of Kendall's stature should have been. Their Manchester City writer, Peter Gardner, had long been used to travelling on the team bus. Kendall asked him to make his own arrangements for away games and felt Gardner had responded with some match reports he considered vitriolic.

Even in 2017, two years after Kendall's death, Peter Reid mentioned it as something that his manager took into consideration when he was suddenly offered the choice between remaining in Manchester or returning to Everton.

The Merseyside press corps was famously protective of its managers. In the mid-1990s, a young reporter was appointed to cover Liverpool and Everton for the *Daily Mirror*. When he asked Roy Evans a pointed question at a press conference at Melwood, one of the doyens of the Merseyside press corps tapped the Liverpool manager on the shoulder: 'You don't want to answer that, Roy. It'll be all over the papers.'

Kendall's departure from Manchester City was very quickly all over the papers. 'We had played Arsenal in the League Cup at home and got knocked out. Everton had lost to Sheffield United and Colin Harvey had been sacked,' says Reid.

'We were having a bevvy with Bob Cass and Joe Melling [of the *Mail on Sunday*] at the Copthorne Hotel. You might call it a 'debriefing'. Bob Cass went out to make a call and when he came back Cassie said to Howard, "Do you fancy the job at Everton?"

'Howard had this problem with Peter Gardner at the *MEN* because he had thrown him off the team bus and Peter Gardner's first call had been to Peter Swales. Howard said to me, "Do you fancy coming back?"

I said, "No, you can never go back?"

'We then drew at Sunderland and he pulled me afterwards and said, "I am going to go." I said "Don't," and he just said, "I am going."

'I asked him again and he said, "No, I love Everton too much."

"Well, I am going to stay," I told him. "Do what you can to try to get me the job."

'He should have stayed, but he came up with that quote that Everton was a marriage and the rest were just love affairs. It's a great quote but it was a mistake. He had just changed it around at City. I thought Paul Lake would have been a superstar. We know how the course of history can change; it might have been Duncan Edwards and not Bobby Moore lifting the World Cup. I thought Lake was going to be a star, that the team could be built around him. He was that good.

'The atmosphere at City was good. I thought he had won the battle with Peter Gardner. He had certainly changed the crowd's reaction from being

MANCHESTER CITY IN THE 1990s

'Everton Reserves' to having a good side.

'He'd bought Niall Quinn who was an asset, he'd got Tony Coton, who was a good goalkeeper. He should have stayed. Swalesy pulled me in and said he would give the job to me as a caretaker. I said, "I'll do one game, Leeds, and then you have a decision to make because I want it." I half held a gun to his head but the crowd were brilliant. We got beat, 3-2. Alan Harper missed a penalty but we played well. That made his mind up.'

Everton were in 1990 a bigger club than Manchester City. They would be one of the 'Big Five' that were instrumental in creating the Premier League, the one everyone now forgets. They were a great power in the way that the Austro-Hungarian Empire was a great power before the First World War – its past was its greatest asset. It would take them until 2005 to finish in the top five of the league they created.

'I believe we could have won the league before United, had Kendall stayed,' is David White's view of his manager's resignation. 'I certainly believe we would have won trophies in his time at the very least.'

Kendall returned to Everton to a mixture of surprise and cynicism. When he cleared his desk at Maine Road he walked out to find his tyres had been slashed. When he took Everton back there in May 1993, he helped dismember his former club, 5-2. The dugouts were being replaced and the managers and their staff were sat on chairs. Kendall, just as much as Peter Swales, was a target for any missiles. Dave Watson dived in front of Kendall to take an egg for the gaffer. It was the kind of mateship that made Kendall's Everton sides, the kind of team spirit burnished over so many nights out in Liverpool's Chinatown, hardened over so many sessions at the bar. Mark Ward, a midfielder brought up on the same streets and playing fields of Huyton and Whiston as Steven Gerrard and Peter Reid, describing Manchester City's mid-season break in Tenerife, said 'that everybody knew had been designed as a piss-up'.

Ward had lost £100 to his manager in a game of tennis – a sport at which Kendall excelled. The player wanted double or quits and Tony Book, who had sensibly been retained on the backroom staff, told Ward that if he needed the money back, he should ask to play at two o'clock in the afternoon, 'because by then the manager will have had eight pints'.

Kendall liked Ward and took him to Goodison Park when he quit Manchester City. His description of the Christmas parties during Kendall's time at Everton was vividly retold in his autobiography, *Hammered*.

'The tickets cost £25. It was good value because that got you entry into the nightclub, a buffet, a stripper and a free bar until 11pm. From 9.30pm on the night the management would allow free entry to a select group of attractive women who had been handpicked and provided with tickets in the weeks running up to the event. Wives and girlfriends were banned. That wasn't unusual at Everton players' functions at the time nor on any trips organised by Howard Kendall.'

Ward, like the vast majority of his players, thought Kendall excellent on the touchline and in the dressing room. He thought the booze-fuelled nights served another purpose. During them, his footballers would tell their manager their concerns, their problems, their insights in a manner they would never have done under any other circumstances. Ward said he thought most of his players imagined Kendall would not remember what they had said the following morning. But he did recall and often he acted upon it.

The return to Goodison Park was not a success. Kendall rescued them from relegation as he had rescued Manchester City but Everton finished twelfth in 1992 and thirteenth the year after. Kendall quit after the Everton board refused to sanction the signing of Dion Dublin from Manchester United. Looking back now, failing to land the man who was to present *Homes under the Hammer* does not seem to be the kind of issue worth the sacrifice of resignation.

It precipitated a disastrous decline in Kendall's career, one that by now was wholly destabilised by booze. It was said of George Best that he made the classic alcoholic's mistake of confusing movement with action.

Best would find himself flitting from California, to London, to Florida to Edinburgh without being able to say how this might advance his career or even his happiness, but which 'proved' to himself that he was doing something. Tony Hancock, having fired Ray Galton and Alan Simpson, the two men who made him funny, ended up thousands of miles from the London suburbs that had been his natural home in a flat by Royal Sydney Golf Course. His suicide note said simply: 'Things went wrong too many times.'

In the last five years of his managerial career, things went wrong too many times for Howard Kendall. He was persuaded to go to Xanthi, a small Greek city near the Turkish border whose stadium could be accommodated three times over at Goodison.

He did not speak the language and discovered that, once training was finished, there was virtually nothing to do. They installed him in a hotel above a petrol station and as well as the smell of gasoline he scented the whiff of match-fixing. This was a man who six years before had been the most sought-after manager in Europe.

When he returned to England it was to Notts County, whose chairman was the domineering figure of Derek Pavis, who accused Kendall of being drunk for most of his 79 days at Meadow Lane. At Sheffield United, whom he took to the 1997 Championship play-off final, Kendall demonstrated he still possessed some of the touch that once attracted the board of Barcelona.

While he was at Bramall Lane, Kendall was offered the opportunity to return to Maine Road. It was 1996, the year Francis Lee, now the club's chairman, would see four men try to manage Manchester City.

It would have been an attractive offer. Lee, unlike Peter Swales, paid his managers well. There was unfinished business at Maine Road. Kendall was tempted, but he had loathed Francis Lee ever since Lee had headbutted him when Kendall was a teenager playing for Preston. Lee has always denied it was deliberate but, more than thirty years on, it was enough to prevent his return.

Then Everton called and he made another attempt at a marriage that was broken now beyond repair. They saved themselves from relegation on the final afternoon of the season. Had he relegated them, as Clough relegated Nottingham Forest, it would have been seen as the most hurtfully poetic example of a man killing the one thing he truly loved.

Kendall made one last, disastrous foray into Greek football before retiring from management. He was 52, a few months older than Alex Ferguson had been when he won his first Premier League title with Manchester United.

Manchester City's long-serving secretary, Bernard Halford, regards Kendall's departure from Maine Road as one of the great turning points of his time at the club. 'I remember we both sat on a transfer tribunal at Oldham as it happens,' he says. 'Ged Brannan had signed for Motherwell but they wouldn't pay the signing-on fee and we took them to a tribunal. Afterwards we went to a pub called the Old Cock near Middleton. I said to him, "What a mistake you made walking out on us. What could we have done had you stayed?" I remember him walking out of that pub crying. His face was wet with tears.'

Kendall never stopped loving Everton. He went to their games, wrote about the club for the *Liverpool Echo*, gave advice when it was required and made appearances when Everton needed reminding of what the club had been and what it might be once more.

When, in October 2015, he died at the age of 69, Everton were about to face Manchester United at Goodison. Feelings of sadness, shock and pride were everywhere for the man who as a player and a manager had taken them to heights they sensed they might never scale again.

On his Facebook page, Bryan Ferry published a photograph of the two of them together at Washington Grammar. Two pit-village boys with, to use Kendall's wry phrase, 'such very different talents'.

Peter

IT AMUSED PETER REID TO THINK THAT PETER SWALES CONFESSED that sacking him was the greatest mistake he had made as chairman of Manchester City. Swales had made so many mistakes. It was nice to have been top of the heap.

For Swales the summer of 1993 would have been a bitter one. Manchester United were champions. The long hoodoo that had hung over Old Trafford for more than a quarter of a century had been broken. The campaign by City fans to get rid of him had reached a crescendo. According to his friends he was 'punch drunk' from the abuse.

Swales leaked details that City would respond to United's championship triumph by spending £6m in the summer – Kenny Dalglish mentioned it to Reid when the two crossed paths at Manchester Airport.

The sum was a fantasy; Manchester City's overdraft stood at £3m, which explained why Swales blocked moves to sign Andy Townsend from Chelsea and ensured that Graeme Souness' offer to sell them John Barnes for £1.5m came to nothing.

Pre-season had been spent competing in the Sittard Tournament in Holland. The results against PSV Eindhoven and Sporting Lisbon in Fortuna Sittard's little stadium were quickly forgotten. The headlines of heavy drinking at a nondescript country hotel, whose main attraction for its clientele of pensioners was a three-lane bowling alley, were much slower to fade in the chairman's mind. David White thought the details were deliberately leaked from inside the club to damage the manager.

Reid had hoped that Paul Stewart would have been enjoying Sittard's limited attractions. Stewart was 29 now and Souness, who was in the midst of his bloody-minded determination to rip the past out of Anfield, was prepared to sell him for £2m.

When it became clear Swales would only sanction the arrival of Alfons Groenendijk from Ajax for a tenth of that, a story appeared in the *Manchester Evening News,* written by the paper's chief sports writer, Paul Hince, that Reid would resign if the Stewart deal fell through.

Reid was not quoted in the story but Swales instinctively knew its source. He called manager and journalist into his office. 'If you ever pull a trick like that again, I will fucking sack you,' he told Reid. It was, said Paul Hince, the only time he had ever heard Swales swear.

The language at Maine Road was to get much worse. Swales, wearying of the task of holding Manchester City together, decided to appoint a journalist, John Maddock, as the club's general manager. He, not Swales, would deal with Reid.

It was not the first time Swales would install a buffer between himself and the dressing room. In 1986 he had appointed Freddie Pye, a scrap-metal merchant who had invested in Manchester City as 'director of team affairs'. The manager, Billy McNeill, who in his days captaining Celtic had been known as 'Caesar', found this an affront to his authority.

In his memoirs McNeill wrote: 'I found most of the directors easy enough to get on along with. Some had invested six-figure sums and I saw that as an act of faith in my ability to take Manchester City forward but I was not so keen on Freddie Pye.

'Freddie had a habit of expressing his opinions rather too loudly and had succeeded in upsetting a number of players, in particular Mick McCarthy. So, when the news broke that Freddie had been given the title of vice-chairman and director of team affairs, I was far from pleased.

'I responded by declaring that, if Freddie came anywhere near the team, I would be off. Peter tried to offer reassurances but I was already upset and unsettled by that news and didn't feel I would be able to handle the situation.'

McNeill resigned to join Aston Villa, which he described as the worst mistake of his football life. Both clubs, Manchester City and Aston Villa, would be relegated.

Swales appointed Maddock to deal with Reid because he no longer trusted his judgement. 'Peter didn't get the players he wanted in that summer of 1993,' the club secretary, Bernard Halford, recalls.

'Geoff Thomas was one of them, although how well he would have done I don't know. He also wanted Paul Stewart and he had left under a bit of a cloud for Tottenham in 1988 because he was convinced that clubs had been in for him and we hadn't told him, which wasn't the case.

'Paul would have cost half a million more than we got for him and the board thought that was ridiculous. When we signed Kåre Ingebrigtsen from Rosenborg and we saw him play, Peter Swales turned to me and said, "Bernard, they have done me again," because we'd bought a player who didn't prove to be a player.

'Then we had Groenendijk, whose price from Ajax went up £20,000 overnight because West Ham were supposedly interested. John was a friend of PJ's, they had known each other for years and wanted him to help out.'

'People had better understand that there is a new regime at Maine Road. I have the power to hire and fire,' said Maddock. 'Control has been handed to me.' Maddock was a tabloid journalist. He understood headlines.

He was also immensely well connected. He had been instrumental in offering Howard Kendall the Manchester City job after his return from Spain. It had been at Maddock's house in Sale in 1981 that Ron Atkinson and Martin Edwards had negotiated the deal that would take him to Old Trafford. By then Maddock had been sports editor of the *Sunday People* for five years.

He was from Warrington and had joined the *Daily Express*' vast northern operation in 1960 as an eighteen-year-old. One of his first tasks had been to go through an article by Desmond Hackett, who was then the most famous sports writer in Britain, whose trademark was a brown bowler hat that he wore everywhere. He charged the *Express* for a new one every month on expenses. The teenaged Maddock held up Hackett's copy and pronounced it 'the biggest load of crap I have ever seen'.

Maddock was not a man who ever moderated his language and there were those who thought his appointment risible. James Lawton, the chief sports writer of his old paper *The Daily Express*, commented, 'the only executive decision John Maddock has taken in football has been to fill in a pools' coupon'. It was a good quip but not strictly true. Maddock had worked with Liverpool as their commercial manager and negotiated the club's first shirt sponsorship deal. Nevertheless, derision from Maddock's former profession was near universal.

Swales almost never interfered in team affairs or selection, but Maddock thought it was in his brief. After a 1-0 defeat at White Hart Lane, Maddock went over to Reid and told him that City had done well 'considering they had ten men'. Reid was nonplussed by this, considering they had had nobody sent off. Maddock replied that 'having Rick Holden out there had been a waste of time'.

Reid, like Maddock, employed language so industrial it might have come from a blast furnace. Four years later while filming the documentary *Premier Passions* when he was manager of Sunderland, Reid would break the record for the most expletives ever used on British television. He employed a few of them now in Maddock's direction.

Their last conversation took place just after Blackburn's 2-0 victory at Maine Road, on a Tuesday night in August. Maddock, rather than Reid, came into the press room, banged the table and delivered what most present thought an incoherent rant that was mainly about how much power he now had at the club. Reid was sacked shortly afterwards.

Had he sacrificed his assistant, Sam Ellis, something Swales asked for, he might have bought himself a little time. Ellis was never a comfortable figure at Manchester City. He had managed Blackpool with some success but his reputation was as an iron-hard disciplinarian and a long-ball merchant. It would have given the impression that something was being done at Maine Road without manager or chairman having to give up their jobs.

Reid realised the sacrifice on his part would have been considerably greater. Swales would be saying goodbye to a nodding acquaintance, Reid to someone he worked with every day.

Two years before, the man who would be Reid's next chairman, Sunderland's Bob Murray, had ordered his manager, Denis Smith, to get rid of his assistant, Viv Busby. The two had played together at Stoke, managed together first at York and then at Roker Park. Smith decided to sacrifice his number two, which neither saved him from the sack nor Sunderland from relegation, but which did wreck one of the great friendships of his football career.

In any event, Reid instinctively realised he was finished. In this, he possessed a greater sense of intuition than some more experienced men who never seemed to sense the ground had shifted beneath their feet. You think of Ron Atkinson arriving at the Cliff and wondering why his boots had not been laid out for training. A generation later, in a different technological age at a different United training ground, David Moyes would frantically phone anyone he could think of in the club's hierarchy to find out why there were so many social media reports that a decision had been taken to dismiss him. Only when Sir Alex Ferguson did not return his calls did Moyes believe the reports were true.

Reid knew. He had been to see Ian Greaves, who had been his first manager at Bolton and who since his departure for Everton had remained a father figure to him. Greaves bluntly informed Reid that he should prepare himself for the worst.

'It might look like a panic measure,' Maddock told the press when the dismissal was announced, 'but we had to do something.' Maddock would have known that 'having to do something' is the very definition of a panic measure.

His greatest achievement was ahead of him; to launch the Sunday version of the *Daily Star* and oversee the development of the huge printing operation at Broughton near Preston that was designed to keep newspaper production in the north.

However, as Express Newspapers, which had sold four million copies a day when the teenaged Maddock held up Hackett's journalism for ridicule, continued to decline into an irrelevant parody of itself, the plant closed in July 2015 with the loss of 91 jobs, half its original workforce. John Maddock survived its passing by only a few weeks.

'Looking back, I don't know how I did it,' Reid recalls of his first job in management. It was doubly difficult because mostly he would be playing as well as managing.

Bob Willis used to observe how difficult it was to captain England as a fast bowler. You would be tired, wiping sweat from your eyes, especially under the merciless blue skies of an Australian summer. You would also be trying to concentrate on the next delivery – and Willis' concentration was so intense it seemed sometimes as if he were in a trance. Then you would have to place the field, decide whether to move third slip to gully or protect the boundary. The feelings of a player-manager are roughly the same.

'It was sexy to have a player-manager in those days. Glenn Hoddle did it at Swindon, Graeme Souness did it at Rangers, Kenny won the Double in his first season at Liverpool as a player manager,' says Reid. 'Later, there was Ruud Gullit at Chelsea.

'When I went on to the park, I got Sam Ellis to deal with everything off the park. Everything – substitutions, physio the lot – and we would have a chat afterwards. I don't know how I got through it, thinking about it now. How did I do it?

'It couldn't be done nowadays. Impossible. Then, it was brilliant; now it would be too intense. The media for a start. My managerial career took me from Manchester City to Plymouth and the game had changed to the extent there was more media to do at Plymouth than there had been at City years before. Then you have the other part; dealing with football agents, chief executives. You don't get time to put your boots on.'

There was one other risk with being a player-manager. If you played badly, your respect in the dressing room eroded.

In February 1993 the severe winter weather caused Sunderland's game at Tranmere to be postponed. The board at Roker Park took the opportunity to fire their manager, Malcolm Crosby, despite the fact he had taken Sunderland to the FA Cup final eight months before. Crosby thus became a quiz question, the only manager to be sacked on the basis of a Pools Panel result – they had gone for a home win.

In his place Sunderland appointed Terry Butcher, who like Reid had been on the pitch in the Azteca Stadium in Mexico City when Diego Maradona first cheated and then dazzled England out of the World Cup. Like Reid, Butcher would be player-manager.

He lasted a few disastrous months. The players could put up with his bizarre team-talks. A little over half an hour before the Tyne-Wear derby, Butcher marched into the away dressing room at St James' Park with his head shaved and bellowed, 'We are fucking commandos. I've had this haircut because I'm a commando and you're going to be commandos, too. We are going to parachute in, get the victory, then fuck off out. No surrender.'

Sunderland played more like the catering corps than commandos and in driving, incessant rain were fortunate only to lose 1-0. However, what damned Butcher in his players' eyes were not the ludicrous team-talks nor the terrible results but the fact he was no longer worth his place as a footballer.

In his memoirs of life as a journeyman at Roker Park, Lee Howey recalled the start of the Newcastle game: 'Under no challenge whatsoever, the man who had played in three World Cups showed zero composure when he received the ball. He just smashed it with all his might like Peter Kay would do in a later beer commercial. My heart sank and so did Sunderland.' Reid, two-and-a-half years older than Butcher, never lost his players' faith as player-manager of Manchester City.

Reid had wanted Ian Greaves to be his assistant at Maine Road, just as Bob Paisley had mentored Kenny Dalglish in his first triumphant season as Liverpool's player-manager. Greaves, however, could not commit the time.

Reid, though, was not short of advice. On the payroll were two former Manchester City managers, Tony Book and Jimmy Frizzell, who had somehow survived admitting to Howard Kendall that he leaked information to the *Manchester Evening News*. Bobby Saxton, who had managed Blackburn, Plymouth and York, and who would become Reid's number two at Sunderland, was chief scout. In the summer of 1991 Greaves was brought in as a consultant and so, too, was John Neal, who had spent four years managing Chelsea.

It was, however, Ellis, who attracted most debate. He looked fearsome. It was said you could balance peas on the crevices of his face. Clive Allen, Colin Hendry and Mark Brennan all fell out terminally with him.

'To be honest, some of his treatment of the players was terrible,' Chris Muir, who was a director at Maine Road from the Allison-Mercer years to his resignation in 1992, told the BBC journalists Andy Buckley and Richard Burgess for their book *Blue Moon Rising*. 'He could be very cruel. He would leave people waiting outside the manager's office for hours and wouldn't speak to them.

'Sam was an unusual character. On the one hand he was one of the most intelligent persons I have ever met. He is very interested in world affairs and architecture. He likes to give off this different image to the public and it backfired badly at City.'

Those who liked Sam Ellis adored him. David White says, 'I wouldn't say he was an emotional person, but he was the most genuine giver of praise I have ever worked with. If you were playing well and doing the right things, he was so happy. He would just fling his arms around you.'

Initially, there had been plenty to be happy about. Under Reid, Manchester

City competed with United in a way they never would again until the arrival of the men from Abu Dhabi. In 1991, they finished above Manchester United for the last time until Sergio Aguero's 94th-minute goal snatched a title that, up in Sunderland, Ferguson's men had just tentatively started to celebrate. There had been a gap of 21 years.

The methods Reid used were the ones he had learned from Kendall. Short, sharp five-a-side games on the training ground, plenty of head tennis. Away from the ground there would be booze-fuelled sessions to bond the squad together. Inside the dressing room there would be the kind of fearsome language detailed in *Premier Passions*. By the time he went to Elland Road in 2003 in an attempt to salvage the bloated wreckage of Leeds United, Reid realised how dated all this had become.

'You have always got to manage players,' he says. 'Are there bigger egos out there now than there were back then? Without a doubt, but you have to go with the times. You can't do what I did in *Premier Passions,* effing and blinding at modern players. They would just down tools.

'I don't regret that approach. At the time it was the way. There is nothing wrong with the hairdryer now and again. I learned it had changed very quickly at Leeds. It was at Anfield. I had a go at them and realised you can't do this anymore. Mark Viduka's reaction told me everything. He looked at me as I laid into him and I could see in his eyes that he was thinking that I was a piece of shite. As they were going out, I pulled him over and said, "Listen, I've only made you an example because you're the best player." I had to think on my feet.'

November 1990, when Reid led City for the first time, was an interesting time to be getting into management. The Italian World Cup, Gazza, *Nessun Dorma*, had stoked interest in a game that had been declining for a decade.

The aftermath of Hillsborough had led to a realisation that supporters could not be herded like cattle. The fall of Margaret Thatcher would see a prime minister who had no interest in sport in general and contempt for football in particular replaced by John Major, who loved cricket and supported Chelsea. Half-a-dozen years after the carnage of Heysel, the winners of that season's First Division would be allowed to compete for the European Cup.

The tectonic plates that underpinned English football were shifting. The long years of dominance that had seen the league title leave Merseyside just twice between 1976 and 1989 were over. Everton's brief time of brilliance did not survive Howard Kendall's departure for Bilbao. The Empire of the Kop was to disintegrate more completely and more quickly than anyone imagined possible.

It was not obvious that Manchester United would inherit the crown. Arsenal, the club that did, to use Ferguson's phrase, 'knock Liverpool off their perch', seemed far more likely to be the dominant long-term power. Leeds, mechanically run by Howard Wilkinson, took the title in 1992. Reid thought it was possible to imagine Manchester City winning the Premier League in its first season.

'I remember Alex Ferguson being right under the cosh at the time. I remember having scampi and chips in my office with him after he'd come to Maine Road to watch a reserve game looking completely lost. They were after him,' says Reid. 'They were after Alex. Everyone talks about signing Eric Cantona as the decision that turned it around for him but to me it was dropping Jim Leighton for the FA Cup final replay against Crystal Palace. That took bollocks, that was a massive decision.

'I made one like that. I was at Sunderland, we were beating Manchester United, 2-1, in the FA Cup at Old Trafford and Cantona scored with five minutes to go at the back stick. It should have been the keeper's ball. Alec Chamberlain was our keeper then but I brought in Shay Given on loan and he kept eleven clean sheets. Everyone said, "A nineteen-year old goalkeeper? You are crackers". But I remembered Fergie's decision with Leighton and I related to that. It was one of the reasons why we won promotion in 1996.'

On the surface, Reid should have absolutely understood the football rivalry that divided Manchester. On Merseyside he had grown up in a family split between Liverpool and Everton. His initial allegiances had been to Bill Shankly's team.

Reid tells a story about playing in the Merseyside derby: 'The ball goes out to John Barnes and we haven't had a kick for twenty minutes and I twat him. It was just on the halfway line and I hear, "You Blue-nosed cunt, you big-eared bastard." I looked up into the crowd and went "Uncle Arthur, sit down." On my life. I had got him players' lounge tickets. He was the nicest man in the world and he was giving it to me. He said afterwards, "Don't tell your mum."

'The one incident about Manchester City that I will never forget was in April 1992,' says Reid. 'Leeds and United were going for the title. We beat

Leeds 4-0 at Maine Road and our own fans booed us off because the crowd wanted Leeds to beat United to the title. I remember thinking that it summed up Manchester United and Manchester City rather nicely.

'But I couldn't understand Peter Swales' obsession with United just as I couldn't understand Bob Murray's with Newcastle when I worked for him at Sunderland. Bob wanted his stadium to have one more seat than Newcastle's. I thought: "Why? They are a bigger club in a bigger city. Just concentrate on what you are doing".'

Like Sam Ellis, Reid had an image that was slightly different to the reality of the man. The image was of a footballer who liked a tackle, a quip and a bevvy. A Liverpool street boy made good. That was true, but Reid was also political in a way few footballers are.

His grandfather, Paddy Reid, known as 'Whacker', had been involved in the Easter Rising. As a fifteen-year-old he had been part of Éamon de Valera's grandly-named but poorly-armed Third Battalion of Irish Volunteers which seized the Boland's Mill bakery warehouse that overlooked Dublin's Grand Canal and tore up the railway line to prevent British reinforcements arriving from the port at Kingstown – now Dún Laoghaire.

Boland's Mill held out until the city was surrendered. After the British withdrawal, Whacker found himself on the wrong side of the Irish Civil War, fighting for the IRA against the Free State, and fled to Liverpool, where the 1923 league title had just come to Anfield. He became chairman of the Huyton Labour Party. Its MP was Harold Wilson.

Huyton was a series of estates designed to take the overspill from Liverpool. It bred an astonishing array of people from Rex Harrison, Caesar to Elizabeth Taylor's Cleopatra, to more conventional Scousers like Freddie Starr and Stan Boardman. After his capture trying to get home to Bremen after the German collapse in Normandy, Manchester City's greatest goalkeeper, Bert Trautmann, was kept as a prisoner of war here and later worked in Huyton clearing unexploded bombs.

It produced gangsters, villains and dealers. Mark Ward, who like Reid learned his football on the streets of Huyton and who played for Manchester City and Everton, was sentenced to eight years in prison. Out of football and needing money, he had stupidly agreed to put his name to a rental agreement for a house in nearby Prescot he discovered fairly quickly was being used as a cocaine factory. He kept taking the money. There were plenty of guns in Huyton and not a few shootings.

In Phil Redmond, who produced *Grange Hill* and *Brookside*, and Alan Bleasdale, who wrote two of Merseyside's greatest dramas, *Boys from the Blackstuff* and *GBH*, it had its chroniclers. It produced footballers in the same way the Yorkshire coalfields once produced cricketers. Reid pointed out that, if you included Kirkby, a similar overspill development, three men who lifted the European Cup as club captain – Dennis Mortimer, Phil Thompson and Steven Gerrard – grew up there.

When we met, he was promoting his autobiography at the Malmaison on Liverpool's waterfront, a symbol of the new, gleaming city. The hotel would be well placed for Everton's new stadium at Bramley Moore Dock. Reid had been to watch Everton lose 1-0 at home to Burnley, one of the last acts of Ronald Koeman's disintegrating regime at Goodison Park. He had been a guest in Derek Hatton's box.

The former deputy leader of Liverpool City Council and the sleek-suited public face of Militant was friendly with many in the Everton dressing room in the days when Merseyside appeared to be on the front line of a class war with the Thatcher Government.

It was one of the great ironies that when football on Merseyside reached its zenith, its city would be bankrupt and broken. The streets of Toxteth would burn. Hatton would, to use Neil Kinnock's phrase, 'send taxis scuttling around the city handing out redundancy notices to its own workers'.

I once asked Howard Kendall, who enjoyed Hatton's company, if he had felt the dichotomy between the glory played out at Goodison and Anfield and the everyday suffering that lay beyond Stanley Park. Kendall said no; he and his players lived in Formby and Southport. He talked as if Formby and Southport lay on the far shores of Orion.

'Well, I was from Huyton. I used to go in The Quiet Man (an estate pub on Longview Drive that is now a care home) so I was acutely aware of the social situation,' says Reid. 'It was tough for people to get money to go to games, especially the games when we were winning things. That's why the FA Cup was a massive thing. Football was a release but they couldn't afford the release every week. For the FA Cup they could do.

'It was hard back then. When I was at Everton, I'd been on the piss and stayed at my ma's because I lived in Bolton. I woke up and thought, "It's fucking freezing". There was ice on the windows. I said to my ma, "Any chance of putting the heating on?" She told me she didn't have a boiler. I'd forgotten. I rang a mate and got a boiler put in straight away.'

As a teenager Reid had been coached by Alan Bleasdale. He was part of the Huyton Boys team that, under Bleasdale's tutelage, won the English Schools Trophy in 1971. It is an achievement of which Reid remains inordinately proud. In his autobiography, he devotes as much care over its description as he does to the passage on winning the Cup Winners' Cup with Everton fourteen years later.

'It would have been really interesting if Alan had done a play about Huyton Boys and made it socially aware,' says Reid. '*The Boys from the Blackstuff* was genius. If you watched it now, you'd think, "That can't be right, he has made that up". That was the reality of the time.

'I think grassroots football should have more money off the Premier League. If you go to Germany, every small town has a little stadium and identity. I think schools and their playing fields have been decimated so money has to go into grassroots football. Where do the generation of kids coming up now play?'

You would imagine Reid has no time for the new Manchester City with the Tunnel Club, where for £750 a head you can have lunch, watch the players warming up outside the dressing rooms and have a member of Pep Guardiola's staff give a little tactical talk.

'Manchester City has changed for obvious reasons but the thing that does impress me is that it has still got this Tony Book, Mike Summerbee heart. I like that. Even though it's Hollywood with the Tunnel Club, it's still got the essence of Maine Road. Tudor Thomas (City's honorary president who has supported the club for seventy years) still goes to the game. Every time I go, I see people and think: "That's still Manchester City". Even though it's gone up in the world, it's still got that little bit of difference.'

The Storming
of the
Winter Palace

THE REVOLUTION THAT WOULD SWEEP PETER SWALES FROM power began on a day he must have looked forward to.

It was March 1993; Manchester City would be playing Tottenham in the quarter-final of the FA Cup. It would mark the official opening of the Platt Lane Stand. The game would be screened live by the BBC. Before kick-off Alan Hansen explained to Des Lynam why he thought City would win the trophy.

Mike Sheron opened the scoring for City. Towards the end of the game, Terry Phelan demanded Tony Coton give him the ball and ran the length of the pitch to score. In between, Tottenham had struck four. Had Teddy Sheringham not missed a penalty and had not a goal been dubiously disallowed, they would have scored six.

With two minutes remaining, the crowd began spilling on to the pitch amid Barry Davies' tut-tutting commentary. 'Too many idiots on the pitch,' he said. 'We thought these days had passed.' Hansen wondered what they would make of these pictures abroad while Jimmy Hill talked of how the scenes 'shame the whole of football'.

By the end there were thirteen police horses on the pitch brought in from the stables at Hough End. Within a year, Swales would meet Francis Lee at the

Swan in Bucklow Hill, where England's cricketers used to stay before Test matches at Old Trafford, to hand over control. He would never visit Maine Road again.

Lee was an authentic hero. When he scored the goal that would win Manchester City the championship in 1968, he ran to the away supporters crammed into St James' Park and stood among them, arms aloft.

He had never quite forgiven Swales for authorising his sale to Derby in 1974. The transfer, however, proved a happy one. Lee won another championship with Derby the following year and while he was at the Baseball Ground, Lee developed his business, FH Lee, that converted waste paper into toilet tissue. By 1976 its turnover was double that of Manchester City. He would sell the business for £8.5m (£58m in today's terms).

'He looked like an unlikely revolutionary,' says Niall Quinn, who in 2006 would launch a takeover of Sunderland that was infinitely less bloody and worked rather better than Lee's. 'Small, paunchy and opinionated. I felt his time in charge was a disaster. Top players proved too expensive. The game had changed more than he could have imagined and was on the verge of changing even more violently.

'He seemed to want to be hands on in every aspect of the club's existence, which meant he couldn't leave his manager to manage. One day, to our shock, he came in and gave the team-talk with Brian Horton standing in the corner looking embarrassed and humiliated.'

Lee did not appoint Horton but his choices of manager would be uniformly disastrous, although there was a case to be made for all of them. Alan Ball had just completed a successful season at Southampton and knew Lee well. Steve Coppell was one of the most innovative and intelligent young managers in the country. Frank Clark had been voted manager of the year at Nottingham Forest.

Joe Royle was technically appointed under his chairmanship, but his regime was in its last throes and it was Royle's understanding that Lee wanted Clark to continue. The deal was done by Dennis Tueart, acting on behalf of the club's biggest shareholders, David Makin and John Wardle.

Tueart was brought in by Wardle and Makin because Lee dominated discussions about football in the boardroom and both men felt they could not compete with a man who had won two league titles. When Royle was introduced to the press by Lee, he had the feeling the chairman's time was already up.

At the start of it all, Lee would have long talks with Alan Ball in which he would tell a man he had known all his adult life that 'the golden rule of management was not to criticise your employees until after they have left'.

Lee would also remark that Ball would leave the chairman's house, the Stanneylands Stud, having agreed one course of action and then see Ball implement something else entirely. He seemed to have no rapport with Clark, while Coppell lasted 33 days. Quinn wondered why Lee had never tried to manage the club himself.

It was the time of the fanzines, when supporters who previously had no other outlet to express their frustrations than writing a letter to the local paper, and who saw the matchday programmes as little more than club propaganda, began producing their own publications.

With them came the rise of the radio phone-ins, which became national when the BBC launched *606*, presented by Danny Baker, in 1991.

Noel Bayley ran and edited *Bert Trautmann's Helmet*, which joined *Blueprint* and the most successful of them all, *King of the Kippax*, on sale outside Maine Road. Bayley is now a Labour councillor in Bury and we met near the most beautifully-named stop on the Manchester metro, Besses o' th'Barn.

'Our first issue came out on the day of Hillsborough. We were at Blackburn and were beaten 4-0,' he says. 'People had stopped buying programmes and *Blueprint*, which was the first City fanzine, was revolutionary. It gave ordinary Manchester City supporters a voice.

'The *Evening News* never seemed to give us anything in those days. They led on United with everything, back page, front page. City only seemed to be the lead article when it was something negative.

'It has changed now but, if you know anything about the history of newspapers in Manchester, there were two. *The Evening News* was, broadly speaking, a United paper and *The Evening Chronicle* generally led on City. Naturally, the City paper folded.

'*King of the Kippax* had great cartoons. *Blueprint* was quite intellectual and had articles on European football, which nobody bothered about in those days – continental football it was called. I like to think we had some terrace wit and gallows humour. By the mid-1990s we had five with *Chips and Gravy* and *City 'til I Cry*.

'I used to do everything myself. Write or edit the copy, take the photos with a Nikon F50 or beg, steal or borrow them from elsewhere and take it to be printed in Washway Road in Sale. I never made any real money from it because you had to go to all the games to sell it and, if you were going to somewhere like Charlton, you had to leave at six in the morning.

'The Soccer Shop on Claremont Road used to sell it. So did Sports Pages in Barton Square, News Stand on Cross Street and Sports Pages on Charing Cross Road in London. They have all gone in the space of fifteen years.

'Dave Wallace has been running *King of the Kippax* for 29 years, which is an astonishing achievement. When Francis Lee became chairman, he offered Dave a place on the board as the fans' representative.

'Like a lot of what Francis Lee did, it was a good idea that became a fiasco. The following year, he ran a vote to see who it would be. We were going to press a day before the result was announced so I phoned the club to see if they could give me a steer on who'd won. They said, "The chairman hasn't decided yet." The idea just dwindled away.

'The picture of Francis Lee with his arms aloft at Newcastle was our first cover. We bought into the Francis Lee campaign but we were always on the periphery. You'd meet someone and they would push a leaflet into your hand saying: "Demonstration at such and such a time. Be there". But I've never been a sheep and I wouldn't go and you'd never see the guy again.

'The problem was Peter Swales. He was a politician with no policies whose only mantra was "give me another year and I'll get it right". And a year became another year and another. We had an issue published back to front with Niall Quinn on the cover. It was called "Backwards with Swales" as a pun on the "Forward with Franny" campaign. It was supposed to make a statement but it just ended up confusing people.'

'Francis Lee used to ring me up quite a bit, though he doesn't any more, obviously. He was a narcissist who thought everyone should agree with him. I suppose when you have won two championships, played for England in the World Cup in Mexico and run a successful business you expect to be agreed with.'

In September 1993 Lee was walking towards the reception at Maine Road to watch City beat Queens Park Rangers, 3-0. He was being mobbed by supporters whose watchword was 'Forward with Franny'. The takeover had begun.

By then Swales was cornered, abused and probably knew he was beaten. Chris Muir, his staunchest ally on the board, commented that he looked dreadful. The protests moved from the stadium to his home in Bowdon.

In an interview with the BBC journalists, Andy Buckley and Richard Burgess, for their book *Blue Moon Rising*, his wife, Brenda, said, 'I wouldn't let any of my daughters or granddaughters come round to the house.

'We had security men on the gate, it was really quite frightening. We also had a lot of death threats on the answer phone.'

The last time Brenda Swales went to Maine Road was November 1993, a 3-1 defeat by Sheffield Wednesday. 'I came home and the house was surrounded by security men. I didn't know what was happening, so I went inside and looked out of the bedroom window.

'It was hard to believe but there were police all round the back garden. Apparently, pubs had received maps to our house, asking people to come round and sort Peter out.'

Lee, who was to endure much the same before his chairmanship was two years old, condemned the abuse – although as Tueart remarked 'he wasn't exactly scathingly critical' – but it was the club's shareholders, rather than the mob, who forced Swales out.

At the annual general meeting, they voted 79-52 not to re-elect him as a director. It was overturned on a fresh vote, based on the value of the shareholdings, but Swales resigned as chairman.

In the remaining months, he tried his utmost to prevent Manchester City falling into the hands of Francis Lee. Steve Morrison, the managing director of Granada Television, was his first choice to be the new chairman.

Morrison had been the executive producer of *My Left Foot*, the film about the Irish artist Christy Brown, which had won Daniel Day-Lewis the best actor Oscar. Morrison was interested but decided he could not spare the time.

Mike McDonald, who had made his money from scrap-metal and engineering, was interested when approached by Swales, who said the club was 'absolutely desperate for money'. He offered a £2m loan without any preconditions. 'To be honest, they were having difficulty paying the wages,' he recalled.

However, Swales could not force the appointment past the board. The vote was lost 4-3. Ian Niven, loyal to Swales for nearly twenty years, believed Francis Lee, who appeared the overwhelming choice of the club's fans, should not be thwarted. In February 1994, the club's centenary year, Lee flew back from Barbados to claim his prize. The deal to replace Swales was concluded shortly after midnight.

It had been a messy, protracted, bitter takeover but Maine Road, one of football's great winter palaces, had been stormed. Lee was in expansive mood. 'This will be the happiest club in the land,' he said. 'The players will be the best paid and we'll drink plenty of champagne and sing until we're hoarse.'

As failed campaign promises went, it matched Harold Wilson's pledge that he would 'cut prices at a stroke', a piece of charlatanry that John Sullivan incorporated into his theme song for *Only Fools and Horses*. Dennis Tueart, watching from the sidelines, thought the bluster concealed plenty of self-doubt. Immediately afterwards, Lee had given an interview to Sky Sports in which he said he would resign if Manchester City had not been turned around in three years.

If Lee's promise of champagne and song had been uttered by the rather less ebullient Jack Walker, who was fourteen months away from transforming Blackburn from a second-division backwater into the champions of England, it would have held good.

However successful FH Lee had been, as a business it was not Walker Steel. Lee paid £3m for his shares but he never controlled more than thirteen percent of Manchester City. Just as Peter Swales did, he would be forced to rely on alliances to see him through.

'The club's first public accounts when I arrived showed a turnover of £4m and they had bought two players, from Wimbledon, for £6m,' Lee said. 'Furthermore, they had bought them on hire purchase, £3m for Keith Curle, £3m for Terry Phelan. You didn't have to be Columbo to see things weren't right.'

Lee was faced with immediate bills to pay. One was for £15,000 to replace Maine Road's boiler, which Lee said, 'looked like something out of *The African Queen*'. There were some bigger ones. The Kippax, the biggest stand of all, had to be redeveloped to comply with the Taylor Report's insistence on all-seater stadia.

When it had been torn down, it was discovered the Kippax had been built on a mound of ashes which, classified as contaminated waste, would cost £1m to remove. It would prove an omen.

Moss Side Story

REVOLUTIONS WERE NOT CONFINED TO INSIDE MAINE ROAD. Outside the stadium, in the red-brick streets, Moss Side seemed to some to be turning away from Manchester City. An area that had once been a talent pool on the club's very doorstep was drying up – or had been allowed to dry up.

Andrew Bridge was eight years old and, from his bedroom window, Moss Side was burning. It was unimaginably thrilling.

It was the summer of 1981. For suburban England it was the summer of the Royal Wedding, the summer in which Ian Botham routed the Australians and became the most famous sportsman in Britain. In inner-city England, in the St Paul's district of Bristol, in Brixton, Toxteth and Moss Side, it was the summer of the petrol bomb and the riot shield.

'We were all in the front room when it happened,' says Andrew, whose path out of Moss Side was to include first football and then music. 'When we heard the police sirens, we switched off the lights, there were people running across our garden, petrol bombs were being thrown. Fights were happening outside our door.

'It seemed like something from a television show. Mum was shouting at me to get away from the window, so I went upstairs and watched it from my bedroom. I could see fireworks going off and cars being set on fire.'

A few days earlier, the six-year-old Robbie Fowler had peered through the curtains of his home in Toxteth and been gripped by much the same thing. It was, he said, 'like watching a civil war from your front room'.

The green copper roof of Fowler's local cinema, the Rialto in Liverpool's

Upper Parliament Street, was still glowing red when violence began to flare outside the Nile, Manchester's leading black nightclub, and spread.

Princess Road, less than a mile from Maine Road, became the front line. Lester Williams, a 37-year-old member of what became known as the Windrush Generation, found himself caught up in the violence as he walked his Alsatian, Max, from their home in Raby Street.

A policeman had become stranded from the rest of his line, the crowd was surging towards him. Williams, who was then in a reggae group called Harlem Spirit, shouted to the crowd, 'You cannot kill someone for doing their job'. The surge stopped. The policeman, in full riot gear, escaped by hurling himself through a glass front door.

There were some surreal moments. During the second day, as the crowd milled around, ice cream vans came out to ply their trade. The police, under the command of James Anderton, the bearded, religiously conservative chief constable of Greater Manchester, formed a double line by the vast Royal Brewery that guarded the southern approaches to the city centre. The rioting was contained and subsided.

The year of the riots, 1981, was the year that Alex Williams made his debut for Manchester City. Williams, born in Moss Side, became the first black goalkeeper to play in the top-flight. His school, Wilbrahim High – now called Whalley Range High – had a fearsome reputation in Manchester football. In the four years Williams kept goal they lost one home game.

In front of Williams was Gary Bennett, who was to captain Sunderland and Roger Palmer, who was to become Oldham's record goalscorer. Euclid Wilson, known to everyone as Clive, and who would play for Chelsea, Queens Park Rangers and Tottenham, was on the left-wing.

This young, black talent was initially signed by the club that stood half a mile away from the school. Three of them would play for Manchester City in the 1980 FA Youth Cup final.

Williams thought City's nurturing of black footballers was as good as West Bromwich Albion's with Laurie Cunningham, Cyrille Regis and Brendon Batson. However, given that Ron Atkinson's 'Three Degrees' came close to winning the league title in 1979, City's black footballers received far less publicity.

There were the usual humiliations. Gary Bennett's brother, Dave, who played 54 times for Manchester City and won the FA Cup with Coventry in 1987, was denied entry to the Britannia nightclub. Nicky Reid, who was with him, was allowed in. Both men were wearing suits.

When Williams was running towards the Gwladys Street End at Goodison Park, he saw an Everton fan make a crucifix from two rolled up programmes and set fire to it to mimic the burning cross of the Ku Klux Klan. When Williams turned to his teammates for support, he found them laughing at the absurdity of the scene.

However, when speaking to the Liverpool academic, Emy Onoura, for his study of race in British football, *Pitch Black*, Williams argued that Manchester City had formed deep links with the area that surrounded it.

'We were all from the heart of Moss Side which at that time was very much an Afro-Caribbean area,' he said. 'The club was great. I never thought of myself as a black footballer or a black goalkeeper. It was just a great place to be.'

Those links may have been deep but they were not enduring and, in the years after the riots, they began to fray until many came to believe that Manchester City had turned its back on Moss Side.

'Football was massive in Moss Side, especially the Alexandra Park Estate, where I grew up,' says Andrew Bridge. 'In the middle of Quinney Crescent there was a football pitch and a five-a-side pitch that was loaded every evening. There were five-a-side pitches on Claremont Road, on Maine Road and on the Rec Park.

'There would be challenge matches organised against teams from Longsight or Hulme and the weird thing was that the gangs used to take part in them. When it came to football, the gang divisions ceased to matter.

'You had all these football pitches, all these lads playing football and a massive club on their doorstep. Yet, in my time, I don't think there was one player that Manchester City signed from Moss Side or one that even got a trial. Adie and Leon Mike did play for City in the 1990s but they were signed from Trafford Park which was a club with strong links to Manchester United.

'I played against professional footballers and I know there were players on my estate who were good enough but who did not get a look in. I don't know why City did not engage with the football being played on Moss Side.'

There may have been several reasons for the breakdown in relations between the club and the community that surrounded it. Talent is cyclical.

When David O'Leary inherited the glittering products of Leeds' youth policy – Alan Smith, Harry Kewell, Stephen McPhail and Jonathan Woodgate – he remarked that this was a gift you received once in a managerial lifetime. Moss Side's footballers may not have been as good as they once were.

However, and perhaps more significantly, at the start of the 1990s, Manchester City's scouting system, which had been vastly superior to United's – 'they seemed to be in every school' in Alex Ferguson's words – was in sharp decline.

Ferguson may have inherited the team that had made the 1986 FA Youth Cup final but they had been easily beaten by City. When asked to describe his inheritance from Ron Atkinson, he shouted, 'What youth policy? He has left me a shower of shit.'

Ferguson, appalled that United used only four scouts to cover the North West – his former club, Aberdeen, employed thirteen across central Scotland – ordered a complete overhaul. The balance began swinging back to Old Trafford.

Peter Swales was in the habit of sending his chief scout, Ken Barnes, memos asking why he was offering complementary tickets and hospitality at Maine Road to parents of promising young footballers.

Barnes, who thought Swales 'a shit who knew nothing about football', recalled: 'I wanted to make Maine Road a special place for the young lads and their parents. It wasn't fucking rocket science.

'I can still remember a certain look you would get on a dad's face. You just knew he couldn't wait for Monday, to get to work and tell his mates he had met Colin Bell. Bugger me; I was being asked to justify a few tickets and some sandwiches.'

In 1991, Peter Reid, acting on instructions from Swales, called Barnes into his office and fired him. For Manchester City's new manager, it was an excruciating conversation. 'He asked if I wanted a drink,' Barnes remembered. 'He was a bit embarrassed. I said, "No thanks, but it looks like you could do with one."'

The training facilities they could offer at the council-owned pitches at Platt Lane were becoming hopelessly antiquated. 'We had to give priority to community groups,' Jim Cassell, who took over the Manchester City academy in 1998, recalls. 'Local students had the pitches on a Wednesday afternoon.

Our Under-16s had to train from 9-10pm. If you went on the wrong five-a-side pitch, you'd be playing with the taxi drivers. We had to leave rooms free for Weight Watchers.'

The finest black football talent in Manchester to break through in the 1990s did not come from Moss Side but from the Whitefield Estate in the north of the city. Trevor Sinclair was not spotted by either City or United but joined Blackpool as a sixteen-year-old, just in time, he said, to rescue him from the temptations of criminality. Sinclair would be thirty when he joined Manchester City, a year after delivering some outstanding performances in the 2002 World Cup.

Andrew Bridge was quick, quicker than just about any other footballer on the pitches of Moss Side. He played for Cheadle Town, up front with Steve Bushell, who would sign a professional contract with York and Halifax. Alongside them was Dominic Orange, whose older brother, Jason, had completed the journey from a Manchester break-dance crew to joining Take That.

'It was weird growing up in Moss Side because Manchester City was just over there but it seemed unreachable. The only way out seemed to be to get to Mike McKenzie, who was the Alex Ferguson of Moss Side.'

Mike McKenzie was manager of Astro, a hugely successful Sunday League team that played in the heart of Moss Side and became national champions. In 1994 McKenzie became manager of Hyde United. In his first season, Hyde reached the first round of the FA Cup, the semi-final of the FA Trophy and won the Manchester Premier Cup.

'There was so much natural talent there,' is how Andrew Bridge remembers Astro. 'But you didn't see City much, not even in the schools.' It was the same when the vibrant colours, sights and smells of the Caribbean Carnival swirled around the outskirts of Maine Road.

'I can't remember a time when either club attended Carnival,' he says. 'Clive Lloyd (the captain of Lancashire and the West Indies) and Clive Wilson would come down but, other than that, nobody.'

Moss Side was changing. Basketball courts were slowly replacing the five-a-side pitches. The most famous sportsman to emerge from the area was now Darren Campbell, who would win relay gold in the Athens Olympics.

Andrew Bridge remembers going to church past the five-a-side pitches 'suited and booted' but the churches were weakening, gang violence was increasing, the Afro-Caribbean population began moving out.

Andrew Bridge was among them and his mode of exit was music in a group managed by Lisa Lewis, who was best known for being Curly Watts' girlfriend in *Coronation Street*.

There were gigs at the Night Centre in Rusholme, where *Top of the Pops* was first broadcast in 1964 with the Rolling Stones opening the programme with 'I Want to Be Your Man'. There were recording sessions at Moonraker Studios with Johnny Jay, one of Manchester's leading producers, who had discovered 808 State and overseen remixes for The Human League.

'It wasn't Abbey Road but we did get some attention from Caroline Elleray who worked for BMG Publishing and whose claim to fame was Oasis – and later Coldplay and Adele. We did *In the City* for her which was an event for the music industry looking for local talent.

'There was a contract but they wanted to sign Johnny Jay as part of the group, but we just wanted him to be our producer and manager. We turned it down and in 1997 you didn't turn down Sony Records. That was us pretty much done.'

If Moss Side's black population felt pushed away by Manchester City, others were gravitating towards it.

On March 13 1988, Andy King went to his first game at Maine Road to watch Liverpool beat a young, spirited Manchester City, 4-0 in the FA Cup quarter-final. Aside from the fact that it was the first time City had been beaten by Liverpool in the competition and that a fan ran on to the pitch to confront the referee, Alan Gunn, for awarding a penalty, it was unremarkable. Except for the fact that Andy was a gay teenager.

He still goes and was behind the goal, eleven rows back, 'with fathers and sons all around me in tears', when Sergio Aguero shot past Paddy Kenny to give Manchester City their first title since 1968, the year after homosexuality ceased to be a criminal act, at least in private.

'Like so many City fans, I can barely remember what we did that night. We did end up in a gay pub, where there were loads of City shirts.

'That showed how everything had changed. When I first started going to Maine Road, you knew to be very wary and keep a low profile, but it was the same when you went to Canal Street (which formed the heart of Manchester's

Gay Village). They would ask why you were wearing a football shirt; they were very suspicious of football. They thought it aggressive, macho and nothing to do with us.'

Andy King now watches Manchester City as part of a group called Canal Street Blues, who bring their own banner to the Etihad Stadium, which flies the Rainbow Flag during Manchester's Pride Festival. Given the club is ultimately owned by the government of Abu Dhabi, which prescribes fourteen years' imprisonment for homosexuality, this is a remarkably independent act.

If Manchester United were better at making money – installing corporate boxes and opening a megastore while Maine Road still had its little souvenir shop – City forged the better links with its community.

'Old Trafford still has no LGBT supporters' association and has only just started a women's football team when we have had one for years,' Andy King says. 'I think that shows City are much better at representing modern Manchester, but could I have been comfortable being an openly gay football fan at Maine Road? Not a chance.'

It was not a comfortable time for anyone to be gay and living in Manchester. The chief constable, James Anderton, a Methodist lay preacher turned Catholic convert, was a man whose zeal to rekindle a kind of 1950s morality in Manchester saw him lampooned by the Happy Mondays in their song, 'God's Cop'.

Anderton began with raids on 248 bookshops and newsagents to seize pornography – which included *The Sun's* Page Three Annual. Then he turned his attention to the gay community, already stricken by the AIDS epidemic, which he accused of 'swirling around in a cesspool of their own making'.

One tactic was to send police motorboats up the Rochdale Canal at night. The boat would switch its engines off and then turn on its searchlights to scour the bridges and wharves around Canal Street for evidence of men together. Anderton retired in 1991. Greater Manchester Police is now officially represented at the Pride Festival.

'It was only during the early 1990s that you could feel comfortable going into the village for a night out,' says Andy King. 'Then, you had the breweries investing, the likes of Mofo with its big glass windows that proclaimed that nothing was going to be hidden and the series *Queer as Folk* which was filmed in and around the village. It became commercialised, normal. Before that, you had to be very careful.

'One of the emotions I did have walking to Maine Road was fear. Fear of trouble, fear of the gangs who may or may not have been lurking outside. I remember being very wary going to that first match. I wanted to be deep inside the crowd, anonymous. When I got inside the ground it was astonishingly friendly, especially after the match when Liverpool and City fans walked out together.

'I was bowled over by the atmosphere. Then, the inflatable bananas were being carried everywhere and there was a novelty shop selling them. The crowd would be much younger than you see now. Most of the people I am around now at the Etihad went to Maine Road. The crowd has just got older.

'I lost my dad when I was two but I gather he was a City fan. It was the 1981 team that got to the cup final, players like Tommy Hutchison, that really excited me. I couldn't imagine a footballer then even hinting he was gay. There would have been constant taunting, jokes and songs, even if he were a Manchester City player.

'The culture in the 1970s and 80s was based on emphasising and pointing out differences. It was almost victimisation. Look what happened to Justin Fashanu. He hanged himself.'

In October 1989 Manchester City signed Fashanu on a short-term contract. His manager, Mel Machin, would have known about his sexuality. Brian Clough, who was a socialist but not a libertarian, had warned him about being seen in Nottingham's gay clubs during his time at Forest.

Clough referred to them as 'poofs' clubs'. Frank Clark, who was to manage Fashanu at Leyton Orient, was far more sympathetic. He tried to persuade Fashanu to come out, arguing that the headlines would fade and 'the lads thought the world of him'. Fashanu replied that he was terrified of the consequences.

Machin had been reserve-team manager at Norwich under John Bond when Fashanu, with his back to goal, had flicked the ball up with his right foot and turned to drive it past Ray Clemence with his left, to score the goal of the 1979/80 season. Liverpool had won that game, 5-3, but the goal was remembered longer than the result.

Bond had attempted to sign Fashanu for Manchester City when he left Carrow Road the following year, but he preferred Nottingham Forest and

Clough, a man who did not remotely pretend to understand him.

Eight years later he arrived at Maine Road to a headline in the *Manchester Evening News* that said 'Thanks a Million', a reference to the price Bond had been prepared to pay. Now, he was a free transfer from Edmonton Brick Men, who played in the vast flatlands of central Canada.

He had initially come to Manchester in January and played a couple of reserve games. In the first he had scored against Manchester United after a dozen minutes.

However, his knee had never fully recovered from an injury sustained while playing at Ipswich on New Year's Eve 1983 and Machin allowed him to return to Edmonton, where he was offered the job of player-manager, in front of crowds that never rose above 4,000. He scored seventeen times in 26 matches.

In October, Machin brought him back to Maine Road. 'I only agreed to let him come back out of sympathy,' he recalled. 'I didn't really believe it would work out for him.' However, once more Fashanu dazzled in a reserve fixture. He and Clive Allen scored five between them against Notts County.

A month after the 5-1 rout of United, Machin's regime was close to disintegration. Fashanu was given two matches. The first, at home to Aston Villa, saw him booed on by the away support. There were twenty minutes left and the match was already lost. His second and final game was the 6-0 humiliation at Derby which prompted Peter Swales to start searching for a new manager.

Fashanu's agent, the convicted fraudster Ambrose Mendy, who also managed Paul Ince and Nigel Benn, attempted to arrange a free transfer to Ipswich, which collapsed on Mendy's insistence that they paid a £300,000 signing-on fee for a man who had not scored a top-flight goal in six years.

He joined West Ham. His first game was against Wimbledon, the team his brother played for. A year later, just before he revealed in sexuality in *The Sun*, in exchange for £100,000, John Fashanu would offer his brother £75,000 not to do the interview. 'I begged him, I threatened him,' John recalled long afterwards. 'I did everything I possibly could to stop him coming out.

'I gave him the money because I didn't want the embarrassment for me or my family. Had he come out now, it would have been a different ball game. Now, he'd be hailed as a hero.'

Under the Volcano

'CITY FANS HAVE THIS THING THAT AS LONG AS YOU LOOK GOOD in the kit or sat in the dugout, then it doesn't matter what you're like,' Noel Gallagher once remarked. 'Howard Kendall didn't look cool and neither did Brian Horton whereas Malcolm Allison did. He turned up at Monday morning training in a white Rolls-Royce with a bottle of champagne and some actress in the back of a car. That's football management.'

Brian Horton is driving a Mercedes when we meet. There is no model in the back seat and no champagne bucket by the dashboard, although the surroundings are glamorous enough. San Carlo is the Manchester footballer's restaurant of choice.

On the walls are photographs of some of the more famous customers, David Beckham and other members of the Class of '92. Manuel Pellegrini stares out from a frame. Sir Alex Ferguson has been a frequent visitor. Underneath the white marble surfaces lobsters stand on ice. Malcolm, you feel, would have approved of San Carlo.

Horton was the twelfth and last man Peter Swales appointed to manage Manchester City. He stands with Mel Machin as being the most left-field of his choices. In David White's words: 'We just couldn't believe Brian Horton had been given the job. When we were told, there was uproar in the dressing room. Some of the players literally hadn't heard of him.'

When John Maddock called a press conference to introduce Manchester City's new manager, the first question Horton had to deal with was: 'Who are you?'

'I thought that was poor journalism,' Horton says. 'I'd played in the top flight for Brighton and Luton and I'd managed in what would now be the Championship for nearly a decade. I'd been part of a side that put Manchester City down and they really didn't know who I was? I thought that was nasty.'

Some of Manchester City's supporters should have known exactly who Brian Horton was. In May 1983, he had captained Luton at Maine Road in a game David Pleat's side had needed to win to survive. Manchester City had only required a point to secure their own status.

City's subsequent defeat wrecked all of Swales' plans to turn Maine Road into one of the great stadia of Europe and sent the club into a steepling financial decline. When in the months after his appointment Horton went to supporters' meetings, it was a game that was invariably brought up. It was not the first and it would not be the last relegation in Manchester City's history, but it was probably the most damaging.

The final whistle saw Pleat, in his light grey suit, skip and dance across the pitch hands above his head. 'What an amazing act of escapology this is,' said John Motson into his BBC microphone. The first man he embraced was his captain, Brian Horton.

Pleat had taken an enormous, if considered, gamble. The previous weekend had seen Luton beaten 5-1 by Everton at Kenilworth Road. They had two games remaining – one at Old Trafford, the other at Maine Road. Pleat decided to field a weakened side at Manchester United and stake everything on the final match against City.

Given that United could not win the league and were preparing for an FA Cup final, it seems doubly strange – Ron Atkinson's side lost their last two matches to Tottenham and Notts County before heading to Wembley. However, in its perverse way, it worked.

Luton lost, 3-0, at Old Trafford on the Monday night. Five days later at Maine Road with the game deadlocked, Pleat gambled again, bringing on Raddy Antić, whose desultory performances that season had amounted to one goal. Five minutes from time he scored.

'David Pleat was my mentor throughout my career,' says Horton, who was to manage more than a thousand games. 'He was a superb tactician, well ahead of his time. You look at the Tottenham sides he managed; he had Clive Allen as the lone striker in the days when everybody played two. Spurs were set up like all Premier League clubs are now. He, not Graham Taylor, should have been given the England job when Bobby Robson stepped down.' As it was, Pleat was not even interviewed.

'He is still embarrassed by the film of him running on to the pitch but it was such a fantastic moment. It personifies the emotion of the game. It was a packed house. The pressure was all on Luton but Manchester City were playing for a draw that day and I have always thought to play for a draw is one of the hardest things in football.'

The final whistle had seen a sullen, aggressive pitch invasion of a wearily familiar kind in the early 1980s and the Luton team bus was pelted with missiles. 'As we pulled away the police told us to get down. We lay down on the floor of the coach and we could hear objects hitting the side of the bus. By the time we got to Stafford the beer was flowing and I was struck by the thought that my contract was up that day. I was done.

'I was 34 and there had been no suggestion from Luton that I would be offered a new deal so when I got home I began the process of phoning clubs and, finally, out of the blue, David phoned me and asked if I wanted two more years at Luton.'

His answer had been the kind of immediate 'yes' he had given Maddock when he phoned in the hours after Peter Reid's dismissal. Unlike Reid, Horton both knew and liked John Maddock. They had known each other since he was a player at Port Vale and Maddock had joined them on a pre-season tour of Malta that ended with the players putting the journalist's bed on to the hotel balcony.

Maddock was one of the generation of journalists who printed much, much less than he knew – and he knew an awful lot. In the age of Twitter the reverse is usually true. The number of secrets he kept made him hugely powerful.

Maddock had recommended Horton to Swales as Mel Machin's successor in 1989 but found himself negotiating Howard Kendall's move to Maine Road instead. Now Maddock campaigned for Horton again. 'The professional's professional,' he called him.

As he drove south to interview Manchester City's new manager, Maddock phoned GMR radio's breakfast show to tease them about who he might be meeting. He said he had been on the road since half five in the morning. It was now eight thirty. The fact he was going south killed the fantasy of appointing

Kevin Keegan, who in eighteen months at Newcastle had made himself the most charismatic manager in English football. It was generally assumed he would be driving to Leicester to meet Brian Little.

Instead, he and Freddie Pye, the scrap metal merchant who was one of Swales' closest allies on the board, left the M6 at junction 14, the turn-off to Stafford, and met Horton at Tillington Hall. Three hours to Stafford sounds excessive, even for the M6, but it was an interesting delegation for Swales to send. If Maddock was enthusiastic about the impending appointment, Pye was suspicious. He believed Manchester City needed a 'name'.

There were reasons other than friendship for Maddock insisting they met Brian Horton. Although he had never managed in the top flight, he had never been relegated and in the late summer of 1993 that seemed a valuable claim for any Manchester City manager to have on their CV.

By then the revolt against Swales had grown vicious, ugly and very public and Horton had plenty of experience of dealing with unstable boardrooms. He had worked for the Maxwells. More importantly, he had outlasted them.

Of all the thoughts that churned in Robert Maxwell's mind in the small hours of 5 November 1991, as he stood on deck as his yacht *Lady Ghislaine* steered the passage between Gran Canaria and Tenerife, it is safe to assume Oxford United was not among them.

His sprawling media empire, the Maxwell Communications Corporation, was haemorrhaging £3m in interest payments every day. He had ransacked the company's pension funds and those of Mirror Group Newspapers to stave off bankruptcy and it had not been enough. Collapse might only be hours away. The still, black waters of the Atlantic must have seemed inviting.

Horton had by then been manager of Oxford for three years, all of them testing. He had gone to the Manor Ground as assistant to Mark Lawrenson. In October 1988, an hour and a half before the game against Blackburn was due to kick-off, Lawrenson was in his office sorting out tickets to leave at the gate when Oxford's chairman, Kevin Maxwell, Robert's son and anointed heir, phoned to tell him that his best striker, Dean Saunders, was to be sold to Derby, whose chairman was Robert Maxwell.

On the Sunday, Lawrenson met the Maxwells in London to be told that where Saunders played was 'none of his business'. 'I told them they could stuff the job,' Lawrenson recalled, 'and I drove home in a state of complete bewilderment.' The next day he returned to the Manor Ground to tender his resignation only to be informed he had already been sacked. Nobody resigned on the Maxwells. Horton took over.

In a book of football writing called *My Favourite Year*, Ed Horton, an Oxford fan, described the feverish state of the place a couple of months before Maxwell's death. 'There was an air of poisoned decline about the city whose famous Cowley car works was on the way to closure. The city was losing its pride and its sense of community; the football club reflected the depression.

'The disillusion was dramatically expressed at the start of September in a spate of joyriding displays and subsequent rioting. A city built on cars was stealing them and wrecking them in the dead of night.'

As the club's finances collapsed with the rest of the empire that was to leave Kevin Maxwell as Britain's biggest bankrupt, owing £406.5m, Horton kept Oxford together. They finished one place and two points off relegation in 1992, one position below Newcastle, who had persuaded themselves that Keegan, who had spent most of the last eight years in Marbella completely cut off from football, could salvage them.

Newcastle won promotion to the Premier League the following year but Oxford's performance, finishing in mid-table while struggling against the financial tide, was in its way as worthy of applause.

'It may surprise you but in three years of dealing with him I found Kevin Maxwell to be one of the best chairmen you could ever work for,' says Horton. 'But when his dad died all the funding stopped. The cars had to go back, the mobile phones were cut off and Kevin told me bluntly we had to sell some players to keep Oxford United going.

'I'd spent nearly a quarter of a million quid bringing Paul Simpson in from Manchester City, but he had to go. We sold him to Derby. Mark Stein went, so did Robbie Mustoe.

'I was told we had to sell Jim Magilton, almost on deadline day. I told Kevin that if we sold our captain and best player we would go down. I couldn't do any more in the dressing room. He told me to leave it with him. I hadn't a clue what Kevin did but we kept Jim and won the final game at Tranmere to stay up.'

The call from Maddock came out of the blue. At Tillington Hall, Pye found Horton's enthusiasm engaging. 'Freddie was totally sold on the idea of bringing in Brian,' Maddock recalled. 'I knew him as a straight, honest, good manager which he proved to be at City without any proper backing.'

Horton's first taste of Maine Road was the 1-1 draw with Coventry on the Friday night. He sat in the Umbro Stand, as the Platt Lane Stand was now called, enveloped by what City's goalkeeper, Tony Coton, thought one of the most unpleasant atmospheres he had ever encountered in a football ground. Once more Tony Book had put himself forward when Manchester City had most needed him. In Coton's words, 'he dredged a performance out of the team'.

Swales and Maddock were targets for most of the abuse inside the ground while, outside it, there was a vast protest that required police horses to be called up from the stables at Hough End.

It was probably something of a relief that Horton's first game as manager of Manchester City would be away. Swindon would come to the aid of a few managers in their one season in the Premier League.

They never recovered from Glenn Hoddle's decision to abandon them for Chelsea in the summer he had won them promotion. Swindon would go down conceding 100 goals. Both because of their proximity to Oxford and because they had long been in the same division, Horton knew them well. City won, 3-1.

There was not to be much respite. On 8 September, Francis Lee announced his bid to take over the club. John Maddock was persuaded to resign, depriving Horton of a valuable ally. His first home game was against Queens Park Rangers. It was won 3-0, with Garry Flitcroft playing and scoring from right-back, although the football did not make the headlines.

Lee made a very prominent return to Maine Road, the first since he had been sold to Derby by Swales in 1974. The atmosphere was feverish and messianic but when the crowd turned on their chairman, Maine Road became a bear pit.

For the next five months, there would be open civil war at Manchester City with Swales desperately attempting to stave off what seemed a defeat long foretold. It was nothing Horton had not seen before. The Manor Ground had seethed with anti-Maxwell sentiment and when his two clubs, Derby and Oxford, met the two sets of supporters serenaded each other with choruses of: 'We hate Maxwell more than you'.

There is, however, little doubt his players were dragged down by the conflict. When, on 4 February 1994 Swales met Lee at The Swan in Bucklow

Hill to sign the surrender documents and hand over control of the club, Manchester City were in the relegation zone, two points clear of Swindon in last place. They had won just a single Premier League fixture in four-and-a-half months.

The day after Swales left, Manchester City played Ipswich. Ten Thousand balloons were released to celebrate the new era, then Garry Flitcroft played a lazy, shrug-of-the-shoulders, diagonal back-pass straight to the Ipswich striker Ian Marshall and City were behind. Much had changed but, where it mattered, everything appeared the same.

Then they rallied. David Rocastle set up the equaliser and Flitcroft slid in the winner to earn redemption. It seemed a metaphor for a new Manchester City and so it was for a time.

One of Horton's most pressing concerns was the dressing room. 'It was full of senior players and if senior players don't want you, they can make or break a football manager.' When Frank Clark inherited the Nottingham Forest dressing room in 1993, a place where they had known only Brian Clough's voice and presence, he realised he was only likely to survive by winning over the captain, Stuart Pearce.

He did and for a while it seemed there could be glory at the City Ground without Clough. For Brian Horton, the key figure was Niall Quinn, who was at the very centre of that dressing room. When Swales had refused to pay for Paul Lake's girlfriend to accompany him to California for the surgery that might salvage his career, Quinn had organised a collection to pay the air fare to Los Angeles. Curiously, when Uwe Rösler joined Manchester City he, too, felt Quinn was the key player in the dressing room. He had to win his confidence.

At both Manchester City and Sunderland, Quinn was to be fiercely loyal to Peter Reid. After a toothless 2-0 defeat in the Tyne-Wear derby in September 2002 had put Reid very close to dismissal, Quinn went into the press room at St James' Park, sat on the stage, and accused the Sunderland players of betraying their manager.

The execution, however, was not long delayed. 'When Sunderland got rid of Peter Reid, I wasn't going to be involved with that,' he says. 'I didn't feel it was the right exit and so I left the club quickly.' Howard Wilkinson, Reid's successor, was unable to persuade Quinn to remain on Wearside and what had once been a tight dressing room disintegrated. Sunderland were relegated with nineteen points.

After Reid's sacking at Manchester City nine years earlier, the Dubliner had felt the same. He thought it was a decision Maddock had no right to make and there had been little footballing justification for it. He had publicly demanded a meeting with Swales.

Quinn might have gone. There was an offer to go to Everton to join Howard Kendall, who was in the middle of a frantic search for a big target man that would end in a blocked deal for Dion Dublin which triggered his second resignation from Goodison Park.

He stayed and though he recalls that he and Horton were initially 'never quite pals', certainly not the pals he and Reid had been, Quinn backed the new regime despite his fears that the foundations of the club were 'creaking and cracking'. Later, they became closer.

Tony Coton, too, was suspicious of Horton and his assistant, David Moss, because they had played with Andy Dibble, City's other goalkeeper, at Luton. 'I needn't have worried,' he reflected. 'I found them both to be honourable men who quickly gained the respect of the dressing room because of their openness and honesty with the players.'

Then for the last time, Swales made one of his grand gestures. Quinn was offered a five-year contract, a £750,000 signing-on fee and doubled wages. Two months later, during a 3-1 defeat at home to Sheffield Wednesday, Quinn attempted to turn while chesting the ball down. His studs get caught in the mud and he wrecks his cruciate ligaments.

'The fact is that we had to keep that squad together,' says Horton. 'They were good pros, good people, people like Tony Coton and Keith Curle. They were going to sell Steve Lomas. I kept him. I gave Garry Flitcroft a five-year deal. I signed Peter Beagrie and Uwe Rösler. Nicky Summerbee came in from Swindon. Suddenly, we were starting to play well. Suddenly, we were starting to win games.'

City lost three of their last seventeen matches. There were a lot of draws, many of them goalless, but in April three straight victories against Aston Villa, Southampton and Newcastle pulled them clear of the drop and they finished sixteenth.

It was far from glory but for a man who was supposed to be a nobody, thrust on to a stage thought far too big for him and forced to manage in the midst of a civil war, it was to prove a considerable achievement.

By then Horton had signed two strikers. One was Paul Walsh, who had been with him on the victorious Luton Town bus as it pulled away from Maine Road in 1983, curtains drawn and its occupants crouching down. The other was an unknown German named Uwe Rösler.

'Paul had been a kid when he played for Luton,' says Horton. 'You could never get the ball off him or persuade him to pass to anyone. When he lost the ball in the wrong areas, as his captain, I would have a right go at him. David Pleat would always defend Walshy because he wanted him to express his talent.

'By the time he came to Manchester City he was a better person and a better player. He absolutely shone when we beat Tottenham 5-2. They were his former club and he had such a point to prove.

'He was good in the dressing room, doing the kinds of things that managers don't see. The senior players like Walsh, Quinn and Curle – although not so much Rösler – would go out together which I didn't mind. It bonded them and it was a strong dressing room to begin with.'

As he drove up from Portsmouth, Walsh wondered what the fans would make of a thirty-something signed from a lower division for £750,000. There had been talk of Dean Saunders or Ian Rush. Walsh could never remember playing particularly well at Maine Road. Even in the relegation decider for Luton he had been anonymous.

'When I arrived in Manchester it was dull, miserable overcast and damp,' he remembered. 'The streets around Maine Road were all terraced and Moss Side wasn't the most picturesque area I'd ever visited. I found it all pretty depressing.' While waiting for his press conference, Walsh phoned his agent, Eric Hall, to ask if he could resurrect a move to West Ham.

When Walsh had signed for Liverpool, Hall had stepped in to tell the club's secretary, Peter Robinson, that if he wanted the player to appear on the 1984 Christmas calendar, an extra fee would be applicable. Even Kenny Dalglish posed for free. This time, however, even Hall was unable to overturn the transfer.

In his memoir, *Wouldn't It Be Good,* Walsh confessed that, initially, he and Rösler made 'no impact whatsoever'. Their partnership was launched with two matches at Maine Road. The first was lost 1-0 to Wimbledon, the second was a dreadful, goalless draw with Sheffield United on 19 March. Walsh and his family were being driven back to Portsmouth when they stopped at Sandbach Services in Cheshire.

He was spotted, standing in a queue for food, by a coachload of Manchester United supporters, travelling back from a 2-2 draw at Swindon. Almost at once they began pointing at him and chanting, 'What a difference you have made'.

'Things did start to improve,' he wrote. 'Gradually, the pieces began to fall into place. I could see Uwe liked running into the channels, trying to get behind the opposition's back four, whereas I liked to come in short and collect the ball from deep. A partnership began to form.'

Walsh thought the signing of Peter Beagrie from Everton was critical. It had always been Horton's intention to turn City into a fast, attacking team and with Beagrie and Nicky Summerbee on the flanks and Rösler and Walsh going through the middle, the club began to pack a punch.

In October 1994 came a knockout blow of the kind that was to be cherished as the decade became grimmer. The 5-2 victory over Tottenham stands comparison with the 5-1 defeat of Manchester United as one of the last great triumphs at Maine Road. John Moston thought it one of the best games of football he had commentated on. One caller to the BBC Radio Five phone-in *606* claimed watching it had been better than sex.

At home Manchester City had become a thrilling, daunting proposition. They would not lose at Maine Road until December, when they were beaten 2-1 by Arsenal. The team that destroyed Tottenham was spearheaded by two men with points to make.

Quinn had been infuriated by Manchester City's unwillingness to give the Irish FA reassurances he was fit enough to play in the World Cup in the United States. The summer had seen a move to Sporting Lisbon collapse as a result of what Quinn saw as Francis Lee's financial duplicity. He had become angry, driven and was playing some of the best football of his six years in Manchester.

Walsh had played for Tottenham at the peak of his career and had won the FA Cup with them but at White Hart Lane he had often been a shadow of the footballer he might have been. His time with Spurs had ended with his being substituted in a reserve game at Charlton. As he walked off, Walsh had thrown his shirt at Ray Clemence, Tottenham's reserve-team manager, and when Clemence threw it back Walsh had spun round and punched him in front of 3,000 witnesses.

On the morning of the game both Horton and the Tottenham manager, Ossie Ardiles, woke up in the same hotel, Mottram Hall. More than a year after his appointment, his family were still living in Oxfordshire. 'I had a beer with Ossie and his assistant Steve Perryman on the Friday night before the game,' says Horton. 'I was confident about the game. For some reason when I was at Luton we always seemed to be able to beat Tottenham in a way we never could when we played Liverpool or Manchester United. The football we played that day was fantastic.'

Tottenham under Ardiles were a far more glamorous and far more divided club than Manchester City. Desperately needing an appointment to placate a club in revolt after his sacking of Terry Venables, Alan Sugar had persuaded Ardiles to break his contract with West Bromwich Albion and return to White Hart Lane. Immediately, the Argentine realised the scale of his mistake.

'It was very, very political because the players did not want to play for Spurs,' he recalled. 'Or what I should say is that they did not want to play for Alan Sugar. I'd never had any enemies in England and, suddenly, I had enemies everywhere. A big, big part of the media was against me and so were many of the supporters and the players.'

Tottenham had finished fifteenth in 1994 on the same points as Manchester City. To quell further revolts, Sugar sanctioned the signings of Jurgen Klinsmann and Ilie Dumitrescu, who played in an attacking quintet that included Nicky Barmby, Teddy Sheringham and Darren Anderton. They were dubbed The Famous Five.

Ardiles noted that these were the same tactics that had won Brazil the World Cup in 1970 but, in the event, he might as well have played Dick, Julian, George and Anne while employing Timmy the dog wide on the left. Defensively, Tottenham were disastrously vulnerable.

They were destroyed by the wing play of Summerbee and Beagrie and the finishing of Quinn and especially Walsh, who at 32 played one of the matches of his life. For the fifth he dribbled furiously at the retreating Tottenham defence before squaring for Flitcroft. He had scored twice and made two of the others. The third, a flowing, incisive move featuring Beagrie, Quinn and Walsh would stand comparison with anything conjured by Pep Guardiola's footballers. They embraced the sound of the North Stand, which because the Kippax was in the middle of redevelopment housed the club's most fervent supporters.

This was the second time Ardiles had lost 5-2 to one of Horton's teams. In February 1992, Oxford had thrashed Newcastle at the Manor Ground. The next day at seven thirty in the morning Ardiles had opened his door to find the Newcastle chief executive, Freddie Fletcher, on his doorstep. 'Come in, Freddie,' Ardiles had said. 'Ossie, you're sacked,' came the reply in clipped Glaswegian tones. Not for nothing was Fletcher known as 'The Rottweiler'.

After this 5-2 defeat, Sugar gave Ardiles two more games. The first, a League Cup tie at Notts County, was lost, 3-0. West Ham were actually beaten at White Hart Lane in the next game, but Sugar had seen enough. He did not use the phrase he employs when he fires candidates he likes on *The Apprentice* – 'it is with regret' – but he did admit to being 'mortified'. Horton's own dismissal was six months away.

The following month came the Manchester derby on a Thursday night at Old Trafford. Alex Ferguson had been at Maine Road to see the destruction of Tottenham and he did not expect Brian Horton's tactics to change. Before kick-off, Ferguson turned to his assistant, Brian Kidd, and said, 'They're going to come and attack, they're not going to change. But, if they do attack, they're going to lose goals.' It was accurate enough. City conceded five. It was United's biggest win in a Manchester derby for a century. Andrei Kanchelskis became the first United player to score a hat-trick in the fixture since Alex Dawson had struck three at Old Trafford on New Year's Eve 1960.

Ferguson thought this was payback for the 5-1 defeat he had endured at Maine Road five long years before. In his office afterwards, he talked to Horton about that game and the impact it had wrought on him and Cathy. He kept a diary of that season and in it he wrote: 'Brian is in a difficult situation. A board has come in which didn't appoint him. I just hope it's going to go right because he is a decent lad.' It wasn't anything Brian Horton didn't know.

Horton had liked Peter Swales as much as he had liked Kevin Maxwell. 'I never got a call questioning team selection. He had good people below him. I wanted Tony Book with me. It did not bother me that he had been manager of Manchester City and that he might have been a bigger figure at the club than I was. I wanted his experience with me. I was never afraid of experience.

'I'd been on an FA coaching course with him at Lilleshall and shared a dormitory with him. I would have been 35 or 36, just starting out as manager of Hull City and I was in absolute awe of the man. I put Colin Bell in charge of the youth team. I wanted players at every level of the club to be surrounded by men they could look up to, whose experiences they could share.'

Not one of those names was to survive Francis Lee's tenure as chairman.

The Germans

THERE WERE THREE MEN STAYING IN THE COPTHORNE HOTEL on Salford Quays, a couple of good goal kicks from Old Trafford. All were contracted to Manchester City. Two would be stricken with cancer, one would die from it. One would face a prison sentence. Two would become bit part players at Manchester City. One would revel in the glow of the Maine Road floodlights.

Of the three, all in their mid-twenties, Uwe Rösler seemed the least likely to make it. He was 25 but already his career seemed to be petering out. At Nürnberg he discovered that, though the Berlin Wall had come down, there were still divisions between the natives of the West and those who had grown up under Communism.

Rösler may have supported the brilliant Borussia Mönchengladbach teams of Allan Simonsen and Berti Vogts, but only because his family had adjusted their aerial to catch the Bundesliga highlights on West German television. His local team had been Chemie Leipzig, which was as glamorous as it sounds.

He had returned to what had been the East but a knee injury had cost him his first-team place at Dynamo Dresden. His agent, Wolfgang Vöge, a miner's son who had played for Borussia Dortmund, had arranged a trial at Middlesbrough. There, the promised training session with the first team had not materialised because of heavy snow and he had been reduced to lying on his bed in a hotel room in Stockton watching Oldham and Leeds draw 1-1.

However, Vöge secured him a second trial, this time at Manchester City. Here, the ground was far more fertile. Francis Lee had long believed that the collapse of the Communist bloc would open up a market for relatively cheap, highly skilled footballers. In Uwe Rösler and Georgi Kinkladze the chairman's hunch was to be proved correct.

Rösler was asked to play for the reserves against Burnley. He scored twice. What happened next is a matter of dispute. 'Francis Lee claims he turned to me and said "Sign him up now,"' remembers Brian Horton. 'I would dispute this because I remember saying to Francis, "There are scouts around, let's get him off now."' Rösler, lacking match fitness and suffering from cramp, was only too happy to go to the dressing rooms. He did not know it at the time, but it would be the beginning of an extraordinary love affair.

Rösler scored 22 times in his first full season for Manchester City and, had he not been injured early in the season against Norwich, he might have become the first striker since Francis Lee to score 30 in a season. Unlike Lee, who hit fifteen penalties out of 35 goals in 1971/72, Rösler did not take spot kicks.

'I was surprised by the fact that for my first game for Manchester City – which was a reserve game – there were 7,000 people there,' Rösler says now. 'Maybe some were intrigued and they might have said to themselves: "Let's have a look at this German and see what he can do."'

'I like to think I convinced them with my effort, with the goals. I play with my heart on my sleeve. It was a different crowd at Maine Road to the one you see today at the Etihad. It was a working-class club, a club for Manchester people; people who lived by hard graft.

'They were people with personalities and they wanted people with personalities at their club. The main thing was that they saw a foreign player give everything that was asked of him.

'It's a completely different club now. The move to the Etihad was important to attract new owners and to compete with the upper half of the Premier League, but the atmosphere at Maine Road was always better.

'I didn't come to England for the money, I came for the atmosphere, the passion, for the tempo and the action. Football matches in England to me were like watching two boxers hitting each other repeatedly until one was knocked down. Now it is a worldwide football club, not just something for the people of Manchester.'

As someone who grew up in East Germany, Rösler's second language was Russian. To prove he still has it, he reels off the numbers from one to ten.

Initially, English was a problem. The club's Dutchmen, Michel Vonk and Alfons Groenendijk, translated for him.

Steve McMahon gave advice on the differences he would find in the Premier League, the tricks that certain defenders used. There were invitations to sample Manchester's nightlife which Rösler found easier to turn down than Steffen Karl, another East German contracted to Manchester City.

'In Germany we were taught how to look after ourselves,' says Rösler. 'I liked a beer after the game but I wasn't drinking during the week. I tried to live a clean life, or as clean as you could get in the 1990s.

'I moved into an apartment in Bramhall when I was given a three-year contract. I should have bought a house there but we Germans we always rent property, we never buy it. That was the biggest mistake I made when I was at Manchester City. I would probably have made more money buying a house in the right area than I made from my football.'

Rösler became friends with Francis Lee's son, Gary and when he married Cecilie, he invited him to his wedding. Cecilie had been a receptionist at the Grand Ocean hotel in Horten, which lies at the mouth of the long fjord that leads to Oslo. Manchester City had used it as their base for a summer tour of Norway. Uwe invited her for a date. Michel Vonk was also invited along to translate.

Francis Lee saw the Bundesliga as a source he could mine for high-class, relatively-cheap footballers. As Uwe Rösler says with a smile, £380,000 was good value for the goals he provided Manchester City.

'But I wasn't that keen for there to be five or six Germans at the club because then you would have a group apart from the rest. I wanted to be part of a team which had a British culture and I wanted to play with British players. I wanted to speak English with the rest of the dressing room. I wanted to understand their jokes.

'I came to England when I was 25. Eike Immel and Michael Frontzeck came to Manchester when their careers were on the way down. Immel had played in the European Championships in West Germany in 1988 and Frontzeck had been to the one in Sweden four years later. They had earned a lot of money and had very little to prove. Maurizio Gaudino was something in between. He was still at his best footballing-wise.'

The other two in the Copthorne Hotel initially seemed more promising.

David Rocastle had won two championships with Arsenal, where the club's most influential director, David Dein, had proclaimed him as the nearest thing to an English-born Brazilian he had ever seen. Everyone called him Rocky.

Steffen Karl, like Rösler, had grown up in East Germany but he was nearly two years younger and had played for Dortmund in the 1993 UEFA Cup final. He had been part of the East German *Supertalent* programme.

Rocastle had left Arsenal for Leeds in the summer of 1992 when the championship had returned to Elland Road for the first time since the days of Don Revie. It was a strange move. Howard Wilkinson was not a man who wanted his footballers to play like Brazilians.

At Highbury, Rocastle had been adored by the North Bank but, like everyone who was to manage him, George Graham was presented with what seemed an insoluble problem. Rocastle had suffered a serious knee injury which had meant the removal of his cartilage. If he trained hard, his knee would balloon. If he was nursed through to matchdays, his weight would go up.

One July morning, in the car park at London Colney, the Arsenal training ground, Graham ushered him into the passenger seat of his BMW and told Rocky he was being sold. Rocastle cried. Graham was so overcome he forgot to deliver the homily he had prepared about Rocky being one of the nicest men he had ever met in football.

Leeds had been a disaster. A secret part of his life had been ripped open and exposed. For three years he had been having an affair with a woman called Sharon Edwards, who suffered from sickle cell anaemia. They had had a daughter and while he was at Leeds, struggling to convince Wilkinson of his worth, Sharon had died. Their daughter, Sasha, was taken to live with her grandmother, first in Essex, then in Jamaica.

He had been Leeds' record signing but it took him four months to start a league game. His first goal for the fast-fading champions had come against Manchester City in March.

When he moved to Maine Road, his partner, Janet, perhaps understandably, took herself and their two children back to London, leaving Rocky in the Copthorne with Rösler and Steffen Karl. By the summer of 1994 there was just Rösler left.

In a sky-blue shirt, Rocastle produced flashes of his old ability. There was a stunning display in a 4-1 victory over Leicester in the FA Cup. On the February day in which 10,000 blue and white balloons announced Francis Lee's chairmanship, Rocastle, surrounded by Ipswich players, had dragged the ball back, turned viciously on his heels and produced the run and the cross for Carl Griffiths to equalise at the near post.

It had not been enough to convince Brian Horton. In the summer, he signed Peter Beagrie and Nicky Summerbee. They were younger than Rocky, their fitness had firmer guarantees and their knees were not suspect. Rocastle was sold to Chelsea for £1.25m. The knee continued to burn and the Chelsea manager, Glenn Hoddle, suggested he visit a faith healer he knew called Eileen Drewery.

Hoddle's successor, Ruud Gullit, would not even give Rocastle a squad number. Loan deals took him to the Holiday Inn in Norwich and another at Hull. He ended up in Borneo, playing for Sabah in the Malaysian League, under the management of Ken Shellito, whose career at Chelsea in the 1960s had also been finished by a knee injury.

It was an experience Rocky and his family relished. Then, he discovered a lump under his armpit that signalled the blood cancer known as non-Hodgkin's lymphoma that would kill him at 33.

Karl's departure from Maine Road was rather more self-inflicted. When he was on loan from Dortmund, Brian Horton had arranged a practice game for him at Platt Lane and been deeply impressed by the midfielder. In April 1994 at the Dell, Karl struck the only goal of the game against Southampton, who were managed by Alan Ball.

It had been a classic six-pointer. Southampton were second bottom; Manchester City, two places and three points better off, had not won away since September. Before the match, Ball had been in apocalyptic mood: 'If we don't beat City on Saturday, we are buried,' he had predicted.

They did not beat Manchester City. Two minutes from time, Steve McMahon ran across the face of the Southampton defence and picked out Karl whose low, angled drive settled the match. Matt Le Tissier, a man to whom Ball had entrusted all of Southampton's survival hopes, struck the post in the last moments of the game. City held on for a precious victory.

That match, however, represented Karl's high-water mark as a Manchester City footballer.

His journey from the East had been even more compelling than Rösler's.

Karl had grown up in Halle, which Rösler remarked was as close to Leipzig as Liverpool is to Manchester. Halle was then a drearily-grey chemical town. Football was a way out and in 1988 Karl, like David Rocastle, found himself contesting the European Under-21 Championships. Karl was just eighteen, earmarked for greatness.

The following year, he found himself playing local football in Hettstedt, an agricultural town miles from anywhere, discarded completely by the East German authorities.

In the summer of 1989 the first, fatal cracks in the Iron Curtain appeared when Hungary opened its borders to the West. Karl had been in a nightclub when he heard the news and announced he would travel to the border crossings and look for a contract in the Bundesliga. Unfortunately, he had talked rather too loudly. The conversation was reported to the Stasi and his football career was all but terminated.

By December the Berlin Wall was down and the German Democratic Republic was dying. Nevertheless, some arms of the state, like the Stasi and the *Volksarmee,* were still attempting to function as if nothing had changed. Karl was ordered to go to Rostock on the Baltic coast to begin his national service.

Instead, with the borders open, he travelled west and got himself an interview with the Borussia Dortmund manager, Horst Köppel, who gave him a contract. In Halle, he was condemned as a deserter. Three years later, he was in a UEFA Cup final against Juventus.

It had been a remarkable journey and, but for alcohol, it might have had a happy ending. Köppel's successor, Ottmar Hitzfeld, found he could no longer tolerate Karl's drinking and looked to loan him to Manchester City.

The drinking did not stop. Nineteen days after beating Southampton, two goals from Eric Cantona settled the Manchester derby at Old Trafford. Karl had been substituted and, according to Rösler, 'disappeared'. A note, written on a piece of white tape, told Rösler that Karl was in the bar at the Copthorne.

As Rösler relates: 'Unfortunately for Steffen, there was a get-together planned for after the match, with all the players, the manager and Francis Lee attending – at the Copthorne Hotel. When we arrived, Steffen was at the bar with a whisky and coke. I think that was pretty much the end for him at City.'

The end for Steffen Karl's football career took another decade to arrive.

Things began to go seriously wrong when he was in Hamburg, playing for St Pauli, where he became the victim of a blackmail plot that saw him disappear – and this time it involved more than a trip to the Copthorne's bar.

Karl turned up in Norway, where he won the championship with Vålerenga. A move to Lokomotiv Sofia was less successful, since the club was owned by a Bulgarian arms dealer called Nikolay Gigov and by the time he returned to Germany he was becoming ever more seriously compromised.

While playing for VfB Fortuna Chemnitz in German football's lower reaches, he met Ante Sapina, a Croat who played amateur football in Berlin. Sapina and his brothers had made more than £1.75m betting on results they liked to know before kick-off. They often worked in conjunction with a Second Division referee, Robert Hoyzer.

Karl was offered £22,000 to help the Sapina brothers fix the game between Paderborn and Vfb Fortuna Chemnitz, and he subsequently agreed to underperform in the match. Since Paderborn won 4-0, it is presumed he delivered.

The conspiracy, involving scores of matches outside the top flight of the Bundesliga, was uncovered and, as Germany was due to stage the World Cup the following year, the sense of embarrassment was excruciating. Hoyzer was jailed, Karl received a suspended sentence and a nine-month ban from all football.

By then Rösler was in Norway, recovering from cancer. By a vicious but remarkable coincidence he had been stricken with non-Hodgkin's lymphoma, the same thing that had killed David Rocastle four years before.

He was playing for Lillestrøm and in training Rösler was starting to lose his temper alarmingly. When the club captain, Torgeir Bjarmann, lay down, jokingly trying to prevent him taking the ball over the line, Rösler kept kicking the ball into his face at point blank range until it was covered with blood.

Soon afterwards, he began feeling pains in his chest. He was quickly sent for a scan. When the doctor came back with the news Rösler was outside his house with Gunnar Halle, who had played for Oldham and Leeds during Rösler's time at Maine Road, changing their cars from winter to summer tyres. There was a tumour the size of a tennis ball in Rösler's chest. His life expectancy was measured in weeks, maybe days.

His cancer was slightly different to Rocastle's in that, although it was aggressive, it was treatable. The proviso was that, if the cancer returned after treatment, it would probably be fatal because his body would be too weak to resist. The chemotherapy worked, the cancer did not return. Rösler, unlike Rocastle, survived.

His fight was supported by Cecilie and by his teammates, Gunnar Halle and Jan Åge Fjørtoft. Uwe Rösler was also supported by a phone call from the City of Manchester Stadium. A friend of his, Mark Buckley, raised his phone above his head and urged Uwe to listen. The fans of Manchester City, a club for whom he had not played in a decade, were singing his name. It was unbearably moving, a symbol of unwavering, deathless support.

He remembers the first time they sang his name, the day he felt Manchester City was his home. 7 May 1994.

'We were playing Sheffield Wednesday at Hillsborough on the last day of the 1993/94 season and the crowd were singing my name for what seemed like 90 minutes. Michel Vonk came over and said, "They're singing your name." I told him that they couldn't be because in Germany the crowd never does that. But they were.

'I scored, we drew 1-1 and, because it was the last day of the season we stopped at several pubs on the way home from Sheffield. The supporters joined us and that was the day when I felt I belonged at Manchester City.'

Steffen Karl's failure to make a significant impact on anything but his bar bill did not stop Lee looking at the Bundesliga as a source of reinforcements. That Maurizio Gaudino did not sound German was because his family were immigrants from Naples.

Like Karl he had played in a UEFA Cup final, alongside Jurgen Klinsmann and Guido Buchwald for Stuttgart against Napoli, and he had taken part in the Bundesliga's most dramatic finish.

On 16 May 1992 Eintracht Frankfurt went into the final round of matches ahead of Stuttgart and Borussia Dortmund on goal difference alone. All three were away.

Dortmund won their derby with Duisburg but Frankfurt lost at Rostock and, with a few minutes remaining, Buchwald, with the coolness of a man who has won a World Cup, headed Stuttgart's winner at Leverkusen. Stuttgart and Gaudino were champions. The chairman of Frankfurt's main sponsor threw the £90,000 in bonuses that he had taken with him in cash to

Rostock's Ostseestadion at the assembled journalists.

Within two years Gaudino was at Eintracht Frankfurt, where he had become a desperate embarrassment. He had just finished his appearance on a chat show, where he had roller-skated with Katarina Witt, who had won figure skating gold medals for East Germany at two Winter Olympics.

He had skated rather well. 'That's a pity,' said the chat-show host, the bouffant-haired Thomas Gottschalk, 'I wanted to see you fall flat on your face.' Gottschalk wouldn't have long to wait. As Gaudino returned to his dressing room he found the police there. They wanted to talk to him about cars. Expensive cars. Stolen cars.

Gaudino was accused of being part of a gang that bought luxury cars and then had them 'stolen'. They would be driven to Eastern Europe and sold. Back in Germany they would then claim on the insurance.

Quite why Manchester City would have wanted a footballer facing ten years in a German jail is an open question, but they did. To complicate matters, Gaudino's wife was pregnant with their son, Gianluca, who was to later join Bayern Munich's academy and play a few games for the club under Pep Guardiola's management.

Nevertheless, there were reasons for Lee to believe in the deal. Gaudino had been part of Berti Vogts' squad in the 1994 World Cup. He was a talent and he would be available on very favourable terms.

His debut was nothing if not dramatic, under the lights at St James' Park in the fourth round of the League Cup facing a Newcastle side that for three, brief dazzling years appeared to be one of English football's most irresistible forces. They had not lost at home for fourteen months.

Newcastle under Kevin Keegan may have appeared the perfect cup team but strangely they got nowhere near a League or an FA Cup final, much less a European one. Their lone appearance at Wembley under Keegan was the 1996 Charity Shield against Manchester United in which they paraded Alan Shearer, who had met and rejected Alex Ferguson to become the most expensive footballer in the world. Newcastle were thrashed 4-0 then and they would lose this game, too.

The match was a replay. Rösler's thunderous header had secured a draw at Maine Road and after ten minutes on Tyneside, he scored again. Nicky Summerbee provided the cross and Rösler stabbed the ball home.

Newcastle's response was relentless. Andy Dibble pushed Darren Peacock's header on to the bar. City twice cleared off the line, Andy Cole struck the post and then Summerbee broke away and Walsh scored the second. The reward was a quarter-final tie at Crystal Palace. At Selhurst Park, Steve Lomas broke his ankle and Manchester City were routed, 4-0.

Gaudino enjoyed his time at Maine Road. 'It was really extreme,' he said. 'Sometimes, it felt like a tennis match. It was 90 minutes of pure fighting. The goals often came after the 75th minute when the players were totally exhausted.

'I was absolutely enthusiastic about the way these players lived for football. I have never experienced this attitude anywhere else. Everything was far more relaxed than in Germany when it came to nutrition or flying to Spain to play a golf tournament there.'

The fans took to him in song. To the tune of *'O Sole Mio* or, if you prefer, the Cornetto advert, they sang:

'Just one Gaudino from Germany.
'He has a fetish for your car keys.
'He robs Lamborghinis.
'He is Gaudino of Man City.'

They sang it loudest towards the end of the season when Gaudino found form just as his loan spell was about to expire. First his header proved decisive in the 2-1 win over Liverpool at Maine Road. Then City travelled to Blackburn who were locked in a compelling struggle for the championship with Manchester United.

Strangely, given the enmity that existed between Maine Road and Old Trafford, City regularly helped out United both by losing the Manchester derbies – between 1990 and 2002 they did not record a single victory – and by taking points off Ferguson's principal enemies.

Peter Reid would never forget the boos that poured out over Maine Road after City's 4-0 win over Leeds appeared to swing the 1992 title race United's way. Four years later, City would fight out a breathless 3-3 draw with Newcastle that would cut Keegan's lead over Ferguson to four points.

Now facing a Blackburn side that was seeing its lead eroded by United, Manchester City, playing in the red-and-black stripes that Malcolm Allison employed to remind him of AC Milan, recovered from a 2-1 deficit at half time to win 3-2. It would be the last time for more than twenty years that Manchester City would go in at half-time losing a Premier League game which they would end up winning.

The match was turned by Rösler and Paul Walsh, who having been elbowed by Graeme Le Saux in the stomach as they stood together in the wall, punched the defender hard in the back of the head; something he said he enjoyed immensely. In the press conference room at Ewood Park, Kenny Dalglish wondered aloud why Manchester City had not performed like this earlier in the season.

Uwe Rösler thought that City were finally playing the kind of football they had been capable of all season. 'I thought it was a huge statement we could beat the champions-elect in their own backyard,' he says. 'With one or two tweaks I felt we weren't far off being a top-six side.' Manchester City would not finish in the Premier League's top six for another fifteen years.

The game had been played on a Monday night. Ferguson, believing Blackburn were bound to win, had not even watched it. A friend from his Aberdeen days had made him a bookshelf and installed it in his home in Wilmslow. Ferguson had spent the evening filling it with books. He was interrupted by a phone call telling him that City had won, 3-2. 'I really think Blackburn have gone now,' he said.

They clung on to take the title by a point, but victories over Liverpool and Blackburn were no longer enough to keep Brian Horton his job. He had expected to be sacked. He was not Lee's man and he knew it. On a Tuesday night at Selhurst Park the dressing room knew it too.

In March 1995, City were playing Wimbledon a couple of days after a 3-2 victory over Sheffield Wednesday. They lost, 2-0. Lee came into the dressing room and began berating the players. According to Niall Quinn, 'Brian Horton was standing in the corner looking embarrassed and humiliated.' Horton was also angry, not least because Lee was repeating almost word for word what he had just told his players.

'I knew I was definitely going to be replaced before the Blackburn game kicked off,' he says. 'On our way home, I told the coach driver to go to the Haydock Thistle hotel. I knew the manager there and I told him to get some champagne ready and we would have a bit of a party with the team. Some of the players said, "We need to get home to our wives." So, I told them to invite them along. I wanted to say goodbye properly.'

Uwe Rösler was especially upset. Suddenly, the man who had been voted the club's player of the season began to fear for the future. He was not alone. Manchester City had four games remaining and they played them like any team might knowing their manager was leaving.

They were twelfth when Horton told his players his contract would be terminated but none of their last four matches were won and they drifted down to seventeenth. One of the reasons given by the board for Horton's dismissal was that the slide over the final weeks had cost several hundred thousand pounds in prize money. It was entirely spurious.

Gaudino returned to Germany, where he received a two-year suspended sentence for his role in the car theft ring. Another loan followed, this time to Mexico to play for Club América on the grand stage of the Azteca Stadium. 'He played little and he played poorly,' recounted the website, *Realidad Americanista*. 'He had the class that few others in the club possessed, however, he displayed it intermittently and there were many times when he seemed he did not have the blood in his veins to be a player for Club América.'

By the time he returned to Frankfurt in 1996 they had been relegated. He played in Switzerland and Turkey, opened a restaurant with his daughter and just before the 2006 World Cup found himself at Reading, turning out for a celebrity Germany side facing a celebrity England one. There, he found himself rugby tackled by Boris Johnson for which he became better known in this country than anything he achieved with Manchester City.

Eike Immel's journey to Manchester had also been an intriguing one. When Alan Ball was introduced to Immel in the summer of 1995, he had no idea he had just been signed as Manchester City's first-choice goalkeeper. He made his debut in the opening fixture against Tottenham after just a single training session at Platt Lane.

It would have been impossible for Immel to have matched the impact of the club's previous German keeper at City. When in October 1949 Bert Trautmann was signed from St Helens Town, 25,000 gathered outside to protest at the club's decision to employ a man who, six years before, had been awarded the Iron Cross for his contribution towards the German war effort on the Eastern Front.

Manchester's cotton industry had helped create what, outside London, was the largest Jewish population in the country. The protests were only halted through the intervention of Manchester's chief rabbi, Alexander Altmann.

Trautmann was to become a chapter in the history of Manchester City, forever remembered for his role in winning the 1956 FA Cup final against Birmingham while playing with a broken neck; a story he grew weary of telling. Immel was never more than a footnote.

It was, on the surface, a shrewd piece of business. Immel had been West Germany's first-choice keeper for the 1988 European Championship and, four years later, he had won the Bundesliga with Stuttgart.

However, by the time he arrived at Maine Road, Immel was 34 and was troubled by his hips and a constant need for money. His parents were farmers and one day their Polish farmhand was knocked over and killed by a car. The teenage Eike took over his duties.

'I had to take big buckets full of feed to the cattle and we had more than a hundred animals,' he recalled. 'It was good muscle training but the pressure was all on my hips.' They were always to give him trouble.

By the time he was fifteen, Immel had offers from Eintracht Frankfurt, Kickers Offenbach and Borussia Dortmund. They all offered him much the same thing; an apprenticeship, regular visits from his parents and 300 Deutschmarks a month (approximately £275 in 1975).

The Offenbach manager, Willi Konrad, told the young Immel he could have *Jagerschnitzel* every day after training. Dortmund offered something more than pork in mushroom sauce. They gave his parents 5,000DM.

Immel never had trouble spending cash. A third of his annual income went on a dark blue Porsche Carrera with white leather seats and as his wages increased to the equivalent of a quarter of a million a year in today's terms, his agent advised him to buy houses as a way of avoiding tax. There were other schemes. At one stage, he had eight life insurance policies.

'I had five luxury homes,' Immel told the German magazine *Sport Bild*. 'They had marble floors and fireplaces and cost 485,000DM each (his salary at Dortmund was 300,000DM). Nowadays, I know that when you are buying property only three things matter – location, location, location. Then, I had no idea.

'The houses were in Hagen-Haspe which was the greyest area of the Ruhr.

After ten years, I sold them for 300,000DM each. The total loss was a million marks. Those houses broke my neck.'

Those houses dictated the rest of Eike Immel's career. The only motivation of a move from Dortmund to Stuttgart was that his salary would double. The chief attraction of Manchester City was the lucrative contract Francis Lee was prepared to offer. He lived in the same apartment block in Bramhall as Uwe Rösler.

Immel performed well at Maine Road. Manchester City were eventually relegated from the Premier League, not because they conceded too many but because they did not score enough.

His finest displays came in the two games against Newcastle, the 3-1 defeat at St James' Park that ought to have been a massacre and the breathless 3-3 draw in Moss Side.

On Tyneside in September, Kevin Keegan's side, spearheaded by Les Ferdinand, David Ginola and Peter Beardsley, had aimed 33 shots at Immel's goal. Twenty were on target.

His arrival signalled the end of Tony Coton, who had been voted player of the year by City fans the previous season. He was told by Alan Ball he was surplus to requirements in January 1996. It was a conversation Coton would always remember, not least because Ball was wearing a flat cap, a tracksuit, a pair of flip-flops and reading *Sporting Life* while he spoke.

Coton, who was to end up as Manchester United's reserve keeper, coped with life after City better than Immel. He became a goalkeeping coach under Christoph Daum at Fenerbahçe. In Istanbul he had not lost his habit of making unwise property investments. Already divorced, with two children, he became involved with what he was to describe as some 'unbelievably expensive girlfriends'. One trip to Louis Vuitton set him back €20,000.

Daum was only in Turkey because his contract to manage Germany had been terminated when it was revealed he was a cocaine user. Cocaine was to feature in Immel's life. In 2007, he was arrested and put on trial for allegedly buying €10,000 worth of the stuff.

The prosecution's case was flimsy and collapsed completely when its star witness, the drug dealer, could not satisfactorily explain why he had lured Immel to a nightclub to sell him the cocaine when both men lived in the same apartment block. He could simply have knocked on his door.

'When you are in the shit you will consider anything,' Immel said. By now, acquitted, vindicated and bankrupt, he appeared on the German version of *I'm a Celebrity Get Me Out of Here*.

He earned a welcome €90,000 for his time in the Australian jungle, where he struck up an unlikely friendship with Bata Illic, best described as a German Charles Aznavour. The result, when they got back to Germany, was a single called 'Wie ein Liebeslied'.

It was saccharine enough to make 'Diamond Lights' by Glenn Hoddle and Chris Waddle sound like a Sex Pistols' B-side and was easy enough to mock. However, at a time when depression had driven another German international keeper, Robert Enke, to suicide, Eike Immel's resilience and refusal to be crushed by what seemed overwhelming reverses was very Manchester City.

Brian Horton, meanwhile, would become one of the select few managers who would take charge of a thousand games, although after his dismissal from Maine Road, none would be in the Premier League. There would be backs-to-the-wall salvage operations; keeping Brighton afloat in the years when they were forced to play their home matches 80 miles away at Gillingham, and preserving Macclesfield's league status.

There would be some glamour mixed in. He was assistant manager to Phil Brown at the 2009 play-off final when Dean Windass' goal for Hull rendered obsolete the quiz question: 'Which is the largest city in England never to have staged top-flight football?' The answer now is Plymouth.

However, Manchester City was his moment in the limelight, his taste of wine. 'I never lost my affection for Manchester City,' he says now. 'After I split up with my first wife, I moved into an apartment block in Bramhall.

'Uwe was in the same block, so was Eike Immel and Michael Frontzeck. Uwe would regularly come downstairs to my flat to watch football because I had Sky and he hadn't.

'I still feel close to Manchester City and still have a pretty good rapport with their fans whenever I see them. They wanted their team to attack, to go forward and we did. I don't ever regret going there. It was my taste of the big time.'

We Have all the Time in the World

THE MEN WHO SPENT THE FEVERISH SUMMER OF 1966 IN THE Hendon Hall Hotel or the Bank of England training pitches at Roehampton found Sir Alf Ramsey's magic was not transferable.

Of the eleven who started English football's greatest game, four chose not to go into management at all. Of the rest, Bobby Moore made a futile attempt to make the journeymen of Southend pass the ball as he had once done; Martin Peters relegated Sheffield United to the Fourth Division; Geoff Hurst discovered that the duties of being Telford manager included painting the roof of the stand. He was given a more glamourous job managing Chelsea but could not win them promotion and returned to selling insurance (following a two-year spell at Kuwait Sporting Club).

Bobby Charlton was astute enough to ask the teenage Mark Lawrenson to interrupt his A levels to sign professional forms with Preston, but he was far too diffident to ever inspire the dressing room at Deepdale. One of Nobby Stiles' abiding memories while working as John Giles' assistant at West Bromwich Albion was going to the cashpoint and being told there were insufficient funds in his account to make a withdrawal.

There remains only Jack Charlton and Alan Ball, and Big Jack's triumphs were largely with another country, the Republic of Ireland. That leaves the little fella.

The image of Bobby Moore emerging from the players' entrance at Upton Park and throwing his car keys to a gaggle of schoolboys, one of whom would race to unlock his Jaguar, symbolises the Michael Caine coolness of mid-1960s

England. Alan Ball, who was 21 when Bobby Moore wiped his hands on the cloth on the Royal Box and took the Jules Rimet trophy from the Queen, seemed to represent the sheer wonder of it all.

Years later he could still recall the amazement he felt when on the morning of the final he was handed £2,000 in cash (worth £34,000 now) by an Adidas representative for wearing their boots in the final – half for him, half for his roommate, Stiles. He rushed upstairs to see Nobby, who had been to church, and threw the notes into the air and on to the bed.

At Everton – where he won the league title in 1970 – he played in white boots, boots that his son Jimmy and daughters Mandy and Keely placed in the centre circle at Goodison Park to commemorate his death. He managed in a flat cap that was placed upon his coffin as it was carried into Winchester Cathedral for his funeral. The boots are remembered more fondly than the hat.

'I think Dad would have made an excellent assistant manager,' says Jimmy Ball. 'When they were England manager Graham Taylor and Kevin Keegan both invited Dad to work with the players and the response he got was overwhelming. They loved being with him, they loved his enthusiasm. They loved listening to him talk, tapping his knowledge.

'Then the FA intervened and said Dad had to have his coaching badges if he were to work with England again but he said, "I'm not doing that," and walked away. He could be stubborn like that.

'When I was coaching in Seattle, Manchester United were on tour in America and I had dinner with Sir Alex Ferguson who made exactly the same point; Dad would have been very good as someone's number two.'

When we spoke, Jimmy was coaching the academy at Stoke City. He was the third generation of his family to coach at Stoke. His grandfather, Alan Ball senior, had worked here and his father had managed at the Victoria Ground.

Alan Ball loathed Stoke. 'I didn't like the area and I didn't like the people,' he had written in his autobiography, *Playing Extra Time*. His final game as Manchester City manager had been at Stoke, where both sets of supporters began chanting 'Ball Out'.

He had first gone there in November 1989, initially as assistant to Mick Mills. The fact his father had worked there held an appeal, but there were few others. His first match was a 6-0 defeat at Swindon.

The end came in February 1991 amid the corrugated iron surrounds of

Springfield Park, Wigan. Stoke had lost 4-0. Before kick-off Ball had gone out to assess the pitch and a boy, perhaps nine or ten years old, had run over and spat at him.

As a manager, Ball clung to the South Coast, at Portsmouth, Exeter and Southampton, and yet he was from the north, born like his father in Farnworth, a red-brick suburb of Bolton. As a footballer, his finest hours had been with Blackpool and Everton; Manchester City represented a return to his past.

If the appointment of Brian Horton posed the question 'Who?' then the question asked when Alan Ball arrived at Manchester City was 'Why?'

Francis Lee's search for his first managerial appointment was a series of left-field choices. He phoned Alan Hansen, who had revolutionised the art of punditry on BBC's *Match of the Day*. 'I just told him I wasn't interested in being the manager of a football club,' Hansen said. 'When I left Liverpool in 1991 I was in the frame for the job at Anfield but if I wasn't going to take the Liverpool job, I wasn't going to take any job.'

Lee did make an attempt to bring Ron Atkinson back to Manchester. At City, he would have fulfilled Noel Gallagher's yearning for a manager at home in the back of a white Rolls-Royce with a bucket of chilled champagne at his feet. However, Atkinson had just signed up to manage Coventry for no better reason that it was close to his home in Worcestershire. 'That,' said Lee when he told him, 'is like Sinatra playing Wigan Pier.'

The man Lee targeted most persistently was Brian Kidd. In Manchester he was a man who straddled the divide. On his nineteenth birthday he had won the 1968 European Cup with United and a decade later had scored home and away for City against AC Milan.

There were many in Manchester and beyond who believed that United's resurgence was more down to Kidd than Ferguson. Since his appointment as Ferguson's assistant in the summer of 1991, Manchester United had finished either first or second and made three Wembley finals.

On the training pitches at the Cliff, the players loved him. Andrei Kanchelskis recalled that on the rare days Ferguson took training, often when Kidd had flown out to Italy or Spain to sharpen up his coaching technique, he would be met with mock boos. In the dressing room at Old Trafford he was the good cop to Ferguson's Taggart. Brian Kidd, Ferguson had thought in 1995, 'had every right' to expect to succeed him. Nobody imagined it would be another eighteen years before he took his leave.

However, Kidd had nothing like Ferguson's sense of leadership or decisiveness. When Lee asked if he had approached the Manchester United chairman, Martin Edwards, Kidd replied he had yet to summon up the courage. The moment came and the moment went.

The indecision would gnaw away at him and in December 1998 he left Old Trafford to manage Blackburn saying, 'I did not want to die without knowing I could do the job.' He could not. Ferguson tried to talk him out of it, arguing the club's owner Jack Walker was becoming increasingly volatile. 'He regarded Roy Hodgson a king one minute and a fool the next,' he said. Hodgson had been fired as Blackburn manager immediately after a defeat by Southampton and had left Ewood Park in tears.

Ferguson had his revenge twice over. First, Manchester United relegated Blackburn after a goalless draw at Ewood. Kidd invited Ferguson to his office. They chatted. A few months later, Ferguson published his first volume of autobiography, *Managing My Life*. Ferguson used it to condemn Kidd as a moaner and an intriguer whose judgement was often poor. He had, for instance, recommended United sign John Hartson rather than Dwight Yorke. Howard Kendall, who was usually close to Ferguson, thought it a hatchet job. Kidd thought it contributed to his sacking at Blackburn.

The chatting stopped. A few years later when he was coaching at Leeds, Kidd walked into the dressing room at Elland Road to find Ferguson standing there, looking for David O'Leary. The two men stared at each other like lovers who had been terribly hurt. Neither said a word.

In the long hot summer of 1995, Alan Ball travelled to meet Lee at Stanneylands, the stud farm he owned near Manchester Airport, and he asked himself what he was doing there. In eighteen months at Southampton he had rescued the club from relegation, taken them to tenth in the Premier League – a position they would not better between 1990 and 2003 – while burnishing and promoting the fabulous talents of Matt Le Tissier.

'Southampton had rejected offer after offer for Le Tissier and yet Dad could not understand why they had given Manchester City permission to talk to him,' says Jimmy. 'He felt rejected and he did not really know why the club was willing to let him go.'

Despite his success at the Dell, there had been increasing friction between

Manchester City 5, Manchester United 1, 23 September 1989. (Mirrorpix)

Peter Swales, the Cincinnati Kid. (Getty)

Big Malcolm Allison wore a big coat and a big smile and a blew a big budget. (Offside)

John Bond with another outrageous signing, this one Trevor Francis. (Getty)

Billy McNeill was known as Cesar at Celtic where he played nearly 800 games. He lasted three seasons at City and by the end, supporters at Maine Road were calling him less flattering names. (Offside)

The local left back Andy Hinchcliffe (L) along with Paul Lake (R), one of the brightest talents Manchester City has ever known. (Getty)

Maine Road and Moss Side in the mid-1990s on a match day. (Offside)

Peter Reid managing
and Peter Reid playing.
(Getty)

A new penny-pinching initiative at City, with Niall Quinn ironing his own match-shirt? (Getty)

Brian Horton (right) with Tony Book (left), or as Noel Gallagher would call Horton: "Not cool." (Offside)

The much-criticised Nicky Summerbee brought tumbling down by United's Denis Irwin. (Offside)

Garry Flitcroft, the City supporter who was sold to Blackburn Rovers. (Getty)

Alan Ball with the Germans, Uwe Rosler, Michael Frontceck and Eike Immel. (Getty)

The genius that is Giorgi Kinkladze taking Sheffield Wednesday's Mark Pembridge this way and that. (Getty

He did not hang around, Steve Coppell. (Getty)

Neither did
Phil Neal. (Getty)

Frank Clark brought with him some optimism but he would go the same way as his predecessors. (Getty)

The day at Stoke when City and Joe Royle tumbled into the Second Division. (Mirrorpix)

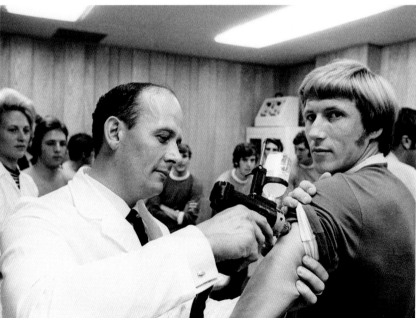

Tony Book and Colin Bell in happier times as players before the fire and fury under Francis Lee. (Getty)

Great player. Crap chairman? Francis Lee. (Getty)

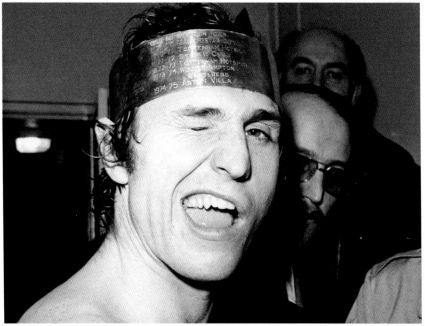

Dennis Tueart another legend turned administrator would divide opinion upon his return to City. (Getty)

Ian Brightwell not mucking about with Eric Cantona. (Getty)

Ian Bishop scoring on his return to Maine Road after a decade away as City return to the Premier League. (Getty)

The last Manchester derby at Maine Road in 2002: Manchester City 3, Manchester United 1. (Offside)

New ground. New players. New aspirations. Yaya Toure leaves the new City. (Getty)

Ball and Guy Askham, his chairman. Lawrie McMenemy, who had returned to the club as director of football, told Ball's biographer, David Tossell, that there had been complaints about Ball's overuse of the company credit card. In the context of the money Alan Ball had made Southampton by keeping them in the Premier League, it was trivial. Askham decided to make a big thing of it.

'There would be a fair amount on Alan's card,' McMenemy said in *The Man in White Boots*. 'He would have gone to Queens Park Rangers or Fulham reserves in midweek, taken a mate or two and then stopped on the way back to have a nice meal and a bottle of wine.'

McMenemy added that the directors did not like the way he invited certain people to the boardroom after matches, especially Dave Hill, who had been a steward at the Dell and was now Ball's driver and general Man Friday.

Big Dave, as everyone called him, was at the family home in Warsash, by Southampton Water, in April 2007 when Ball suffered a fatal heart attack trying to fight a bonfire that had burned out of control. He was almost part of the family.

Ball was emphatically not a snob. He had relished his time managing Exeter or acting as Jock Wallace's assistant at Colchester and the slight to Big Dave would have wounded him. It is also a rule of thumb in most professions that an employee's expense account is only an issue when someone wants rid of them. As a manager whose salary of £72,000 was very modest by Premier League standards, Ball may have thought he was entitled to some perks.

Lee was prepared to more than double Ball's money. At Ascot, Ball met Mick Channon, with whom he had shared a dressing room at the Dell for four years. Channon, who had been a victim of Malcolm Allison's great purge at Manchester City, told him emphatically to stay away from Maine Road.

By the time he met his daughters, Mandy and Keely, who were joining him on a family holiday in Spain, his mind had been made up. He was wearing Southampton shorts when he met his girls at the airport. He said he would drive them to their holiday home in Marbella and then he would fly to Manchester. It was done.

When he reflected on the disaster that was to follow, Ball concluded that his biggest mistake had been not asking Francis Lee any questions or doing any research into Manchester City's financial position, which by then was parlous.

In terms of attendances, they were the tenth biggest club in England, behind

Middlesbrough but just ahead of the champions, Blackburn. As the Premier League expanded its television revenues, getting people through the gate was to become less important economically, but in 1995 it still mattered very much.

'The two clubs he was not successful at were Stoke and Manchester City,' says Jimmy. 'I don't think it's a coincidence that they were both teetering on the financial brink when he worked there. Manchester City and Stoke were clubs that almost needed to go down so they could detoxify themselves, purge themselves to become the clubs they are now.'

Alan Ball was Manchester City's fifth manager in six years. The squad he inherited was a patchwork of other people's choices and the speech with which he addressed them as they began pre-season training at Manchester University was remarkable.

'Let me tell you about me and what I am about. I am a winner. They all go on about winning this or winning that but I am a World Cup winner. None of you can out-drink me and none of you have been to better parties. I have done it all, let me tell you. I am only after success; that all I'll strive for here and that's what we'll get.'

Perhaps it was a sign of Ball's insecurity, the feeling that he should still be at Southampton, but Uwe Rösler thought it a speech that completely misjudged its audience. It was, he said, the sort of thing you would say to someone who had no idea who Alan Ball was.

'He was not speaking to a young squad, he was speaking to an experienced group of footballers,' Rösler says. 'He lost a lot of the English lads in the first weeks I have to say. When you have achieved so much – and Alan Ball achieved so much – you don't need to speak about it. You know what you have done. You let other people speak about it. Franz Beckenbauer doesn't talk about himself. People talk about him. Your history should do the talking for you.

'When you are a world-class player, and Alan Ball was a world-class player, football is natural. Sometimes, they don't understand that for the rest of us football can be a hard, awkward thing. Controlling a ball, seeing a pass is not as natural as it is for them and sometimes, those world-class footballers who become managers find that hard to come to terms with.'

One of the criticisms levelled at Alan Ball during his time at Maine Road was that he would not shut up about the World Cup. It seems unfair. Jimmy says that at home his father brought up the events of 1966 infrequently:

'He used to tell me, "I hope they win it again so they stop wheeling us out every four years, asking us the same questions."'

Jonathan Ross used to say that one of his fantasies was to invite Neil Armstrong on to his chat show and not ask him a single question about going to the Moon. If it seemed the only thing the Boys of '66 ever talked about was the World Cup, it was because it was what they were asked about whenever they were interviewed.

And in 1996, when England staged their first major football tournament since the World Cup and when Baddiel and Skinner sang about 'thirty years of hurt' and 'Jules Rimet still gleaming', they were interviewed rather a lot. Even Kenneth Wolstenholme took himself out on the road to talk about his 'people are on the pitch they think it's all over' commentary.

Ball was destroyed by the first three months of the season. On 28 October, Manchester City were annihilated, 6-0, at Anfield. Their total from eleven games were three goals and two points. They were seven points, eight when goal difference was taken into account, from seventeenth place and safety, a position occupied by Southampton. After a goalless draw with Wycombe in the League Cup there were livid arguments in the dressing room.

There had been injuries, most damagingly to Peter Beagrie and Rösler, who had broken down in pre-season. Eike Immel who had won the Bundesliga with Stuttgart, mentioned a young fitness coach at his old club who might be able to help. His name was Ralf Rangnick, who later would promote Hoffenheim from the depths of German regional football to the Bundesliga and then take Schalke to the semi-finals of the Champions League.

With Rangnick's help, Rösler made and scored in the opening game, a deceptive 1-1 draw with Tottenham, but it would take him several weeks to become match-fit, weeks in which only one other City player managed a goal. Ian Brightwell would be injured against Leeds.

When Jorge Valdano was director of football at Real Madrid, he warned his chairman, Florentino Pérez, that three transfers in every five fail. However, even by Valdano's rule of thumb, Manchester City's transfers were dreadful.

Rösler resented the sale of his strike-partner, Paul Walsh, who was to be sold back to Portsmouth in exchange for Gerry Creaney, a man whom Ball would come to regard as a 'boat-rocker' off the pitch and a 'disappointment' on it.

Of the seven players Ball and Lee brought in during the season, none at all were from the Premier League. Creaney and Kit Symons arrived from Portsmouth, who would avoid relegation to the old Third Division on goal difference. Creaney's declaration that playing in the Premier League would prove 'no problem' was answered by statistics – he started six games that season.

Some £500,000 was gambled on Martin Phillips, a teenager Ball had worked with at Exeter whom he predicted with typical flamboyance would become 'the first £10m footballer'. A good lad, said Rösler, but not quite good enough.

Someone who broke into professional football on the South Coast did indeed become the first £10m footballer less than twelve months after Ball made his prediction, but that was Alan Shearer. Phillips returned to Exeter in 1998 and with transfers to Plymouth and Torquay completed a tour of Devon's football clubs. At Plainmoor, he was diagnosed with myalgic encephalomyelitis, also known as chronic fatigue syndrome, which in the words of one sufferer makes your body feel 'as if unseen weights are pulling it to the floor'.

Georgi Kinkladze danced on air. Ball was thrilled by skill in a footballer. At Southampton he had nurtured Matt Le Tissier and indulged him to the extent that some thought his only tactics at the Dell had been to give the ball to the boy from Guernsey. The reward was 45 goals in 65 matches which first saved Southampton from relegation and then established them in the Premier League's top ten.

Ball imagined Kinkladze could replicate those performances at Maine Road even to the extent of signing Ronnie Ekelund on loan, who at the Dell had established a fabulous rapport with Le Tissier. It was something he never came close to repeating at Maine Road with Kinkladze, and he soon moved on to Coventry.

Ball adored Kinkladze, revelled in his ability. 'He loved that spark of genius in a footballer,' says Jimmy. 'With England he loved playing alongside men who seemed to him to be truly brilliant; Bobby Charlton, Jimmy Greaves, Bobby Moore.

'He loved their company. Sunday afternoons in our house in Hampshire could be extraordinary. I would grow up surrounded by the gods of football. Booby Moore or Kevin Keegan would be there more often than not and I would be sat there as a young boy watching them watch a match on television. They would have arguments about the game, the salt and pepper pots would come out to help with some tactical point.

'He saw that quality in Matt Le Tissier and at Manchester City the player he loved working with the most was Kinkladze. All he wanted was for the ball to go to Georgi, but whether Kinky was the right player for a relegation dogfight is debatable.'

In those awful early weeks, Ball attempted every formation he could think of to accommodate Kinkladze, even to the extent that once Rösler and Niall Quinn found themselves on the right and left flanks respectively, with Kinkladze going through the middle.

'He would take defeat badly and he took it home with him,' Jimmy continues. 'It would spill over into Sunday and it would be down to Mum [Lesley] to get him out of the house. We would go over to the Plough and Flail in Mobberley and have Sunday lunch there.

'He found management hard, much harder than playing. He had been a world-class footballer; he had never needed to think about his game or what he needed to do. When he was a manager he had to think all the time.'

Like Oscar-winning actors becoming great directors, relatively few great footballers shine as managers and Alan Ball was not about to join the ranks of Eastwood, Guardiola, Clooney or Beckenbauer.

There were no Oscars, but Ball was given an award in the form of the November manager of the month trophy. Suddenly Manchester City had clicked. Bolton, Wimbledon, Aston Villa and Leeds were all beaten. Mixed in was a 1-1 draw with Sheffield Wednesday at Hillsborough. City had by the first week of December broken clear of the relegation zone.

Manchester City were not necessarily doomed by their beginning, but it would be a hard, relentless slog to survive. The breakout was spectacular but lacked power – they scored only one goal in each of those four wins and by the end of the season no team would have scored fewer. The highest they clambered was fifteenth after a 2-1 victory over Southampton in which Kinkladze scored perhaps his most sublime goal for the club.

Of the 25 sides to have been bottom of the Premier League after eleven matches, none made a worse start than Manchester City and none was further adrift. That they would go down on goal difference was a tribute of sorts.

Theirs was almost the greatest escape.

Ten of those 25 teams survived. Three clubs – Everton in 1994, Blackburn in 1996 and Crystal Palace, twice in 2013 and 2017 – did so from positions that were similar to the one Ball found himself in the late October of 1995. They had between three and four points and were each six points adrift of safety. All survived. All sacked their manager.

For Francis Lee, it would have been far too much to have got rid of the little fella four months after appointing him. They were Bolton lads, Lee from Westhoughton, Ball from Farnworth. As schoolboys they had trained with Bolton Wanderers, although Lee had been given an apprenticeship at Burnden Park and Ball had not.

They had been together at the Hilton in Guadalajara in the summer of 1970 as the horns sounded and the klaxons screeched the night before England played Brazil. Lee had first floated the idea of Ball managing Manchester City when he launched his bid to take over the club more than twenty years later. There were too many ties.

The only time they looked likely to snap was over Garry Flitcroft. The call came at the end of March, just before deadline day. The Kinkladze-fuelled victory over Southampton had been followed by a 4-2 defeat at West Ham. City had slipped one place to sixteenth, three points clear of the drop.

Lee told Ball he needed him to phone the Blackburn manager, Ray Harford, and sell him Flitcroft. When Ball protested that selling their captain was senseless, Lee replied, 'I need £3.5m by Friday or the banks will foreclose. He's got to go, he is the most saleable player we've got.'

Blackburn under Walker were the kind of club who could pay straight cash but their terms of £1.75m immediately, followed by twelve instalments of £145,000 could not satisfy Manchester City's need for immediate money. Ball claimed Blackburn offered a single payment of £2.8m, which he believed the club accepted. Their indebtedness had cost £700,000, although in Flitcroft they would lose far more.

Then came Easter and the Manchester derby. It would be the last for four years. Ball played both his Georgians, with Mikhail Kavelashvili making his debut alongside Kinkladze. Kavelashvili scored, so too did Rösler, but this was the season in which Eric Cantona swept all before him and he marked his final appearance at Maine Road by scoring one goal and making two more.

The third, a vicious drive from Ryan Giggs into the top corner, settled matters. Rösler had celebrated his goal by running over to the bench, pursued by Nigel Clough, who was attempting to stop him, to taunt his manager. After the match he was interviewed by *Match of the Day,* which is usually an exercise in blandness, with neither interviewer nor subject making eye contact. Not this time.

'There is a massive problem between me and the manager,' he said. 'I'm playing for this football club, my team and our supporters but not for Alan Ball.' When he saw the interview on television Rösler felt only embarrassment. This was an age before press officers took control of Premier League footballers, a time before media training. Rösler confesses that now he would not have been allowed anywhere near a microphone.

He expected to be fined, dropped or bawled out, probably all three. Ball did nothing. Perhaps he needed Rösler too much. Perhaps he could rise above it. When Ball was sacked, Rösler, curiously, felt sadness that it had come to this.

Rösler has since spent years in management in Norway and England. His greatest achievement was leading Wigan to victory over Manchester City at the Etihad Stadium to take them to the semi-finals of the FA Cup, which was only lost to Arsenal on penalties.

'I have been a coach and I know what it is like and how it feels,' he says. 'To the outside world when they see someone lose their job they think, "Oh, he will get a pay-off; it will be okay. There will be another job."

'It's not like that. You have family, you have kids. They will be affected. When the fans start singing, "You'll be sacked in the morning", I don't think that is right because they do not know what being sacked feels like. I know it is English banter but I don't like it.'

Nothing quite summed up Manchester City in the 1990s like their final game in the Premier League. When Francis Lee made his comment about the club winning only 'cups for cock-ups' this is the match that was recalled.

The one that saw Ball ordering Steve Lomas to run down the clock believing a draw would be enough to survive while Niall Quinn, who had been listening to a radio in the dressing room and knew they needed to win, ran to the touchline in his shirt and trousers to urge his teammates to start attacking.

For a club that had begun the season appallingly, whose dressing room was split between the young players who looked up to their manager and the old sweats who derided him and his obsession with Kinkladze, Manchester City had done remarkably well to be in this position at all.

Their struggle has echoes of what was happening at the other end of the table. Newcastle, led by one of Ball's successors as England captain, Kevin Keegan, had seen their vivid dreams dissolve of a first title since the days when the Quayside was known for its wharves and coal barges rather than nightclubs and boutique hotels.

Each was undone by a game against Liverpool. For Keegan it was the 4-3 defeat at Anfield in which Faustino Asprilla and Stan Collymore, brilliant centre-forwards who were to fall prey to depression, shone with a brightness they displayed too seldom. For Ball, it was this 2-2 draw.

There was one relegation place to fill and there were three teams who could fill it. The two other candidates were Coventry and Southampton, clubs that throughout the decade would pull off the kind of great escapes the average inmate of Stalag Luft III dreamed of.

As the season reached a crescendo, Manchester United went to Southampton and lost 3-1. It was the afternoon in which Ferguson ordered his players to change their kit during the interval. Ferguson had read something about peripheral vision and argued that United's disastrous first-half performance had been down to their grey away shirts.

They came back in blue and white. It made no kind of difference to the extent that when Le Tissier was stopped by a journalist in the Dell's car park he confessed to not having realised Manchester United had changed their kit at all.

At Maine Road, United's defeat fell like a blow upon a bruise. The air of fatalism deepened after the penultimate game which had seen Manchester City win 1-0 at Aston Villa. Michael Brown, part of Ball's midfield that afternoon, recalls the aftermath of that victory: 'When we came into the dressing room at the end, the atmosphere was brilliant. It was as if we had stayed up. But then somebody said both Coventry and Southampton had won as well and we were just shattered. All the elation just evaporated within seconds.'

For the finale, Coventry, Manchester City and Southampton would all be at home, although Ball's task appeared considerably harder than either Atkinson's at Highfield Road or Dave Merrington's at the Dell. City had to better one of their results and they would be playing Liverpool, who in their two previous encounters had put ten past them. Coventry had Leeds, Southampton would face Wimbledon.

Nevertheless, as the game approached there was a sense of optimism around Platt Lane. Wimbledon would be cussedly awkward. Leeds had beaten Coventry, 3-1, at Elland Road earlier in the season. The following week, Liverpool would be playing in the FA Cup final and, away from Anfield, they had not won since February. The previous month Coventry had beaten them at Highfield Road.

After 41 minutes, City were two down; Steve Lomas had put through his own net and a deflected shot had given Ian Rush his 346th and final goal for Liverpool.

Manchester City kept attacking, they had no other option. Quinn and Rösler went close. Neil Ruddock brought down Kinkladze. Rösler scored from the penalty spot. Then Kit Symons improbably stabbed the ball into the roof of the net from three yards out. There were a dozen minutes remaining. Then the attacks stopped and time was allowed to seep away until Quinn's frantic arrival on the touchline.

Two years later, Alex Ferguson was walking back to the Old Trafford dressing rooms. It was half-time against Bayern Munich and he asked if anyone knew the other scores in the Champions League. Bayern's press officer, Markus Hörwick, fished out his phone and read the scores out. Ferguson was astonished. This was technology he had never seen before. He wondered why the Germans always seemed to be the first to have it.

In Moss Side in 1996 they relied on the transistor radio pressed to the ear. Someone with one shouted out that Wimbledon had scored. Twenty-two years later, a study by the Massachusetts Institute of Technology would find that on social media fake news travels six times faster than the truth. At Maine Road it travelled to the home bench with giddying speed.

The transistor radio was in the directors' box. Michael Horwich had resigned as a director in 1992 when he reached 70 but he had been made a club vice-president and was watching the game with his son, David.

'Just in front of me was a couple who I think were from Oldham,' David recalls. 'She always had a radio and would constantly give out the scores in every game. The guy next to her was the one responsible for the fuck-up.

'He shouted out to Francis Lee that Southampton were losing. Francis shouted the news to Martyn Margetson (the reserve goalkeeper) who was standing behind the City dug-out. Martyn passed the message on that we only needed to draw.

'Shortly afterwards, I tapped the woman with the radio on the shoulder and asked, "Are Southampton losing?" and she replied, "No. Definitely drawing."

"Definitely?"

"Definitely."

'I then grabbed Franny Lee and said, "Southampton are definitely drawing." His face absolutely fell. Almost at that moment we looked down and we could see Niall Quinn in his suit running down the touchline urging City to attack.

'After the game I was due to meet some clients who were Liverpool fans in the Royal Oak in Didsbury. It was quite emotional; the pub had only just opened and I was telling everyone the story of how "this wanker" had cost us relegation when this guy walked in and said, "I am so sorry." I told him it probably hadn't made any difference.'

Ball was to describe relegating Manchester City as the worst moment of his managerial career. The other error he turned over again and again in his mind also involved playing for a draw.

In April 1985 his Portsmouth side met Manchester City at Fratton Park. Both were going for the last available promotion place. The match was deadlocked at 1-1 but Ball urged Portsmouth forward only to see the eighteen-year-old Paul Simpson lead a breakaway and seal the match for City with a lob.

Portsmouth won their final three games and, had they closed up and ground out a draw against Manchester City, they, rather than Billy McNeill's side, would have been promoted. It was something Alan Ball never quite forgot and perhaps subconsciously it played on his mind now. Perhaps.

'He wasn't bitter when Franny sacked him,' says Jimmy. 'He understood the game. Franny called him over to his house and he knew what was coming. He had needed to win and he hadn't won. When he arrived at Franny's house he told him, "I know what you're going to say". Franny just said, "This can't go on, mate." When it was done they talked through things over a brandy and a cigar.

'It hurt him, though. Looking back, he would say that he didn't start quickly enough. When you're a manager at a new club you tend to have to make quick judgements. At Manchester City he didn't find out about people quickly enough, he didn't get people in or out quickly enough and he paid the price in those first eleven games.

'Maybe he should have taken fewer risks, been more boring, put Kinkladze on the bench and brought him on late. The other signing he was proud of was Paul Dickov. He signed him the week he was sacked. He took me with him to Arsenal to scout him. He came on as a substitute in his last game, here at Stoke.

'City had an ageing squad some of whom he frankly didn't get on with. But he did think that, below them there was a good young side waiting to take shape. That's why the Garry Flitcroft sale hurt him so much. He thought he could build a side around Garry with the likes of Nicky Summerbee, Steve Lomas, Kit Symons, Richard Edghill and Kinkladze. He thought this next crop would have had the energy to have done well. He never got to see it, though.

'He was offered a six-figure sum to tell his side of the story and turned it down. He was old-school like that, proper. He didn't buy into the hype that the modern Premier League was something amazing. Put Eden Hazard on to the kind of rough, heavy pitches of the late 1960s or early 1970s and have Johnny Giles chasing him down and then see what happens.

'Is the game quicker? Inevitably, because the ball is not rolling through mud. Is it better? If you asked Dad, he would roll through a list of names – Moore, Best, Beckenbauer, Platini, Charlton, Pelé – a and he would say, "I'm not sure, son."

'There is one moment from his funeral that really sticks in my mind. There were football fans from everywhere around the cathedral paying their respects. I looked up and saw someone in a Manchester City shirt.'

George

FOR NOEL GALLAGHER, SATURDAY, 19 AUGUST 1995 HAD BEEN the end of quite a week. The previous Monday had seen the release of Oasis' first single from what would become their masterpiece; *What's the Story, Morning Glory*.

'Roll With It', which was a very long way from the album's best track, was released simultaneously with 'Country House', the first single from Blur's new album, *The Great Escape*. It was Britpop's cup final, pitching the Gallagher brothers, who had been brought up in Burnage by an abusive father, against Damon Albarn, whose mother was an artist and whose father was a musician.

On one record cover was a photograph of Neuschwanstein Castle in Bavaria, the other had Manchester's likely lads wrapped up in duffel coats by the pier at Weston-super-Mare. It was North v South, Beatles v Stones.

The rivalry made it on to *News at Ten* and Gallagher decided to relax by taking himself off to Maine Road to watch Manchester City's first game of the season. Sitting in the directors' box, next to Terry Venables, who was then England manager, he had his first sight of Georgi Kinkladze, playing against Tottenham.

'I thought, Jesus, this is either the most frightening thing I have ever seen or the best things I have ever seen,' he said of Kinkladze. 'I couldn't decide which it was. It was typical City.' The match finished 1-1. Blur beat Oasis by 274,000 records sold to 216,000.

If Noel Gallagher couldn't make up his mind, Joe Royle could. Maine Road's second game of the season saw City host Everton. Royle was enjoying his time in charge of Goodison Park. They had won the FA Cup a few months before, he had just broken the club's transfer record for Andrei Kanchelskis.

Maine Road meant a return to a former club, conversations with Alan Ball, with whom he had won the championship at Goodison in 1970. Everton won 2-0 and afterwards Royle sought out another of his former team-mates, Tony Book. The subject of Kinkladze came up. 'He's a wonderful talent,' said Joe. 'But he'll get you the sack, Bookie.'

Seen from the Kippax, he was proof that, even in decline, City still valued pure ability. Songs were composed in his honour.

As a team player, he was unimaginably disastrous. In his three seasons at Maine Road, Manchester City were relegated twice. The season in between saw them end up fourteenth in the old Second Division, which was then the worst finish in their history – a record that would take twelve months to break.

When Kinkladze embarked on his second stint in English football, at Derby in 1999, Francis Lee called Jim Smith to congratulate him on the signing. 'He will win you matches that cannot be won. If you get two more players who are on the same wavelength, you will have a devastating team.'

There were very few footballers in England who were on Kinkladze's wavelength. By the time he left Pride Park, Derby had been relegated once and had narrowly escaped collapsing into the third tier of English football.

The game that changed Georgi Kinkladze's life came on a rain-spattered afternoon in Tbilisi in November 1994. Georgia had been an independent nation for three years and they had yet to score a competitive goal at home. They were playing Wales.

Ryan Giggs had predictably withdrawn from the trip – he would start Manchester United's next match, the 5-0 Andrei Kanchelskis-inspired demolition of City – but he would play only twice for Wales in their attempt to qualify for Euro '96.

They were, however, still able to field a formidable squad. The Welsh forward line consisted of Mark Hughes, Ian Rush and Dean Saunders. Gary Speed and Barry Horne were in midfield while Neville Southall kept goal.

It was, however, a squad that was deeply suspicious of travelling into the unknown fragments of the old Soviet Union. The previous month had seen them in Moldova. Training sessions had to be arranged around the two-hour spells the Cosmos hotel in Chişinău had hot water.

The mattresses had mould, the rooms had their quota of cockroaches and when it seemed their return to Cardiff would be delayed, the team said they would sleep on the plane. It may not have been coincidence that when things went against them in Georgia, they collapsed completely.

Their hotel in Tbilisi was luxurious, but the afterglow of Georgia's civil war still lingered. The team passed a burned-out UN armoured car on the way to the stadium and, in the evening, they could hear gunfire coming from the suburbs.

To compound matters, Wales had done virtually no research on their opponents and many players regarded their manager with derision. The squad adored Terry Yorath, who had taken Wales achingly close to qualifying for the 1994 World Cup but who had resigned when the Welsh FA would not give him a pay rise of £5,000.

His successor Mike Smith was, in the language of the dressing room, a 'civvy' who had never played professionally. They called him 'The Verger'.

There should have been plenty to research. Since breaking away from the Soviet Union, Georgia had nurtured some thrilling talents. Alongside Kinkladze were Temuri Ketsbaia and Shota Arveladze, who would play for Newcastle and Glasgow Rangers respectively. Between them they annihilated the Welsh defence.

Ketsbaia scored twice but, seen through Southall's eyes, Kinkladze had been unplayable. Power shortages in Tbilisi meant that it was hard to make out the numbers on the electronic scoreboard, but the certainty was that the 5-0 defeat was Wales' heaviest since 1953.

In June came the return at Cardiff Arms Park in front of a pitiful crowd of 8,000. The match was notable for Vinnie Jones belting out 'Land of My Fathers' in an attempt to prove his tenuous right to wear a Wales shirt, which consisted of a grandfather born in Ruthin. It demonstrated his ability to remember a script – even one in Welsh – which would serve him well when his career turned to acting.

Within half an hour, Jones had demonstrated why so few in Wales had wanted him to research his family tree by stamping on Mikheil Kavelashvili. It was his third dismissal in a year. Seventeen minutes from time, Kinkladze ran, unchallenged, at the Welsh defence and chipped Southall from more than twenty yards.

Southall had not left himself obviously exposed – he was standing on his own six-yard line. He was left helpless. Lee had sent both Colin Bell and Jimmy Frizzell, then Manchester City's chief scout, to Cardiff.

A few weeks after the triumph in Cardiff, Lee made his move for Kinkladze, who had just turned 22. For Robinzon Kinkladze, Georgi's father, this was everything he had trained him for.

His work had begun early. To build up his stamina Robinzon would tell his son to walk around their flat on his knees. He signed him up to study Georgia's national dance, the *mtiuluri*, for the same reason.

By 1991, the year Georgia declared itself independent, he became part of the nation's most famous team, Dinamo Tbilisi, the club that had knocked Liverpool out of the European Cup in 1979 and won the Cup Winners' Cup two years later, thrashing West Ham 4-1 at Upton Park on the way to the final in Düsseldorf. Because their opponents, Carl Zeiss Jena, were from East Germany, fewer than 5,000 watched the game.

The boys who had destroyed Wales – Ketsbaia, Kinkladze and Arveladze – all played for Dinamo and possessed an instinctive understanding of each other's game. However, Dinamo Tbilisi was changing. In the Soviet Union, the club had been funded by the Red Army and given special privileges by the Georgian Communist Party, whose most famous member had been Josef Stalin.

Now the Red Army no longer existed and what soldiers did remain in Georgia were fighting a civil war between the country's first president, Zviad Gamsakhurdia, and the man who replaced him, Eduard Shevardnadze, who had been Mikhail Gorbachev's foreign secretary. On New Year's Eve, 1993 Shevardnadze won. Gamsakhurdia, a nationalist whose slogan had been 'Georgia for the Georgians', found himself cornered in a village in his home province and was found with a gunshot wound to the head. His wife said he had committed suicide.

While Georgia burned, Dinamo Tbilisi attempted to protect its greatest assets – its footballers. Dinamo's president, Merab Jordania, ruled they had to be got out of the country, either on loan or sold.

Ketsbaia went to Cyprus, to Anorthosis, a club he would eventually manage in the Champions League. Arveladze was loaned out to Trabzonspor in northern Turkey. Kinkladze, Dinamo's most valuable player, went furthest of all from the front line.

It was a bizarre itinerary. Saarbrücken, Madrid, Buenos Aires. Saarbrücken were in the second division of the Bundesliga. Kinkladze loathed its physicality, played eleven games, scored no goals.

He was offered to Atletico Madrid for £200,000, a tenth of what Francis Lee would pay for him, and had a trial at Real, who thought him tactically naïve. However, Boca Juniors had a scout in the Spanish capital looking for talent that might not be good enough for the Bernabéu, but who might shine at the Bombonera.

In Buenos Aires, Kinkladze was introduced to Diego Maradona, who had just had his contract with Newell's Old Boys terminated. A group of journalists had gathered at the gates of his home in the plush suburb of Moreno and he had answered by firing an airgun at them. He was spending his time shark fishing and losing weight for the World Cup in the company of a bodybuilder, Daniel Cerrini, whose use of ephedrine would be uncovered after a group game in Dallas.

The meeting would have been the only high point of Kinkladze's time in Argentina. When he arrived, Boca Juniors were in convulsions. The regime of César Luis Menotti, the man who had managed Argentina to the 1978 World Cup, was disintegrating. Boca were making panic signings from everywhere in an attempt to halt a slide that would see them finish thirteenth.

It was not a surprise that Kinkladze failed to settle, and what convinced him to leave was that all the talk amongst Boca's players was of securing a move to Europe. Kinkladze found himself back in Tbilisi, on the edge of Europe, winning his final trophies for Dinamo. The war was done; it was time for Jordania to cash in.

Alan Ball was presented with Georgi Kinkladze as a gift and it was one he cherished. He relished the skill, the possibilities that he would bring. Just before the opening game against Tottenham, Ball was confident enough to state: 'Statistics tell me that City had no problem scoring goals last season and there is no reason why they are going to stop.'

In this he was completely mistaken. Manchester City fell from being the tenth highest goal-scorers in 1994/95 to the lowest. Ball imagined that Kinkladze could transform Manchester City in the same way Matt Le Tissier had transformed Southampton. They were both fabulous individualists but Kinkladze had nothing like Le Tissier's talent for putting the ball in the net.

In his 443 appearances for Southampton, Le Tissier scored 141 goals, more than a goal every three games. After leaving Tbilisi, Kinkladze played 260 matches for clubs ranging from Manchester City to Rubin Kazan and scored 35 times – once every seven-and-a-half matches.

'He did not score enough goals,' says Uwe Rösler. 'Le Tissier would score 25 goals a season and Kinkladze would score four or five. When you build a team around an individual he needs to be the main man in terms of goals.

'Technically, Kinky was the best footballer I ever played alongside. But when people say who was the best player I played alongside, I always say, "Do you mean the most effective player or technically the best player?"

'Now he would have been like David Silva, but we didn't play like that in 1995 and we didn't have the players around him to be able to play that kind of football. It was very, very difficult to integrate him into the team without losing some of the aspects that are required to win games.

'Alan Ball tried everything. Two up front, played Kinkladze on the wing. Then he played him in a diamond as a ten. Then he played split strikers when Niall Quinn played on the right wing and I played on the left wing and Kinkladze played through the middle. Niall had played for Ireland in the World Cup and now he was being asked to play right wing.

'Because I came from Germany and was a European footballer, I found it not too difficult to read Georgi's game but a lot of the British lads found it hard to anticipate his runs and to accept that he didn't do anything off the ball.

'There were a lot of players who found it hard to accept a free role for one player – the Keith Curles, the Niall Quinns, the Tony Cotons – but Kinkladze is part of the history of Manchester City. People came to Maine Road just to watch him. He made Manchester City exciting.'

If you ask Uwe Rösler to name the best goal he scored for Manchester City, it would be the opening goal in the FA Cup tie against United at Old Trafford in February 1996. The pass from Kinkladze was perfect, made on the turn, spotting the gap between three red shirts. Peter Schmeichel sprinted out, Rösler lobbed him and the ball just brushed the tips of the Dane's gloves, struck the inside of the post and rolled in.

Rösler sits back and ponders the tantalising question. How would Georgi Kinkladze have fitted into the fabulous Manchester City side managed by Pep Guardiola? The answer is that he wouldn't.

'When you watch Manchester City under Guardiola, everybody works very, very hard,' Rösler says. 'He would not have played for Guardiola because he would not have worked as Guardiola likes his footballers to work. It doesn't matter how much talent he has.'

It took until late November for Kinkladze to show why Lee and Ball had been so enthused by his ability. It was the time Ball won his manager of the month award, three victories and a draw at Sheffield Wednesday. The finest of the wins was against Aston Villa at Maine Road.

The Aston Villa manager, Brian Little, had chosen a three-pronged attack against a club that had spent most of the autumn staggering blindly from defeat to defeat.

However, Kinkladze proved so adept at ripping through space in Villa's midfield that Dwight Yorke was pushed back in attempt to plug the gap. Then five minutes from time came a one-two with Quinn and Kinkladze picked his spot from an acute angle. 'Give him the ball and he will blossom,' said his manager in what was to become Alan Ball's mantra at Maine Road. On that late November day it seemed obvious, but few things at Manchester City ever were.

That performance was followed up with another 1-0 win, this time at Elland Road. Gary McAllister, the creative heart of the Leeds midfield, confessed to Francis Lee after the match: 'He turned me one way, he turned me the other way and I turned back and nearly screwed myself into the ground.'

Then, there were the fourteen seconds of genius against Southampton. When Kinkladze is remembered, it is usually for taking the ball on the right flank, skipping past Simon Charlton and dancing towards the goal.

He never quite loses Charlton, there are times in those fourteen seconds that he would feel the midfielder's hand on his shoulder, his breath on his neck. In front of them are three covering defenders. Ken Monkou meets him on the eighteen-yard line and almost trips himself.

Neil Heaney, having done almost a full circle in the area, slides in from the right and misses. Suddenly, there is daylight and just the vast 6ft 4in frame of Dave Beasant. But the goalkeeper has already gone down, is already on his knees, when Kinkladze chips. The ball brushes Beasant's glove on its way to the net.

It is a goal that stands comparison with Diego Maradona's against England in Mexico ten years before. That was in a World Cup quarter-final. In a fabulous study of Kinkladze for *FourFourTwo* magazine, the journalist Seb Stafford-Bloor regrets the fact that it came in a match between Manchester City and Southampton, two unremarkable sides – 'A watercolour in a cheap frame'.

However, for Kinkladze and for Manchester City, this was a desperately serious afternoon. Ball had called it the most important fixture the club had faced since his arrival. City had begun it in seventeenth place, two points clear of Southampton in the final relegation spot, although Ball's former club had two matches in hand. It was mid-March; the clocks would soon be going forward and now matches had to be won.

Kinkladze delivered for the man who had staked everything on him. After fourteen minutes he had struck the crossbar. Like Maradona's slalom through England in the Azteca, his dance through the defence had been his second goal of the game. The first had been a tap-in after Beasant had parried Nigel Clough's shot.

The win lifted Manchester City to fifteenth, five points and three places above the relegation slots. They were in a place of greater safety, although like so much about Manchester City, the feeling would be delusional.

Kinkladze was loved far in excess of the goals he produced or the success he brought. In Stafford-Bloor's words: 'He arrived at a time when differences were unusual and when consequently they were most appreciated. English football was about power, size and gelled centre partings and he was an impish player with the feet of an angel and a chorister's haircut.'

It was perhaps unsurprising Georgi Kinkladze started slowly. Manchester City was the fourth club that had tried to take him on in the space of less than two years. He spoke barely any English. Unlike Uwe Rösler, who had Michel Vonk to tell him what Brian Horton was saying, Kinkladze found no one in the City dressing room able to translate for him – very few in Alan Ball's squad could even place Georgia on a map.

Few at Platt Lane became closer to Kinkladze than Nicky Summerbee. 'When he first came over, he couldn't speak a word of English, but we seemed to hit it off as mates. We'd go out and he wouldn't speak much – it was odd because it was just the two of us.

'When you got to know Georgi, he had a really good sense of humour – very sarcastic. He could cut you down as well as anyone else. When he first came, nobody knew about him so there was no pressure to perform but, as soon as the fans saw what he could do, they liked him straight away.

'I think Alan Ball knew how to play him best. He had a real go with him. Georgi needed a bit of an arm around him to show he was needed and Ball definitely did that.'

After two months living in a hotel, the club found Kinkladze a house on a modern executive estate in Wilmslow. He was joined by a fellow Georgian, Nataly, who had learned English at Hastings and had been employed as an interpreter. Then, just before Christmas, 1995, they were kept company by his mother, Khatuna, who worked as a history teacher at a time when Georgia suddenly had a lot of history to teach.

Khatuna's journey from Tbilisi to Wilmslow had been a chaotic one. Nataly had failed to show up and Mrs Kinkladze, armed with a photograph of her son, stopped strangers at Heathrow, employing the only English words she knew: 'Mother of Georgi. City football.' With that, she made her connection to Manchester to prepare a Georgian Christmas dinner of aubergine, chicken in walnut sauce and honey cake.

Her son liked cars. Fast cars, parked haphazardly. 'He had a nasty habit of leaving his car anywhere in Manchester,' Frank Clark recalls. 'My secretary, Julia, had to pay his parking tickets. I told George, "This has to stop. You can park where you like but, if you get a parking ticket, it is your responsibility to pay it."'

It was a Ferrari which in 1997 almost ended his career. It was a Testarossa that cost £150,000 and it was parked in the Four Seasons Hotel not far from the airport. Next to it was Summerbee's BMW.

Both men turned out of the hotel bound for Princess Parkway, the dual carriageway that leads to central Manchester. They didn't get very far. There was a screech of tyres, Kinkladze lost control, the Ferrari, which he had owned for less than a month, struck the wall of an underpass. Kinkladze was propelled through the sunroof, which fortuitously, given it was late October was open, and on to the tarmac. He required 30 stitches in his back.

It was gift to the headline writers. Underperforming footballers in overperforming cars, racing while Manchester City careered towards the third division – the club had taken one point from its last four matches, and that a goalless draw at home to Reading.

Summerbee was adamant they were not racing. Kinkladze was simply not a good enough driver to handle a Ferrari Testarossa, but they were prosecuted for dangerous driving, a case that cost the pair £15,000 between them in fines, although by the time the court convened, Summerbee was at Sunderland and Kinkladze was playing his football in Amsterdam.

'I never saw the enigma called Georgi Kinkladze,' Frank Clark says now. 'He was a lovely kid. When we first started work at the club, I saw him eyeing me up, wondering how I was going to treat him.

'We played four at the back, four across midfield with Uwe Rösler up top and Kinkladze free behind him. He could go wherever he wanted in the hope that we could get him on the ball in and around the opposition penalty area, where he could be lethal.

'The last home game of the 1996/97 season the players did a lap of honour. Well, it wasn't a lap of honour, it was to thank the crowd for their support and the reception Kinkladze got was incredible. I turned to my assistants, Richard Money and Alan Hill, and said, "We can't sell him."

'In fact, we did receive a bid for him that summer for £5m. I won't tell you who it was from but the board were horrified. They did not understand that if you had Kinkladze in a good team he would have made them into a great one, but in an average team he was a luxury.'

Francis Lee was astonished when Clark asked him where he thought Kinkladze should play. Clark had then been manager of Manchester City for three months. 'I thought, "Bloody hell, you're supposed to be the manager,"' Lee said. 'He had a coach there, Richard Money, and he was supposed to be a good coach and they didn't know what Gio's best position was.' The truth was that nobody did.

The lap of honour after the 3-2 win over Reading stuck in the throats of some players, not least Uwe Rösler. Kinkladze, who was carrying an injury, had not played in that game. The stadium announcer that day was Vince Miller, a man without whom no sportsmen's dinner in Manchester was complete.

Miller revelled in the title of 'the king of comperes' and, though he was a City fan who had delivered the eulogy at Bernard Manning's funeral, he worked the lounges at Old Trafford until in 2017 he was asked to leave for putting his arms around a waitress and calling her 'love'. He was 82.

Twenty years before Miller was in charge of organising the closing ceremony on what had been Manchester City's worst season in their history. Francis Lee had told him to take Kinkladze alone to the centre circle and 'let him wave to the crowd'.

Interviewed by Kinkladze's biographer, David Clayton, Miller recalled: 'Uwe Rösler took exception to this and came over to me to make his feelings known and we exchanged a few heated words. He thought it wasn't right – to single out one player – but I did what I was asked and led Gio to the middle of Maine Road. The fans had Georgian flags everywhere and messages written in his own language... I am quite sure Gio was planning to leave before that day.'

He should have gone. All the banners, the flags, the pleas written in Georgia's impossibly ancient script, the fan presenting him with a cuttings book devoted to his career, achieved was to ensure Kinkladze shackled himself to a corpse.

Jim Whitley broke through to the City first team in January 1998, in time to see the last few months of Kinkladze's Manchester City career. 'His fitness by then was laughable,' he says. 'But I'd been part of the set up for a long time before that and had watched him train. Alan Ball would ask him to do sprints and he would go 'nah' and walk off. Your Niall Quinns and your Garry Flitcrofts were having to do it. If anyone else had done that they would have been fined, but not Gio. He was separated from everyone else.

'He would go past two players, produce one little shimmy and be voted man of the match, despite the fact we had basically played with ten men. When he was on song he would drag away three or four players and I and everyone else in that midfield would suddenly look very good but, as that season wore on and we slipped closer to the edge, he lost interest.'

Despite the adulation he received from Alan Ball, Kinkladze himself thought Frank Clark had handled him best. But in February 1998 Clark was gone and he was succeeded by Joe Royle, a man whose first view of the player had convinced him that Georgi Kinkladze was a man who got managers the sack. He was not about to put his own theory to the test.

There was a dreadful match against Port Vale, which convinced Royle his prejudices were correct. He considered Kinkladze's contribution 'abysmal'. He was cast out.

There was one last coda. If Manchester City won their last two games, they would escape. The first was at home to Queens Park Rangers, who in danger of relegation themselves, had signed Vinnie Jones as a player-coach. His brief, according to his manager, Ray Harford, was 'to raise the spirits and get the fighting qualities shining through the team'.

Kinkladze was brought back to face the man he had humiliated in Cardiff three years before in the game that had persuaded Francis Lee that this might be the boy who would change everything at Maine Road. Now, Jones would again attempt to bait Kinkladze. This time, he would have more success.

The pressure on Manchester City was now so intense that they no longer warmed up at Maine Road but used the primary school opposite the ground to avoid the jeers. Jamie Pollock was one of those in the school grounds.

The game would be recalled not for Kinkladze's final display of beauty to those that had loved him, but for one of the most bizarre and balletic own-goals ever scored.

Sport is an innately superstitious business. During the Lord's Test against Pakistan in 1982, David Gower, Allan Lamb and Robin Jackman all went out for dinner. All went against the cricketer's unspoken code that you do not order duck. The next day each was dismissed without scoring.

The evening before the Queens Park Rangers game, Jamie Pollock was at home watching a DVD of own-goals and footballing gaffes. It had been given as a Christmas present but for superstitious reasons Pollock had never, until now, wanted to watch it.

Now, for reasons he did not properly understand, he opened the case, pushed the disc into the machine and began watching. His wife, Lizzie, came into the room and asked what fate he was possibly trying to tempt.

The next day, with the scores level at 1-1, Pollock found himself running towards the edge of his own box to cut out a long ball from QPR's right-back David Bardsley. Fully aware that Rangers striker Mike Sheron and a covering teammate were just yards away from him, Pollock calmly lifted the ball over the pair and headed it back towards Martyn Margetson.

It was something Paolo Maldini might have done, except that Maldini might have cushioned his header rather than sending it high over Margetson and into the net. Almost as much as the image of Alan Ball's side playing for a draw in a match they needed to win, this encapsulated the view of Manchester City, a man with an empty revolver and a bloodied, blown-off foot.

Pollock said he could 'feel the silence' all around Maine Road. In the dressing-room, Royle and his assistant, Willie Donachie, offered their support. This was the goal that effectively relegated Manchester City to the third tier, but the fatal damage had been done long before.

Fifty miles down the M6, the drama would be played out at Stoke. The day before, Kinkladze would be playing in Tunisia for Georgia.

Tunisia were preparing for the 1998 World Cup that would pitch them against England in Marseilles, a match remembered more for the rioting that wrecked the Old Port rather than for anything that happened on the pitch. This match, in Sousse, was a 1-1 draw. Kinkladze scored for Georgia, a gorgeous lob from thirty yards.

Francis Lee, who had stepped down as chairman two months before, had arranged a private plane to bring Kinkladze back to Manchester. Bernard Halford and the club's fixer, Layachi Bouskouchi, who was brought up in Tangiers, ran a newsagents' in Chorlton and had spent years helping out Manchester City and their players, were the ones charged with the mission.

After the match, Halford went to the away dressing room. There, the Georgia manager, David Kipiani, who had been part of the Dinamo Tbilisi side that had won the Cup Winners' Cup in 1981 and was probably his nation's greatest footballer, was debriefing his players. Bernard beat a hasty retreat.

Eventually, Kinkladze emerged and the three of them boarded the plane. 'He knew it was probably his last game for Manchester City,' Halford recalls. 'He had played not to get injured in the friendly and he knew this was pretty much the end of the road. When we touched down, I drove him to his house to pick some clothes up and we set off for Stoke, where we joined the rest of the team at the hotel. It was around midnight.'

The irony was that he was scarcely needed. Manchester City won 5-2, a victory rendered irrelevant by other results. Kinkladze played the final seventeen minutes.

In the World Cup summer of 1998, Kinkladze was 25. He had signed for Ajax, a club that more than any other values technique and undiluted skill. They had won the Eredivisie by 39 points. The new, gleaming Amsterdam Arena, rather than the scruffy stands of Maine Road was where Kinkladze should have played out the peak years of his career.

He would share a dressing-room with Shota Arveladze. They had been friends since childhood, Arveladze had spent a first, highly-successful season at Ajax and had named his new-born son Giorgi. It should have worked.

However, the championship-winning side was being broken up. Edwin van der Sar was sold to Juventus, Ronald and Frank de Boer were agitating to join Louis van Gaal at Barcelona. Van Gaal was due to have signed Jari Litmanen as well, but he remained in Amsterdam. If Kinkladze was to win a place in the heart of the Ajax midfield, this is the man he would have to dislodge.

Litmanen was the finest footballer Finland produced but his greatest impact was in Holland, where he won five Eredivisie titles and three Dutch Cups. To gauge how highly he was regarded, in 2016 the Finnish newspaper, *Helsingin Sanomat*, produced an entire team of young Dutch professionals called Jari, which is not a Dutch Christian name. Something similar happened in Germany to the name Kevin when Keegan won his two European Footballer of the Year titles with Hamburg. Kinkladze was relegated to the left wing or the bench.

The Ajax manager, Morten Olsen, who had persuaded him to come to Amsterdam, became embroiled in a dispute with the De Boer, twins who refused to train unless they were granted a move to the Nou Camp. In December 1998, after Ajax were knocked out of the Champions League at the group stage, Olsen was sacked.

Six months after moving to Amsterdam, Kinkladze was dividing his time between living with Arveladze or going back the hotel. He had been Ajax's record signing and he felt lost, redundant and angry.

The fanzine editor, Noel Bayley, who went to pay homage to Kinkladze at his new club, glimpsed the Georgian's precariousness while in Amsterdam. 'I first met him at Platt Lane. He was with Francis Lee, who was fussing over him and telling him that he should be wearing a vest because he'd catch cold. It was like seeing a father and son together,' he says. 'When Kinkladze first came to Manchester, he would have known nobody and I think Francis looked after him; he had him round to tea at Stanneylands and he may even have stayed with them before they sorted him a house.

'When he moved to Ajax, the Prestwich and Whitefield supporters branch ran a trip to Amsterdam to see him play. The information they printed said the ferry would leave from Horwich, which was unlikely since it's in Bolton.

'We set off for Harwich at two in the morning from Heaton Park and, on the way, we were told there were problems there so we took the van to Dover but it meant that by the time we reached Amsterdam the game we were supposed

CAUGHT BENEATH THE LANDSLIDE

to be seeing Kinkladze in was at half-time so we gave it a miss.

'The next day some of the lads went to the Amsterdam Arena for a look round and saw Kinkladze at the training ground. They told him there were some City supporters in town and would he like to meet them?

'We went to this long, narrow bar which had a pool table in the back. Kinkladze was standing by the pool table, wearing a City away shirt from the 1999 play-off final against Gillingham, which somebody must have given him because he wasn't involved in it. He wasn't drinking, he was just standing there, very shy and alone.'

Ajax questioned his mental state and like so many Manchester City managers, Jan Wouters, who had replaced Olsen, could not understand how a footballer could make so little defensive contribution. The club finished sixth, behind Roda and Vitesse Arnhem. It was their worst finish since 1965, the year Johan Cruyff broke through at the old De Meer stadium.

'Personally, I believe Gio could play in any position but he was determined he only wanted to play in the centre,' Shota Arveladze told David Clayton. 'I remember once at Ajax, Olsen was taking a training session and he wanted to get him putting in crosses from the right. That was no problem for him but he kept putting in awful balls. Olsen was really annoyed.

'Later, Kinky told me he did it one purpose so they would make him play in another position. He never got the chance to play in his best position for Ajax. Gio hated everything there, he even hated Amsterdam, which is crazy really. As a player when you are not getting to play everything can seem wrong.

'But he was stuck at Ajax. Having paid out all that money for him, they needed to get some of it back. You can understand their position – it was a business transaction – but it was very tough for him. All he wanted to do was to come back to England.'

Derby seemed a good place to start, initially on loan, then on a full £3m transfer. The deal was brokered by Derby's chairman, Lionel Pickering. His manager, Jim Smith, who was to sign Fabrizio Ravanelli and Igor Štimac, had a taste for an exotic gamble.

Kinkladze could go back to his home in Cheshire and marry his fiancée, Louise. They would have a son, Sabba, together. He bought a Porsche Carrera with the number plate: K11NKY and on Boxing Day 2000 he returned to Maine Road. The ovations he received were more memorable than the goalless draw.

However, in 2002 Kinkladze was relegated with Derby just as he had been with Manchester City, although by then he was a far more peripheral figure at Pride Park than he had ever been at Maine Road. Gerald Mortimer, the *Derby Evening Telegraph's* chief sports writer, remained unimpressed.

Mortimer was a magisterial writer whom Brian Clough had asked to type his resignation letter in October 1973. He could be acerbic – he once placed a two-pence piece in a colleague's leaving collection and asked for change – but he was never one for bullshit. Seen through Gerald's eyes, Kinkladze lacked the pace and the edge he had possessed at Manchester City and he was becoming involved in a lot of relegations.

Accompanied by his lawyer, Daniel Izza, Kinkladze had arranged a meeting to ask why Smith's successor as Derby manager, Colin Todd, was no longer starting him. Twelve months later, Derby, like Manchester City, were staggering towards the third division. Mark Lillis, who had spent a season at Maine Road under Billy McNeill, was now his caretaker manager.

Lillis had been a coach at Pride Park when Kinkladze first arrived. 'Soon after arriving at Derby, I took training and started singing 'Blue Moon' at Kinkladze who just looked at me as if I were off my head,' he says. 'He didn't know I'd played for City before him, but we stayed behind kicking a ball and talking about City.

'We had both moved on from Manchester City but we hadn't, if you know what I mean. I enjoyed working with Kinky; he had some great talent but I am still not sure what his best position is.'

Derby survived but Kinkladze did not and he began being passed around like a plate of stale sandwiches to increasingly unsuitable clubs.

At Portsmouth, Harry Redknapp played him in a single pre-season friendly. Dundee were interested in taking him to Scotland. Their chairman was Giovanni di Stefano, a convicted fraudster, an all-round fantasist and a friend of the Serbian war criminal, Arkan.

Eddie Gray, attempting to stop Leeds United's collapse into bankruptcy, offered Kinkladze a trial at Thorp Arch. He turned up late for training, his weight was a problem and his wage demands were a problem. Given Leeds' slide towards insolvency, any kind of wage might have been a problem.

He ended up in Cyprus playing under Temuri Ketsbaia at Anorthosis

Famagusta. Ketsbaia, who he had played alongside as a teenager in Tbilisi, with whom he had destroyed Wales all those long years ago. His journey was full circle.

The Year of the Four Managers

IN ROME THEY CALLED IT THE YEAR OF THE FOUR EMPERORS, THE year that Nero, the last surviving heir of Julius Caesar, was deposed and three other men wore his bloodstained laurel wreath before being assassinated or committing suicide.

Manchester City had the Year of the Four Managers. The body count was lower, but the sense of chaos and despair was broadly similar.

Rome got a new stadium out of it. Three years after the bloodshed, Vespasian, who was the last man standing in the power struggle, ordered the building of the Colosseum. Three years after the Year of the Four Managers, Tony Blair, another of history's great survivors, laid the foundation stone at the City of Manchester Stadium.

The summer of 1996 was the summer of Cool Britannia, the summer when football came home. It was the summer that began with Oasis playing Maine Road in front of 40,000; Noel opening the evening playing a guitar with a Union Jack motif. Liam, dressed in a lumberjack shirt and holding a cigarette and tambourine, then wandered on to sing the opening lines of 'Acquiesce': 'I don't what it is that makes me feel alive. I don't know how to wake the things that sleep inside. I only want to see the light that shines behind your eyes.'

The lights were dying inside the club the Gallagher brothers had supported since Liam's teacher – 'Mr Walsh, I think' – would take a few of his kids with their packed lunches to watch City train at Platt Lane.

At Maine Road it was the summer of relegation, a summer of asset stripping, the summer when the club shop at the Arndale Centre was wrecked by the

Manchester bomb. A summer dealing with a debt of £26m.

The desperate need for immediate cash had meant the club had already taken a £700,000 hit on Garry Flitcroft's sale to Blackburn. Keith Curle was sold to Wolverhampton Wanderers for £650,000. Terry Phelan and Tony Coton had already left. The loss they would make on Niall Quinn would dwarf what Manchester City had lost on Flitcroft. Alan Ball thought the Irishman might be worth £2.5m. The trouble was, Quinn had what Ball described as 'a seriously lucrative contract' that ran until 1998. He had to be got off the books.

Quinn was so disenchanted with Manchester City that he had taken himself off to Malaysia, where Selangor were prepared to deposit a million pounds in his Bank of Ireland account if he signed. First, they wanted him to play a pre-season friendly against Middlesbrough. Curtis Fleming, a teammate with Ireland, asked Quinn what on earth he was doing in Kuala Lumpur. Quinn said Selangor had asked him to play.

He thought he had better inform Colin Barlow, the managing director of Manchester City, the club he was still contracted to. Barlow, who answered the phone in the small hours, asked if he was mad. Quinn scored, Selangor won, 2-1 and Quinn was a hero. However, his wife, Gillian, had been reduced to tears by the way officials at the club had spoken to her.

She was four months pregnant and women were not supposed to ask questions in Malaysia. Quinn was angered by that and suspicious of how real the million pounds might be. He walked away.

Sunderland, who had just been promoted to the Premier League under Peter Reid, offered £1.3m for Quinn. It was half of what he should have been worth but Manchester City were no longer in a position to haggle. Quinn went to Wearside just before his 30th birthday. The next six years would see him play some of the best football of his life.

Ball's final press conference, after the 2-1 defeat to Stoke, was not a dignified affair. He claimed that Manchester City's problems were down to one man and pointed at Paul Hince, the chief sports writer of the *Manchester Evening News*. The Friday night headline had been: 'Fans Want Ball Out'. Two days later, they had their wish.

The players wanted Ball's deputy, Asa Hartford, to take over, although any hopes he might have had of managing the club he had played for were swept away on a September night in Lincoln, where Manchester City opened the scoring after 40 seconds and still managed to lose the League Cup tie 4-1.

John Beck, Lincoln's manager, remarked that Manchester City 'needed organising and directing'. He added prophetically that 'they might have to be relegated before they sort themselves out'.

George Graham knew how to organise and direct. Graham had been Francis Lee's first choice to succeed Brian Horton and, had he not faced a one-year ban for financial impropriety at Arsenal, he might have taken over. Lee offered him the job now but suddenly Graham didn't return his phone calls. Suddenly, he was unveiled as the manager of Leeds, who would endure one of the most stultifying seasons in their history, scoring 28 goals in 38 games. Graham's brilliance when it came to organising a defence ensured this would be enough for Leeds to finish eleventh in the Premier League.

It would not be the first conversation Lee and his deputy, David Bernstein, would have where there needed to be subtitles to determine what people really meant.

Dave Bassett had taken Crystal Palace to the play-off final in 1996 and they had just beaten City 3-1 at Selhurst Park. He had promoted first Wimbledon and then Sheffield United to the top flight. He was good with the media. For all of these reasons he was interviewed by Lee and Colin Barlow the day after the humiliation at Lincoln.

Not only did Bassett agree to manage Manchester City, he told Bernstein and Lee whom he wanted as his first signing. However, as Bassett, who had never played league football, turned to leave, he said, 'I am a Southern League player who became a manager. I have never played the game at your level or perhaps know it at your level.' Lee thought it an extraordinary way to end a meeting.

What Dave Bassett found extraordinary was hearing that Manchester City were organising a press conference to announce him as manager when he had asked for time to weigh up the offer. 'I just thought: "fuck you".'

The next morning, at half-past six, Lee received a call from Bassett. He would be staying at Crystal Palace. Lee had spent a lot of time trying to negotiate with investors from the Arabian Gulf, whose money was to prove rather more elusive than it would be in 2008.

He was tired, he said, of 'talking to idiots and clowns'. He was flabbergasted by Bassett's call. 'I asked him if this was his final decision and when he said yes,

I told him I was looking forward to thrashing him 5-1 when he next came to Maine Road.' That would be in January 1997, by which time Lee would have appointed two more managers and a caretaker. It was a 1-1 draw.

Less than two months later Bassett resigned as manager of Crystal Palace to make a futile attempt to save Nottingham Forest from relegation from the Premier League. He was replaced by Steve Coppell, who had started the season at Selhurst Park as Palace's technical director. All this might have been in the normal order of things had Coppell not become Manchester City manager in between.

'I am an animal who tends to roost wherever he stays,' Coppell said when unveiled at Maine Road in October 1996. 'I was at Manchester United and Crystal Palace for nine years. I hope City is a long-term move.' A month later he would call another press conference in the same room to explain his resignation.

Steve Coppell's 33 days at Maine Road are in their own way as intriguing as Brian Clough's 44 at Leeds. In each case the question is what might they have done had they stayed? David Bernstein, who met Coppell at his home in Finchley, thought the house might one day have a blue plaque proclaiming that the great revival of Manchester City began here.

Both Clough and Coppell had their careers ended by a knee injury and both entered management young; Clough was thirty while Coppell was 29 when he first became manager of Crystal Palace after Dave Bassett had resigned after four days at Selhurst Park in 1984.

Nevertheless, they were very different people. One was shy, self-effacing, believed in new methods like video analysis and had a degree in economics from Liverpool University. The other was impersonated by Mike Yarwood.

However, both Leeds and Manchester City were the biggest clubs either Clough or Coppell managed. Derby and Nottingham Forest were provincial teams where expectations, initially, were low. You could say the same of Crystal Palace and Reading, where Coppell enjoyed his greatest successes. Manchester City was not provincial and the expectation was suffocating.

Both Coppell and Frank Clark, the man who succeeded him, appeared full of belief that Manchester City, initially, represented a vast opportunity. Coppell said in his inaugural press conference that he 'did not view the club as the poisoned chalice it's been described'. Clark remarked that managing a club that could take 6,000 supporters to Barnsley 'did not sound like the job from Hell'.

Coppell soon discovered he was drinking strychnine. The results were not disastrous, but neither were they impressive. In his six matches, Coppell's Manchester City had taken seven points and had slid to seventeenth in the second tier. Four of those games were away and, after a 2-0 defeat at Swindon, he took the train back to London.

The stress was hollowing him out. His marriage to Jane, whom he had loved since they were both teenagers, was under pressure and there were the endless miles of the M6 between himself, his home in Surrey, and their son, Mark. The distance seemed to grow with every week.

It is significant that after this experience, Steve Coppell, who like John Lennon, Joe Royle and Les Dennis, had attended Quarry Bank Grammar, who had played all his football on Merseyside or in Manchester, limited his career to the south of England. He would never again want to roost far from his family.

He looked ill. Ron Noades, his chairman at Crystal Palace, said he was surprised how much the club seemed to be taking out of him. 'I think he found Manchester City too enormous.'

Paul Hince attended the press conference to explain the manager's resignation, where no questions were allowed and security staff prevented journalists approaching Coppell after he had left the podium.

'He looked physically ill. Really ill,' Hince told Coppell's biographer, Stuart Roach. 'He had lost a great deal of weight in a short time and I am not talking a pound or two; he looked skeletal.

'We were told there was no point asking a question because it wouldn't be answered and that, coupled with how ill he looked, was what led to the rumours there was something seriously wrong with him. All sorts of rumours started to circulate, not least AIDS.

'Our news-desk reporters were phoning all the AIDS hospitals and asking "Can you put me through to Mr Coppell?" hoping that one of them would say, "Certainly sir, he is in room 28." It was completely unfounded.'

The club was toxic, poisoning everyone from within. Bernstein, the man who had brokered the deal, was mortified. He had tried to persuade Lee to stall Coppell and arrange a meeting between the three of them. He was told it was impossible. The only concession Lee had wrung out of his manager was that Coppell agreed to front up at what proved to be an excruciating press conference.

Money, or the lack of it, played its part in Coppell's demise. The club's financial results were released on the day he announced his resignation. A profit of £203,000 had been turned into a £3m loss.

Coppell made only one signing, Eddie McColdrick, whom he had managed at Crystal Palace and who had won the Cup Winners' Cup with Arsenal in 1994. However, it was the signing he did not make that would have a longer-term impact.

He wanted a goalkeeper and Mark Schwarzer appeared to fulfil many of Manchester City's requirements. At 24 he was young, already an Australian international, and he played for Kaiserslautern in the Bundesliga, a league Francis Lee had long seen as a market City could exploit. At £250,000, he was cheap. Coppell arranged a behind-closed-doors friendly against Wrexham to judge him. The deal fell through. He joined Bradford.

The following year, Schwarzer would move to the north-eastern edge of Yorkshire, to Middlesbrough, for whom he would play in four major finals. On the last day of the 2004/05 season at Eastlands he would save a penalty from Robbie Fowler that ensured Middlesbrough would play European football and Manchester City would not.

Twelve months later, Schwarzer was keeping goal for Middlesbrough in the UEFA Cup final against Seville. By then, he ought to have been Manchester City's goalkeeper for a decade.

Coppell has been described as a shy, sometimes secretive individual. Even though both men were working at Selhurst Park at the same time, he did not approach Dave Bassett to ask why he had turned down the Manchester City job or whether he harboured any suspicions about the club. Bassett would have told him he thought that, compared to Ron Noades, Francis Lee was an interfering chairman who had too many spies in the dressing room.

Coppell seems to have had a reasonable, if brief, relationship with Lee. Once Coppell returned to Surrey, he received a letter from Francis Lee, offering him a payment of £30,000. Given that Coppell had resigned, there was no obligation on Lee to pay anything. Coppell wrote back, saying he appreciated the gesture but that he had not earned the money. On both parts, there was a touch of magnanimity amid the chaos.

It was entirely in character that Coppell did not inform his deputy, Phil

Neal, that he was resigning. Neal turned up at Platt Lane on the Friday morning to be told that the manager had tendered his resignation and that he would be taking training.

Neal might have expected to have been offered the job permanently. He thought he should have succeeded Joe Fagan as Liverpool manager in the grisly aftermath of the Heysel disaster. It had, after all, been Neal as club captain who had addressed the fans inside the stadium knowing there had been deaths. The job went to Kenny Dalglish. Neal described it as 'the most devastating week of my life'. Dalglish gave the captaincy to Alan Hansen and by December 1985 Neal was at Bolton as player-manager.

If his playing career at Liverpool had been one of soaring peaks – 23 trophies and five European Cup finals – Neal's time as a manager had been a flatland. Still, he had taken Coventry to eleventh in the Premier League in 1994, which was a fair achievement considering the lack of resources at Highfield Road. That had followed a spell as Graham Taylor's number two at England, attempting to manage Paul Gascoigne when he was both desperately needed and out of control. 'You would pick up a coffee cup and it would stink of brandy,' he recalled years later.

However, Neal was never to enjoy the full confidence of the Manchester City board. He was not invited to the annual general meeting, which as first-team manager would have been his prerogative. He confessed that he found out most of his news about what was going on at the club from supporters who watched training at Platt Lane.

Very soon those supporters would be demonstrating outside Maine Road against Francis Lee's regime, much as they had demonstrated against Peter Swales. Things, however, were far worse. Of the ten games Manchester City played under Neal, they lost seven. It was not how many they lost, it was who they lost to. They lost to Oxford, to Tranmere, to Oldham, to Port Vale, to Barnsley. By the time Neal made way, Manchester City were 21st in what used to be called the Second Division.

Of all the people sucked into the mess Manchester City had become, arguably none suffered more than Frank Clark. In 1995 he had been voted manager of the year; two years later the only job offer he would receive was from Southend United.

He had been part of the Newcastle side that the Manchester City of Malcolm

Allison, Joe Mercer, Francis Lee, Colin Bell and all the other immortals had beaten 4-3 at St James' Park to take the title from Manchester United in 1968.

'I remember the game very clearly,' he said half a century later. 'I had to deal with Francis Lee because Joe Mercer and Malcolm Allison had decided to play Francis on the right and push Mike Summerbee through the middle, which was the opposite of what we expected.

'My abiding memory is when the final whistle went and they had won the title Tony Coleman has got me around the throat trying to smack me. I said, "Tony, you have just won the title, why don't you take your hands off me and go and celebrate?" He was a hard man was Tony.'

A year later, in 1969, he lifted a trophy of his own, the Inter-Cities Fairs Cup – the last major piece of silverware Newcastle would parade for generations. Then, in July 1975, a couple of months before his 32nd birthday, Clark was given a free transfer to Nottingham Forest, who had just finished sixteenth in the Second Division behind Blackpool, Notts County and York. It would have been a gentle retirement had Brian Clough not also arrived at the City Ground.

Within four years Clark was part of a team that won promotion, the league title, two League Cups and the European Cup amid the most spellbinding transformation of a football club ever achieved by one man.

After the victory in Munich that sealed Nottingham Forest's first European Cup, Clark left to become Sunderland's assistant manager, working under Ken Knighton. In their first season at Roker Park, they took the club back to the top flight.

However, Sunderland's chairman was Tom Cowie. 'Imagine a cliched, identikit picture of a hard, self-made millionaire, and you'll have a good idea what Tom Cowie was like,' says Clark. He had begun his career selling motorbikes on a piece of waste ground in Sunderland and by 1980 he controlled car dealerships across the North East.

On Boxing Day, Sunderland were due to play West Bromwich Albion at home. Knighton suggested the team stay at a hotel on Christmas night. Cowie replied the club could not afford it. Knighton, who knew the hotel would accept £10 a room, offered to pay for the hotel himself and leaked the details to the local press. It was something Cowie, who felt he had been exposed as a skinflint, never forgave. The club's chief executive stood over them as Clark and Knighton cleared their desks.

They pitched up at Leyton Orient. For away games, Clark would load the skips filled with kit on to the train or drive the team bus himself. Knighton was expected to use his credit card to guarantee hotel reservations. In 1983 Clark became the manager at Brisbane Road. Six years later, they won the play-off final to gain promotion to the Third Division. He became the club's managing director.

Then, in 1993, came the call to replace a legend, the task that was to prove so completely beyond David Moyes when he succeeded Sir Alex Ferguson at Old Trafford twenty years later. In many respects the task Clark faced at the City Ground in succeeding Brian Clough was far harder, harder than the job he would be given at Maine Road or the job Moyes walked into.

Moyes inherited a Manchester United side that were champions of England. Nottingham Forest had been relegated. Roy Keane, Nigel Clough and Gary Charles were leaving. In terms of personality all Clough and Clark had in common was a North East accent. Every word he said to his players in the dressing room of the City Ground would be compared to the language Clough had used. Every action would be judged against the master.

'In some respect it was easier,' Clark says. 'Nottingham Forest were a fabulous football club, full of lovely people, many of whom I knew. As soon as I walked into the club, I felt at home. I never felt that way at Manchester City.

'Forest had been relegated; they were depressed. The messiah had gone; they were scared. I knew I could deal with that. I'd been phoned by Fred Reacher, the chairman, who had been a director when I'd been a player.

'When I picked up the phone, Fred said, "Have you heard that Brian's gone?"

"Yes, I've read about it in the papers."

"Do you want the job? It's just that five people have turned me down already and I'm desperate."'

Three months after Clark had taken over at Nottingham Forest, the club were 20th in the Second Division. After one defeat the Forest team bus found itself on the M1 by the turn-off for Mansfield alongside a coach carrying its supporters who banged the windows and gestured obscenities at their players.

The turning point came with a touch of Clough. A room was booked in a pub called the Griffin, the players were served fish and chips with plenty of wine and told to air their grievances.

Then, Clark did something Clough would not have done. He employed a fitness trainer, a karate black-belt named Pete Edwards who had worked with Lazio and Parma in Italy. In April at Peterborough, Stan Collymore scored the goal that returned Nottingham Forest to the Premier League.

The following year, Forest finished third. Not since they were second to Liverpool in 1979, the year they beat Malmö to win the European Cup, had they been higher. On their return to Europe, Malmö were their first opponents. They reached the quarter-finals of the UEFA Cup only to be overwhelmed by Bayern Munich.

Then came the slide. Collymore was sold to Liverpool. Steve Stone was injured, Bryan Roy's second season in Nottingham was a shadow of the first. New signings like Dean Saunders and Andrea Silenzi, brought in from Torino, did not work. Forest finished ninth.

On 17 December 1996 Nottingham Forest were beaten 4-2 at Anfield; Collymore scored twice. They had not won a game since the opening weekend of the season and were bottom of the table, with ten points from seventeen games. The club was in the throes of a takeover. Everything appeared to be in a state of paralysis.

Brian Clough used to tell any manager contemplating resignation that they should sleep on it and keep sleeping until they changed their minds. Clark became convinced that if something did not change at the City Ground, Nottingham Forest would be relegated. He resigned.

The news sparked a brief panic on the Stock Exchange when one broker thought Ken Clarke, then Chancellor of the Exchequer and a prominent Nottingham Forest fan, had resigned and began dumping thousands of shares. Having quit, Clark took himself off to a Status Quo concert. Clarke would have chosen a jazz club.

A few days later, Frank Clark was at home in the snowbound Nottinghamshire countryside when Francis Lee phoned from Barbados offering him an immediate return to management. With hindsight, it was far too soon. Clark should have taken a break, perhaps joined Lee in the Caribbean, taken stock and waited for the offers to come as they would. His managerial career was still in credit.

When Brian Clough was fired by Leeds in 1974, he could joke he had won the Pools. The pay-off would, financially, set him up for life. Clough, however, was an exception. Even twenty years later, managerial settlements were generally modest. Frank Clark had resigned from Nottingham Forest, he was 53, had two kids and could not afford to retire. He was from Rowlands Gill, a village you meet just before County Durham folds into the sprawl of Tyneside. There, you did not turn work down.

The work Francis Lee was offering was well paid. It was more than the salary he had earned at Nottingham Forest. Manchester City was still big and its language was bold. Behind the scenes, however, everything Frank Clark saw was small and shabby.

'My first day should have given me an idea of what to expect,' he says. 'When I accepted the job, Phil Neal was still the manager and I told the club they should settle his contract before I arrived. I travelled up to Manchester the night before and David Bernstein picked me up from the hotel and drove me over to the training ground.

'Platt Lane had a huge car park and, when we arrived, David drove to very furthest corner of it and parked up. "What are you doing, David?" I asked him.

"We will have to wait a while here," he said. "Phil Neal is still inside the training ground, saying his goodbyes."

'So, I spent my first day as Manchester City manager hiding in a car park, hoping that Phil Neal doesn't see me. I should have known this was the way it was going to be.

'To me, Manchester City seemed to be a commercial enterprise masquerading as a football club. By that, I mean the players were a secondary priority. I inherited a squad of between forty to fifty professionals, all on good money, which made it difficult to move them on. There were 24 players who knew they were not going to get a game at the weekend.

'Manchester City had some wonderful supporters' clubs who, naturally, wanted players to attend their meetings. I was all for that but not on a Friday night, which is what the club had agreed to.

'Platt Lane had one big training area, one pitch that you didn't want to use too often because they were used on Saturday mornings for the A and B teams. Anyone could watch; it was wide open. The canteen and dressing rooms were also open to the public. I tried to encourage the players to eat there but when you sat down there could be anybody at your table. They served a lot of chips.

'The team coach was a disgrace for a supposedly big club. It was small and had no microwave so the only food you could offer the players were sandwiches. I would be sat in the front seat and the players would be all round me and coming back from games you didn't have the space to think.

'I complained to the chairman and the chairman complained to the coach company, who were just around the corner. The managing director came to see me and said they were desperate to keep the contract with Manchester City. I said: "Go down to Nottingham Forest and have a look at their bus. That is what I want".

'I take full responsibility for what happened at Manchester City but I make those points because you cannot afford to give footballers excuses for playing badly. They could say that, though they might have been crap, look at the bus they travelled on, look at the canteen where they ate and the pitches they trained on.'

Initially, the results were good. Frank Clark lost just one of his first fourteen league matches in charge. For the first time since 1992, Manchester City won four games on the spin. There was a run to the fifth round of the FA Cup, where they narrowly lost to the eventual finalists, Middlesbrough.

For the first time in a decade, Manchester City staged a staff Christmas party. It was held in the new hospitality suites at the top of the refurbished Kippax. It was held in February. Alan Hill, who was Clark's number two, hoped it might have the same impact as the fish, chips and booze night at The Griffin had at Nottingham Forest.

'We arrived on New Year's Day and we were astonished to hear City hadn't had a Christmas party in ten years,' says Clark. 'We hired a Beatles tribute act called The Fab Four, who I think are still going. I brought my guitar and sang a couple of Beatles songs with them and I finished with an old skiffle song. I looked at Francis and said, "Mr Chairman, this one's for you. It's called 'Worried Man Blues'."'

The Legends Depart

IT WAS BOXING DAY 1996 AND THE MANCHESTER CITY OFFICES in Hart Road were deserted save for two men. Both had given their lives to the club, both loved Manchester City more than it was possible to love a football club. One had come to fire the other. That is what Manchester City had come to.

Getting rid of Tony Book was the most gruelling day's work Bernard Halford ever did and, given that Halford was Manchester City's secretary for 39 years, there had been many, many days at the club.

The year before, Nelson Mandela had rung him and asked if he would become head of the South African FA. Halford had, very politely, but very firmly turned down the President of South Africa. He already had the best job in the world. Why would he ever want to leave Maine Road?

You might say the same of Tony Book. He was a Somerset bricklayer and part-time footballer with Bath City whose life had changed forever when he looked down to see the club's new manager, Malcolm Allison, climbing up the scaffolding to talk to him. He wanted Book to start training four days a week rather than two and follow some new methods. This was 1963. Book was 29.

Allison took Book with him everywhere. First to Toronto – Book had never before flown in an airliner – then to Plymouth and finally to Manchester City. There, he captained the side to the championship, the FA Cup, the League Cup and the Cup Winners' Cup.

He managed them to the League Cup in 1976 and then, when Allison returned, he stepped aside to become his assistant. He had been youth team manager. His official title now was kit manager, although he was worth far more than that. Francis Lee asked Bernard to fire him.

'It was done on Boxing Day afternoon in the offices on Hart Road,' Halford recalls. 'There was nobody else in the building because they were all on holiday. It was the hardest thing I have had to do in 58 years of football. Tony was a man of fantastic integrity, a superb man.

'I'd played my part in getting him back to Manchester City. When John Bond succeeded Malcolm Allison in 1980 I tried to get him to allow Tony to stay, but he wouldn't have it and I didn't know John Bond well enough to force the issue. We had bit of a party for him, laid on some sandwiches. At the end of the night he didn't want to leave Maine Road and eventually we had to take him home.

'Tony then went to work for Cardiff but nine months later we had a problem with the youth-team squad and needed someone to help out in administration with Ken Barnes. I said I knew someone who would sort this out and we approached Tony Book.' In 1986 he had managed them to the FA Youth Cup, brushing aside Manchester United in the final.

Book was angry. Angry that he was being sacked. Angry that Francis Lee had asked Bernard Halford to do it. Angry that it was being done in some rented club offices rather than at Maine Road.

He was not, however, angry with the man who had told him to his face to go. When he left Maine Road for the second time, the club laid on a rather more stylish party than they had when Book was first asked to leave Manchester City.

'Bookie was on the stage and in a voice loud enough for everyone to hear, he asked me and my wife to join him on his table,' says Halford. 'He wanted the room to know he did not hold it against me. Now on a match day we do the supporters lounges together at the Etihad Stadium.'

Francis Lee claimed that the instructions to fire Tony Book had come from his freshly-appointed manager, Frank Clark. He would be bringing in his own backroom staff and there would be no place for Skip.

That version of events is disputed by Clark: 'When I took the job, I told Francis I would be bringing in two people – Alan Hill, who had been my assistant at Nottingham Forest, and Richard Money as a coach.

'I told him that, if he wanted anyone sacked, he should do it before I arrived.

He sacked Tony Book and told him that it was me who had ordered it. When I got there, we didn't even have a kit man. The kit was chucked on the floor from a big skip and whoever was first in got the best kit. It is unbelievable, I know.

'I met Tony a couple of months afterwards. I said, "Tony, on my kids' life I had nothing to do with it."' Eventually, Book made his peace with Francis Lee, the man he had captained to all those trophies. It was at another dinner. Lee held his hand out, Book took it. A truce of sorts was arranged.

There will never be a truce with the other giant of the club who departed in the 1996/97 season that saw Manchester City finish fourteenth in what would now be the Championship. No sooner was it all over, with City recovering from being two goals down at home to Reading to win 3-2, than Clark fired Colin Bell from his role with the youth team.

This time the execution was carried out at Platt Lane. However, the bullets had been loaded at Old Trafford. In the summer of 1995, Alex Ferguson had sold Paul Ince, Mark Hughes and Andrei Kanchelskis and put his faith in the boys who had won the FA Youth Cup three years before. David Beckham, the Neville brothers, Paul Scholes and Nicky Butt. The Class of '92.

The *Manchester Evening News* carried out a poll to determine whether its readers thought Ferguson should be sacked. The verdict, one that Ferguson never forgot, was yes. He referred to the paper, which he thought hopelessly biased towards City, as the 'Manchester Evening Blues'. Manchester City did enjoy better relations with the media but this was because Manchester United, even under Matt Busby, let alone Ferguson, were often morbidly suspicious of journalists.

After an opening day defeat to Aston Villa, Alan Hansen told *Match of the Day* viewers that United would 'win nothing with kids'. They won the Double and in 1997 they retained their title. One of the highlights was of Beckham scoring at Wimbledon from the halfway line.

Eight years before, a Manchester City team with a core of young, locally-bred talent had destroyed United at Maine Road. The future should have been theirs. Instead, the future had slid away. Lee demanded radical measures to wrest it back.

Soon after becoming chairman, Lee had appointed Neil McNab, who had captained Manchester City to promotion in 1989 and played in the 5-1 defeat of United, to head up the youth programme. Lee thought the centre of excellence 'a shambles'. Alan Hill, Clark's assistant manager, said in evidence to an industrial tribunal, that Colin Bell and his assistant, Terry Farrell, thought they were 'untouchable and beyond reproach'.

Bell found McNab abrasive, especially when it came to releasing boys not deemed good enough for the club. 'He had a different approach to me. I didn't approve of the way he talked to the boys,' Bell recalled. 'He seemed to resent me, which I couldn't understand, and there were a series of incidents that seemed designed to embarrass me. For the first time in my life I dreaded going into the club.'

In May 1997 he went to Platt Lane for the last time. Leeds had just won the FA Youth Cup and Paul Robinson, Alan Smith, Jonathan Woodgate and Harry Kewell would form the core of the side David O'Leary would take to the semi-finals of the Champions League four years later.

Farrell was fired first, then Bell was told by Clark – coldly and clinically is how he remembers it: 'We are dispensing with your services.' Neil McNab was also sacked. Lee, said Bell, made no attempt to contact a man with whom he had shared so many dressing rooms. Unlike for Tony Book there was no farewell do. Bell asked if his England cap he had lent the club to be put on display could be returned. Lee was on holiday in Jersey at the time. Conveniently, Bell thought.

Lee had been in Barbados when Book was fired. Like Macavity the Mystery Cat in TS Eliot's poem, Franny was never at the scene of the crime. Lee said he had expected his deputy, David Bernstein, to have offered Bell an ambassadorial role with Manchester City, although once the deed was done, he did not try to get in touch.

'Francis had told me the youth-team set up was not good enough,' says Frank Clark. 'Alan Hill had a lot more experience of youth football than I did. He looked at the set-up for a month and said Terry and Colin Bell were not good enough.

'We did some digging around and the name that kept cropping up was Jim Cassell, who had been chief scout at Oldham. His name was always top of everybody's list. His salary amounted to what we paid Terry and Colin Bell, although Colin wasn't paid very much. I went to Francis and he said, "Okay sack them." I said, "Francis you are talking about sacking a legend, surely we can find something for him, have him around the club and, if you want to sign a kid or a player, you can have their photo taken with him."

'Francis said, "Nah, I want them out."'

Bell and Farrell took Manchester City to an industrial tribunal for the sole reason of getting Francis Lee to appear before it. Bell did not succeed even in this aim. The tribunal convened in October and after one day the club offered to settle out of court.

The resentment lasted forever. Francis Lee and Colin Bell have not spoken since. In 2013 James Lawton, who had ghosted Malcolm Allison's autobiography, *The Colours of My Life*, decided to write his own account of the extraordinary Manchester City team that so dazzled England between 1967 and 1972 called *Forever Boys*.

Bell told Lawton: 'I can tell you that if Franny came today with a wagon filled with £20m and tipped it on my front garden, I would fill the wagon back up and send it on its way.

'I might be short of cash, I might need it very much but I wouldn't touch a penny of it. I still see him at City games but we do not speak; occasionally he gets up from his seat and says, "Excuse me, Mr Colin Bell, can I get past?" I just let him go. I have nothing to say to him.'

Bernard Halford has known both men for more than forty years: 'That is a rift that will never be repaired and it is sad when things like that continue,' he says. 'That enmity will last as long as they are alive and it is not going to change. Colin doesn't even get involved with the Former Players' Association.'

Although his regime would not last long enough to benefit, Clark's appointments were good ones. Les Chapman, 'a real old-fashioned Lancastrian', in Clark's words, would become Manchester City's kit manager for the next seventeen years, by which time the club was utterly unrecognisable.

Chapman, who had been sacked as reserve-team manager the previous year, proved hugely popular. He came dressed up as Santa Claus for Antoine Sibierski's children and had T-shirts printed for Mario Balotelli, proclaiming: 'Why Always Me?' before Manchester United had been destroyed, 6-1, at Old Trafford.

Some footballers, Chapman found, were more demanding than others. When Peter Schmeichel returned to Manchester football, this time to play for City, among his requirements were that, before a game, his gloves be taken to the dressing room and hidden from the rest of the team. Nobody was to touch them. He also required a separate kit for the warm-up, the first and the second half.

Jim Cassell would transform Manchester City's youth teams. He oversaw the development of Micah Richards, Stephen Ireland, Daniel Sturridge and Joey Barton. There was also the beautiful, enigmatic talent of Michael Johnson, whose ability was said to match that of the young Colin Bell.

Johnson was from Urmston – Manchester United territory – but he supported Leeds and captained Manchester City to the 2006 FA Youth Cup final, which was lost to Liverpool. Rafael Benitez bid £12m for him.

Then came the injuries; hamstring, double hernia, a ruptured cruciate ligament. Then came the depression. Then came the drink and then the headlines. There were two drink-driving offences, a spell in the Priory and finally a statement announcing his retirement from football that came with a plea to be 'left alone and allowed to get on with the rest of my life'. He was 24.

Cassell's boys won the FA Youth Cup in 2008 but relations with the manager, Mark Hughes, had become very strained and when the Abu Dhabi takeover arrived, the youth team no longer mattered in quite the way it had. Cassell was packed off to a sinecure working in the Arabian Gulf.

Sheikh Mansour built fabulous facilities for the club's youth team footballers, who would parade their talents in their own stadium. Very few, however, could expect careers at the Etihad Stadium. Michael Johnson remains the last Manchester-born footballer to play for City in a Manchester derby. That was in 2007.

For Bernard Halford there were many better days than the ones that saw Tony Book and Colin Bell leave Manchester City. His uncle Harry had first taken him to Maine Road in August 1948. The London Olympics had just finished, the two Manchester clubs were still sharing Maine Road because Old Trafford had not yet recovered from wartime bomb damage. It was Frank Swift's final season as Manchester City's goalkeeper. They were playing Portsmouth. City won, 1-0.

It was an early indication of how deceptive football can be. Portsmouth became league champions and Manchester City were relegated. It was a good lesson for someone who would make Maine Road their life.

'Frank Swift had this tremendous presence about him,' Halford recalls, seventy years later. 'He was, after all, England's goalkeeper. I remember seeing him play a testimonial at Oldham, who had a player called Ray Haddington who was to go to Manchester City and who reputedly had the hardest shot in football.

'He took a penalty which Frank saved, one-handed, and, joker that he was, Frank turned to the crowd and shook his hand as if it were still stinging from the power of Haddington's shot.

'He had a part-time job for Smallman's who did a lot of catering for the cotton mills. My dad was really into his football and said to me, "Frank Swift is coming to the canteen today at lunchtime." He took me. I would have been about six. The thing that fascinated me about Frank Swift was the size of his hands. To me, they were like shovels. I never forgot his hands.'

Bernard's sport was rugby league, playing centre or full-back. He had hoped for a career with Oldham but when he was eighteen, he was released; informed he was too slender for rugby. He was told that if he ever faced Billy Boston, Wigan's greatest-ever try scorer, he would be 'snapped in half'. He never kicked a rugby ball for Oldham or anyone else again.

'I'd been working in a mill for the Lancashire Cotton Corporation since I was fifteen. They were sold to Courtauld's and six weeks after that happened I saw an advert in the paper saying Oldham Athletic wanted an assistant secretary. I thought, "I'll have a go for that".

'I got it and in 1965 Ken Bates bought the club. He had been there three months and on the Friday night he called a board meeting and sacked the secretary. I came in at ten to nine and he was standing there, wearing a long, black coat. He put his hands in his pockets and pulled a bunch of keys out and threw them to me. "There you go, Bernard, it's all yours." I found out he had sacked everybody except me and the groundsman.

'He had me doing everything and it was the makings of me. He supported and encouraged everything I did. He was a hard man to work for. Ken's moods would change. Sometimes, he could be the joker but the jokes could change just like that. People were frightened to death of him.

'He hated complimentary tickets. I remember when we first started out just me and him – because he had sacked everybody else – we had a little assistant groundsman called Albert Edwards. Ken put him on door of the players' entrance and he told him, "Albert, if Jesus Christ comes to this door without a ticket, you don't let him in." Albert just stood there shaking.'

Halford left Boundary Park for Maine Road in 1972. 'When I got the job at Manchester City, I was so overwhelmed, I decided to stay for life. I had turned jobs down in the 1960s so I could be available for City. My mentor was Paul Doherty, who was the head of sport at Granada.

'He was close to very many people in Manchester. He had brought Colin Bell to Manchester City, Ron Atkinson was very pally with him so were John Bond and Malcolm Allison. He had an ability to make contacts and after he left Granada he went to live in Cape Town.

'In 1995 I got a phone call from Nelson Mandela asking if I would run the South African FA. I turned it down because at Manchester City I already had the best job in the world.

'If I had gone to South Africa, I would have been constantly asking myself how City were getting on and the corruption in South Africa would not have sat well with me. Life is simpler if you do things right.'

The year Bernard Halford joined Manchester City, 1972, was a pivotal one for the club. Their drive for the title destabilised by the signing of an overweight and unfit Rodney Marsh, who was supposed to add style and panache to a championship-winning side. It saw the final split between Joe Mercer and Malcolm Allison and the opening of fissures in the boardroom that would lead to Peter Swales taking over as chairman.

'I have been in the game since 1960 and worked with thirty managers, including five at Oldham,' says Halford. 'The only one could I not get on with was Ron Saunders, who was an absolute nightmare to be around. He was here five months, which was six months too long, especially as far as the players were concerned.

'My favourite player was Bobby Johnstone, one of the Famous Five forward line at Hibernian who knocked Rangers and Celtic off the top in the early 1950s. We signed Bobby in March 1955; he was the first player to score in consecutive FA Cup finals – against Newcastle and Birmingham.

'He was signed by Oldham in 1961 and I have never seen a player transform a club in the way he did. If he played, the crowds would be all the way down Sheepfolds Lane. Not only did he double the gate, he kept the crowds season after season. He cost £3,000 (£65,000 in today's terms). We had 18,000 the first day he came and that was six times the previous gate. When we played Liverpool in the FA Cup we had 42,000 at Boundary Park.

'At City, we never got over the financial situation that accompanied Malcolm's second coming. Everything after that was a real struggle. Malcolm was great company. He would always have a camelhair coat over his shoulders; he almost never wore dark suits and he would never carry any money or even a chequebook.

'He would be drinking champagne in a bar, holding court and then he would suddenly sweep out, looking for somewhere else to go. Out of the corner of your eye you would be able to see the barman starting to panic and then Malcolm would turn around and say, "Oh, Bernard, sort the bill out."'

He wonders what might have been; if the club he loved really had to endure the long years of decline. There was for Bernard Halford one sliding-doors moment in his time at Manchester City – the resignation of Howard Kendall.

'I do think that if Howard had not gone back to Everton, Peter Swales would have survived. The players loved him and in Peter Reid he had an extension of himself on the field. It was a brilliant combination and, between them, they turned the place around.

'We had lost five matches in eleven months when Everton surfaced again. I had no idea just how strong Howard's love for Everton was until then. Peter Swales would have lived a lot longer had Howard not gone back to Goodison.'

Bernard Halford appears to have been one of the very few who tried to keep Manchester City at Maine Road rather than move to what was to become the Etihad Stadium after the 2002 Commonwealth Games. Its history was in the tight streets of Moss Side rather than among the light industry and empty spaces of Eastlands. The club had spent vast sums refurbishing the Kippax. There were good reasons to stay.

'I tried to get Maine Road expanded but you couldn't do it,' he says. 'Carlton Avenue was the road behind the North Stand where the social club was. You couldn't buy the street because there was one guy who had done a lot to his house.

'I went to see him and, yes, he had done a lot to the house and he would not sell it. They were indoctrinated; there was no chance they were going to sell us the house. I was on a lost cause.

'The other end backed on to Thornton Avenue which was a long road and it was mission impossible to buy it up. I was on a lone mission more or less to keep us at Maine Road because Manchester City Council were wedded to the Commonwealth Games project and turning that into our stadium.

'But we had just spent a fortune redeveloping Maine Road – the new Kippax Stand, alone, had cost £11m in three phases which was a lot of money at the time. When the Taylor Report made it compulsory to have all-seater stadiums, Francis had just come in as chairman and he thought he could get dispensation to retain the terraces for an additional year, but he found he couldn't and the capacity was chopped to 21,000.'

Bernard Halford survived the move to Eastlands and the arrival of the men from Abu Dhabi, whose money would transform the club. He handled the paperwork that would bring Robinho from Real Madrid on the day of the takeover.

In 2011 he stepped down as club secretary. It was a different club in a different stadium with very different owners from the one he had joined, but its sense of community had remained. His last match was the FA Cup final against Stoke. When Roberto Mancini's side won, he was asked to climb the steps and lift the trophy.

A few days after we met, Bernard would go back to the training ground to have his picture taken with the signings he made who were still at Manchester City – David Silva, Vincent Kompany, Sergio Aguero and Yaya Touré. It was a run of transfers the club had not seen since Colin Bell, Mike Summerbee and Tony Book were brought to Maine Road from the backwaters of Bury, Swindon and Bath, rather than from football's front line in Valencia, Hamburg, Madrid and Barcelona.

Downfall

THERE WERE THINGS THAT FRANCIS LEE SAID THAT WERE TRUE and there were things he said that were untrue. He told Frank Clark he would have money to spend. That was true. He told him the board at Maine Road was united. That was untrue.

Manchester City's worst finish in their history – fourteenth place in the second tier of English football in 1996/97 – had prompted a rash of action. Some of it was needed. The club would receive the biggest cash injection until the arrival of the men from Abu Dhabi. The club's merchandising operations would be overhauled. Some of it was rather peripheral. There would be a new club badge and a new Latin motto. There would be disagreements about the Latin.

Not since Malcolm Allison's return had so much money been pumped into Manchester City. The £11.5m put in by Stephen Boler, Lee and the new investors, JD Sports, owned by John Wardle and David Makin, was, in real terms, the equivalent of the £4.14m Allison had squandered in 1979. Eighteen years later, the money would go the same way.

Boler's investment was £5m but the injection was made with a degree of apprehension. Lee invited Boler, who now spent most of his time in South Africa, to meet Frank Clark. When Clark had left the room, Boler turned to Lee and said, 'Don't let that bugger waste my money.'

Clark found the Maine Road board difficult to gauge. At Nottingham Forest he had worked under an almost unique system designed so that no one man could take control, creating a power vacuum Brian Clough had exploited brilliantly.

'The club had 211 shareholders who had paid a fiver or maybe a pound for their shareholding,' Clark says. 'Three of the board had to stand for re-election every year. It meant anyone wanting to take control could be voted out on a whim. Nobody at Nottingham Forest had any power which suited Brian because he could run the club how he wished and everybody was scared of him.

'The best set-up in football is when you get a benevolent dictator. Unfortunately, you don't get many benevolent dictators in this game. The problem was there was no majority shareholder at Manchester City. Francis Lee, who was the chairman, the figurehead and the spokesman for the club, was not even the main shareholder.

'The main shareholders were Stephen Boler, who owned The Mere, where the club did a lot of its business, and John Wardle and David Makin from JD Sports. I went to a board meeting and John Wardle had just joined the board. He said that Dennis Tueart would be coming to work at the club. Everyone began looking at the floor.

'I knew Dennis. He had been at Sunderland when I was at Newcastle. I'd kicked him a few times and he'd kicked me back.

'I asked John, "What's he going to do?"

"He's coming in to look after our interests."

'It occurred to me that the men sitting round this table should have had only one interest – the well-being of Manchester City. I told them this.

"Ah well", said Wardle, "there are a few things that have been going on that I am not happy about. It's nothing to do with you. Don't worry."

'I believe Dennis had been brought in by John Wardle to examine some old transfers, though even to this day I don't know why. He had an unfortunate habit of opening his mouth to the press. I brought him in one day and told him to shut up.

'I have the utmost sympathy for Francis Lee because he was placed in a very difficult position. He was the chairman, the one who would kop it from the fans, but he had no real power.'

There was a new chief executive. Mike Turner replaced Graham Barlow on a salary of £100,000 a year. The club changed shirt sponsors. Umbro, who had supplied the kit for the 1937 championship-winning squad and every Manchester City side after that, were discarded in favour of the

Italian firm, Kappa.

The shirts were no longer 'sky blue' but 'laser blue'. The souvenir shop which in the words of Manchester's celebrated photographer, Kevin Cummins, contained nothing at all you would ever want to buy was replaced by the City Superstore, which stood were the old Social Club had once been.

The badge was changed. Out went the red rose of Lancashire and the boat on the Ship Canal to be replaced by a vaguely fascistic design featuring an eagle (a bird not native to Manchester) and some Latin, a language that had not been spoken in Manchester since the Gorton Monastery closed for worship. It looked like something that might have been designed for Benito Mussolini.

The motto was *'Superbia in Proelio'* or 'Pride in Battle'. However, the club could not agree whether the correct spelling should be *Proelio or Proelia* – pride in battle or pride in battles. In 2012, five years before they changed it back to something that looked remarkably similar to the old badge, they decided it would end in o. By then the language of the dressing room was Spanish and the currency was the dirham.

Clark remarked that a manager is judged on his first big signing. At Nottingham Forest it had been Stan Collymore. At Manchester City it was Lee Bradbury. At £3.25m, it was the most expensive signing the club had ever made. It proved disastrous. He would cost the club £295,000 for every goal he scored. As a signing it was up there with Steve Daley. In 1998 Bradbury was sold to Crystal Palace for half of what City had paid for him. Portsmouth then bought him back for a tenth of the fee they had accepted from Francis Lee.

'He was an ex-squaddie, tough as old boots who had never had an injury in his life,' Clark recalls. 'In the first weeks of the season I thought he and Uwe Rösler could play off each other. Then, he went off to play for England Under-21s and came back with a stress fracture of the spine. He was never the same player again.'

Frank Clark had appointed Richard Money as his first-team coach. Money had a brief but eventful career at Liverpool, playing in the 1981 European Cup semi-final against Bayern Munich and watching the final against Real Madrid from the bench. Two years later, he had been part of the Luton side that had relegated Manchester City. He would go on to manage in Sweden and Australia.

'The mistake I made was letting Richard do nearly all the coaching. I didn't get close enough to the players. I was bruised by the last three or four months at Nottingham Forest, probably more than I'd realised. I should have been out there on the training pitch, in amongst them. It's what I had always done but now I always found excuses to be in the office.'

The season began in front of 30,000 at Maine Road. Portsmouth fought back to draw 2-2. They were knocked out of the League Cup by Blackpool on penalties. Bradbury missed the fateful spot kick. Clark began wrestling with the problem that had dogged and dragged down Alan Ball; where and how to play Georgi Kinkladze.

Uwe Rösler was badly injured playing against a behind-closed-doors friendly against a team of Italian footballers hoping for a contract in the Premier League. This hit Manchester City twice over. It derailed a potentially lucrative transfer to Everton and cost Clark his best and most reliable striker for three months.

They travelled to Sunderland to become the first side to play a league game at the Stadium of Light. Niall Quinn scored the first goal. Manchester City were beaten, 3-1. They overcame Nottingham Forest, who would end the season as champions, at the City Ground but not Bury or Tranmere. They put six past Swindon with Paul Dickov giving Bradbury a tap-in for his first goal rather than score and complete his hat-trick. Only one of the next nine games was won – and that a home game against Crewe. There was no consistency, no pattern. Nicky Summerbee was exchanged for Craig Russell.

Russell was adored at Roker Park. He described himself as 'a cup-final baby' born precisely nine months after Sunderland won the FA Cup in 1973. 'I think Mam and Dad had a good celebration.' He ended up playing and scoring for the club he loved, although when Quinn and Kevin Phillips came to Wearside, the boy from Jarrow found himself third choice centre-forward.

An earlier attempt to bring Russell to Maine Road foundered when, after an offer of £1.6m had been accepted, he failed his medical. He ought to have gone to Middlesbrough but his manager, Peter Reid, refused to sell to a local rival. The weekends ticked past. He still wasn't getting a game at Sunderland; Manchester City were still sliding towards relegation. The deal was resurrected. The golden, history-laden name of Summerbee left Maine Road.

His mother, Tina, had never wanted her son to go to Manchester City. Mike Summerbee, her husband, Nick's father, had been one of the gods of Maine Road. She knew Nick would be judged, she feared he would be found wanting.

Like Jimmy Ball, Nicky Summerbee had grown up among footballers like a border collie grows up around sheep. At the age of nine he found Bobby Moore sleeping in his bed – the explanation was entirely innocent.

In 1989, precisely thirty years after Mike had played his first game at the County Ground, Nicky made his debut for Swindon. Middlesbrough were interested, more interested than Manchester City. They were sponsored by ICI and Bryan Robson made the firm's private jet available to fly the family up to Teesside. Francis Lee sent Brian Horton and Bernard Halford to talk to Nicky. The family was more impressed by Robson and his private jet. Nicky chose to follow his father. He chose Maine Road.

He was exactly the same age as Mike, 22, when he played his first game for Manchester City. At first the omens had seemed favourable. He drove home a fabulous volley from outside the area as Queens Park Rangers were beaten 4-3. He dazzled in the astonishing 5-2 victory over Tottenham. He loved Manchester and the way people would stop him in the street, ask about football and how his dad was doing.

However, he was not like his father. He was diffident, self-contained, shy. Despite his family, his idols as a boy had been Jimmy Greenhof and Norman Whiteside. As a child, his teddy bear had been called Jimmy. Rumours began to grow that he didn't kiss the badge because his heart belonged to Manchester United. Why else had he performed so badly on the Thursday night when Andrei Kanchelskis had run amok and United had scored five?

It was nonsense. Dennis Tueart had grown up supporting Newcastle, helped Sunderland win the FA Cup and, inadvertently, caused Craig Russell to be conceived. Three years later, Tueart's overhead kick at Wembley had denied the team he supported the League Cup.

Nicky did not get on with Alan Ball, could not stand the constant criticism in training and, although they were to become close, he could not fathom why Kinkladze was mollycoddled. His sister, Rachel, was a talented horsewoman. One day, in the spring of 1996, as Manchester City were staggering towards relegation, a fan appeared at her yard, asked if she were related to Nicky Summerbee and then began a tirade of abuse, how he was nothing like his father. Rachel asked the yard manager to escort the supporter from the stables. The family stopped taking the *Manchester Evening News*.

Nicky sought refuge in booze, bars and women. They were not the sort of women his father would encounter when he accompanied George Best to the Brown Bull in Salford in the years when the *Manchester Evening News* would no more write about the private lives of its city's footballers than they would print election results from Sweden.

The women Nicky Summerbee encountered were more than happy to tape his conversations and take the recordings to the *News of the World*. Summerbee was portrayed as a Manchester United-supporting playboy who partied while Maine Road burned. When he was substituted during the humiliating 4-1 defeat at Lincoln, the away fans greeted the decision with a standing ovation.

By now it was autumn 1996 and the mood across the blue half of Manchester had darkened until it was bible black. When Frank Clark had taken over a relegated Nottingham Forest, its fans had worn T-shirts, proclaiming the club was 'on loan' to the Football League. By now, Manchester City's fans realised that not only were they not on loan to the lower reaches of English football, they were likely to become permanent exhibits.

'The problem you find when you have tremendous backing from the supporters, as we did at Maine Road, is that when things are not going well, they can very quickly turn,' Clark remembers.

'You need big, strong characters to deal with it and we didn't have enough. You would talk to the opposition managers after the home games and they would nearly all say the same thing. They had told their players that, if they could keep the crowd quiet for half an hour, they would turn. They were booing Kit Symons who was the club captain. Kit was magnificent away from home but at Maine Road he could not deal with it.'

The derby was no longer with Manchester United but with Stockport County. On 29 November 1997, they met at Edgeley Park. Stockport were three up in half an hour. Symons was howled down. The following month, they faced Wolverhampton Wanderers at Maine Road. Symons tried to clear an innocuous ball and succeeded only in slicing it over the head of his goalkeeper, Martyn Margetson, for what proved the only goal of the game.

It was, he confessed, 'the lowest I have felt in football'. He was relieved of the captaincy. Twenty years after being part of a Manchester City side that reeled, punch-drunk from the Premier League to the third division, Symons would find himself as assistant manager of Sunderland, a club that did exactly the same thing.

'In those last months, Malcolm Allison used to come to the home games and he and Francis would be drinking in the boardroom after the match with Malcolm slaughtering the team,' Frank Clark recalls. 'By the time I got up there, the atmosphere would be pretty tense. It grew worse and worse and it was almost a relief when they sacked me, although the way it was done was typical of Manchester City.'

The coup began on Valentine's Day, 1998. Manchester City had lost another derby, this time at home, this time to Bury. The only goal had been scored by Paul Butler, a centre-half who had grown up in Moston in north-east Manchester and supported City. He said he would be having a quiet night in. A Manchester City fan had run on to the pitch and publicly torn up his season ticket.

After the match, three thousand fans gathered outside Maine Road for a demonstration against Francis Lee that carried as much vituperation as the ones against Peter Swales that had carried Lee to power. Uwe Rösler was confronted after the final whistle and as he tried to leave the ground.

David Makin was a fan who had a season ticket on the Kippax. He was also a millionaire, a director of JD Sports and a director of Manchester City. He was at Mottram Hall hotel and had not seen the defeat to Bury, though he had listened to the commentary on BBC GMR radio.

He phoned Wardle and asked if the game had been as bad as it sounded. Wardle replied that it was worse. He told Wardle he would contact the station's post-match phone-in and say what he thought of Frank Clark and Francis Lee. Wardle told him to go ahead.

The phone-in was presented by Jimmy Wagg, who was a Manchester City fan and knew precisely who Makin was. When he saw his name on the call sheet, Wagg asked for Makin to be put straight on. What he came out with would surpass any radio producer's wildest dream. It would see both Clark and Lee removed from their posts.

'I think there is a massive chemistry problem within the club, I really do,' Makin said. 'He [Francis Lee] overrides everybody. He tries to be dominant. I am in business and know that, if you haven't got a happy workplace, there are problems. I don't think City is a happy workplace and, frankly, there is a problem.

'Everybody is looking at Frank. Yes, I'll be honest, so am I. His tactics have left a hell of a lot to be desired but by the same rule the problem is upstairs and I think Francis should do us all a favour and live up to what he said.'

Lee had announced in 1994 that he would resign if Manchester City had not won a trophy within three years of his takeover.

'I have had enough,' Makin continued. 'I will be doing my best to remove the chairman because he is staying there and I don't know if he is bloody minded or stubborn. He is being proud. If I was him, I would put on a moustache and a cap and hide. I know for certain that there are people behind the scenes ready to take over.

'It can happen and I think it should. I have seen enough and I know the fans are hurt. I still go to the Kippax. I've been in tears with the best of them. The first thing I would do when Francis is gone is to find the guy who has probably been barred for throwing away his season ticket on the pitch and put him in the directors' box. It sums up how the fans feel.'

Three days later, the board met at Maine Road and voted to dismiss Frank Clark and appoint Joe Royle. They told one but not the other. Both were travelling to Sunderland. Royle to have a few drinks with Peter Reid, Clark to watch Sunderland's opponents, Reading, who they would be playing soon. Royle was contacted and told to turn around. Clark was allowed to keep driving.

'I got home at two in the morning and then got up to go to training,' Clark says. 'I put the radio on in the car. It was tuned into GMR or something like that and almost the first words I heard were, "Manchester City are expected to announce Joe Royle as their next manager."

'The phone went ten minutes later. It was Francis. "Can you call into my house on the way over?" I said, "I wonder what that's about, Francis."'

Joe Royle had also taken a phone call, this time from Dennis Tueart, the man with whom he had won the 1976 League Cup at Wembley. Tueart, Royle and Wardle all met in Rochdale at the home of Royle's agent, Phil Black.

The negotiations did not go well. Royle was taken aback to discover that Frank Clark did not know he was about to be sacked. He was shocked at the fact that he was offered a four-month contract. His wife, Janet, was firmly against him accepting any kind of offer from Manchester City.

He was emphatically the appointment of John Wardle and David Makin. David Bernstein did not even attend the interview that saw Royle's appointment. Lee was for keeping faith with Frank Clark. It was, however, JD Sports' money and their shareholding which told.

Royle had been out of work since resigning as Everton manager in March 1997, but he was still a major player in the English game. He had taken Oldham to promotion and two FA Cup semi-finals, saved his former club, Everton, from relegation and won them the FA Cup in 1995. The following season Everton had finished sixth, their best finish between 1990 and 2005. His salary at Goodison Park had been £250,000. He accepted half of that at Maine Road.

Royle had fifteen games to save Manchester City from the greatest humiliation in their history. They took eighteen points from fifteen games, which if repeated over the course of a season would have seen them finish fifteenth with 55 points. It was not quite enough.

Royle did two things. He decided there was no use indulging in the debate of where to play Georgi Kinkladze that had dragged down Alan Ball and Frank Clark. He dropped him entirely. His first match was at home to Ipswich. Kinkladze created the opening goal for Kit Symons and then proceeded to ignore every instruction delivered by Royle and his assistant, Willie Donachie. Ipswich won, 2-1. Royle attended his first board meeting the following week and demanded Kinkladze be sold.

'He was not a team player,' Royle reasoned. 'He was a man with no defensive instincts whatsoever.' He was too introverted to be a forceful character on the pitch and Royle disliked the whole 'Kinkladze cult phenomenon'. The players had cars supplied by Honda. Kinkladze was given a Mercedes.

The other decision Royle took was to dispense with Uwe Rösler. His final match as a Manchester City player had been on 28 March, 1998 – a 2-1 defeat at Bradford that left the club third from bottom. He had played alongside Shaun Goater, whom both Royle and Rösler himself thought too similar a player for them to have been an effective partnership.

There was, however, money as well as football behind the decision to do away with the team's most consistent striker. Manchester City's last away game of the 1996/97 had seen them travel to Norwich. Rösler had a year remaining on his contract. 'In that situation, you either expect a new deal or you expect to be sold,' he says. He was injured but travelled to Norfolk with the team and suggested his agent, Jerome Anderson, join Frank Clark for dinner.

'We agreed a four-year contract,' Rösler continues. 'I went on holiday and came back for pre-season but there was no contract. There was nothing. After two months I began asking about the contract and I was told, "Don't worry, we are just sorting out the paperwork." Francis Lee's son, Gary, was one of my best mates. I never imagined for a moment the club would not keep their word.

'Then, suddenly, Frank Clark was gone and the alarm bells began ringing for me. I had a slight injury at the time, nothing major but I straight away went to the new manager, Joe Royle, and said, "Francis Lee knows that we agreed a deal for another four years."

'Joe Royle said, "No, you have to prove yourself to me."

'I said, "I have been here three-and-a-half years, I have been the leading goalscorer at this football club for three seasons. You know what you get. I am fit, I am motivated, I am not 35."

'He said, "I cannot do a deal with you."'

Rösler now began to worry. His first son, Tony – named after Tony Book – had just been born and the future appeared very uncertain. 'I realised that only Kinkladze and myself remained from the old team. They were planning to sell Kinkladze to Ajax and they were letting my contract run down."

Then, the soon-to-be champions of Germany wanted to talk to him. Kaiserslautern had endured an even more remarkable journey than Manchester City. Like City, they had been relegated from the top flight in 1996, although they had won the German Cup, the DFB Pokal, on their way down. Like Manchester City, they maintained a vast support in the lower leagues. There were no other similarities.'

Under the leadership of Otto Rehhagel, who would manage Greece to the European Championship in 2004, Kaiserslautern were promoted straight back to the Bundesliga and now they were in the process of winning it. '

'It was March 1998 and they invited me over to Kaiserslautern. It was a day off, I didn't miss training. When I came back, Joe Royle said, "Were you in Germany?"'

"Yes."'

"Well in that case, we don't need you any more."'

"If you don't need me to stay in the league, then fine."'

There were six matches remaining. Manchester City won the first and the last, putting four past Stockport and five past Stoke. In between, there were a couple of 2-2 draws and two 1-0 defeats, to Birmingham and Middlesbrough.

Manchester City were relegated by a point. Their goal difference was vastly superior to the teams around them. Had Uwe Rösler scored in any one of those four matches, Manchester City would have survived.

The final match was at Stoke. Rösler was at the Britannia Stadium but he was in the away end rather than the away dressing room, a baseball cap pulled down over his head. The equation was even worse than it had been two years before. Reading were doomed to finish last, but two of four clubs could join them in the third tier.

Manchester City were second bottom, a point behind Stoke, Portsmouth and Port Vale, but with a significantly better goal difference. Portsmouth, managed by Alan Ball, were at Bradford. Port Vale were at Huddersfield. Stoke and Manchester City would play each other.

Because Portsmouth and Port Vale both won and because Stoke's goal difference was so poor – they had conceded seven at home to Birmingham and five at Oxford – what happened at the Britannia Stadium was rendered irrelevant. It was, however, a glorious irrelevance. Manchester City won, 5-2. Their fans launched into choruses of 'Are You Watching Macclesfield?'

Uwe Rösler joined Kaiserslautern and found himself playing Champions League football while his former teammates prepared for Wycombe Wanderers and Walsall. 'I didn't speak to Joe Royle for a long time after that,' he says. 'Then last year we met and cleared everything up. We met in Majorca. Joe has always taken people to Majorca who were part of the Manchester City set-up when he was manager – people like Jim Cassell, Asa Hartford and Willie Donachie. I was in Majorca at the time and he invited me over.

'We had a long talk about how I came to leave Manchester City. We parted as friends. I have been a coach. I can see both sides now.'

Postcards from the Edge

THERE ARE FEW PLACES TO HIDE IN A DRESSING ROOM. MICHAEL Brown thought the showers at Loftus Road were as good a place as any to seek sanctuary.

He was seventeen and had just made his first-team debut for Manchester City. He had been on the pitch for a dozen minutes and been sent off. City had lost 1-0.

Michael had been brought up in Hartlepool, where Brian Clough first tried his hand at management. Clough would stare out at a sea the colour of battleships and declare Hartlepool 'the edge of the world'.

For young Michael Brown it was a springboard. He was a prodigy – by the time he was fourteen, there were offers from clubs as far flung as Newcastle, Sheffield Wednesday and Southampton. Manchester City had offered him a six-year contract, two as a schoolboy, two on YTS terms and two as a full professional.

'Neil McNab was my youth coach at City,' he says. 'You probably wouldn't be able to put his methods into practice now; it would be a bit tough for some. He was strong with people and some couldn't handle that.

'I thrived on it and one thing Neil taught me was, "Whether you're having a good game or a bad game, always make someone knows you're around." Perhaps I took that advice too much to heart. One of my earliest games was in a testimonial against Manchester United and I began putting a couple of their players into the stand. Alex Ferguson was on the touchline going absolutely crazy.

'My first team debut was out of the blue. Neil rang me and said, "You'll be travelling with the first team to Queens Park Rangers tomorrow. I'll get you a tracksuit. Enjoy the day." I travelled down to London and when we gathered to leave the team hotel I thought, "Shall I ask to help with the bags?"

'We got to the ground and, as Alan Ball read out the substitutes, I thought, "Did he read out my name?" I imagined I was going along for the ride. I don't think I even took my own boots. They may have had to sort me out a pair. Instead, I was on the bench in the Premier League.

'The game wasn't going well, we were one down and after about 65 minutes Alan Ball turned to me and told me to warm up. Then, I was sent on for Steve Lomas, who probably thought who was this kid that was coming on?

'I tried to follow Neil's advice and put a few tackles in when, suddenly, Andy Impey began running away from me towards goal. I gave his shirt a little tug and he fell down. I could see Alan Kernaghan coming round to cover.

'The referee came over and I thought I'd get a yellow card. Instead, he produces a red. I just thought, "I'm dead at this club."

'As I walked towards the dressing room, I heard one of the coaches' voices: "You fucking idiot. Why have you done that? You have absolutely killed us."

'I went and sat in the shower room. I was seventeen and in bits. From the shower room I could hear Bally doing his post-match team talk. "You've got no fight, no pride and that kid who's gone on . . ."

'I just waited for Alan Ball to destroy me. Instead he said, "That kid has shown more fight than all of you lot."

'I didn't speak to anyone on the coach back to Manchester but I was at my digs in Bramhall when at about eleven o'clock on Sunday morning the phone rang. I was told Alan Ball wanted to speak to me. I thought, "I'm dead here", because Alan Ball was now going to tell me what he really thought of me.

'His voice came over the phone: "Don't worry about yesterday, son. You were unlucky. Get yourself ready for Tuesday because you're playing against Everton." I was up against Andrei Kanchelskis and it was then I realised how quick the game is.'

This was August 1995. Michael Brown's first-team career began when he was seventeen and he played on until he was forty. For longevity, his career stands comparison with Ryan Giggs'. However, while Giggs played under only two managers, Brown reckons on around '28 or 29'.

By the time he was 21, Brown had been at Maine Road for six years and

Manchester City had got through eight managers, if you included caretakers.

It is one of those ironies of sport, that Brown played some of his best football for the man who wanted him least. Looking back now from the lounge at the Alderley Edge Hotel, he is convinced he probably saved Joe Royle his job.

December 1998 was the month in which Manchester City fell to the lowest point in its history. The month began with a 1-1 draw to Darlington in the second round of the FA Cup. Gary Bennett, once of City but now 37 and Darlington's player manager, would have put them through to the third round but for a late equaliser from Paul Dickov. Willie Donachie said the abuse directed at his players made him feel physically sick.

A few days later, in front of 3,007 supporters, the lowest attendance recorded at Maine Road, the club was knocked out of the Auto Windscreens Shield by Mansfield. They were then beaten 2-1 at York to leave the club twelfth in the third tier of English football.

In the middle of all this, the training ground at Platt Lane was robbed by intruders armed with baseball bats. Janet Royle's intuition that her husband should not have accepted the Manchester City job was beginning to look horribly accurate.

On Boxing Day, Manchester City travelled to Wrexham. They played appallingly. Richard Edghill, operating in the heart of Royle's defence, thought it 'one of the worst games of football I have seen or played in. We were literally sat in the dressing room laughing at how shit we had played.' They were able to laugh because Manchester City had won, 1-0.

Michael Brown, a footballer Joe Royle saw little long-term future for, had dug the victory out. Later, he would be joined by Terry Cooke, who had been part of the Manchester United side that had won the 1995 FA Youth Cup final, a group that, Phil Neville apart, would fade away.

Brown and Cooke had both played for England at Under-21 level and now formed a midfield partnership for Manchester City when they desperately needed it. They would lose only twice more, against Oldham and Wycombe.

'The game at Wrexham saved his job, it was that brutal,' Brown says. 'I was properly ill. I wasn't part of his plans and he only started playing me in November. Later on, I discovered from two very good sources that, if we had lost at Wrexham, Joe would have been sacked. Instead, he went on to win two promotions.

'It is hard playing for a club that doesn't really want you. That game at Wrexham was the turning point that took us to the play-offs. I could have thought, "I'm not going to try because you don't want me and, if we lose, you're gone"

'But I was playing for Manchester City and I loved the club and its fans. We won the play-offs and I went anyway, like I knew I would.'

Before he won his place back in Joe Royle's side, Michael Brown decided to cheer himself up by going to the Mercedes showroom in Stockport to buy a car. 'I was wearing a tracksuit or a shell-suit, I must have looked like a right scally.

'I walked over to look at the latest Mercedes and a young salesman approached me and said, "I don't think you'll be getting one of those. There's a long waiting list." I tried to talk to him but he turned to me and said, "I'm sorry, I've got another client" and walked off.

'Eventually, I went to another salesman and persuaded him that I wanted a Mercedes and that, despite what I was wearing, I had the money to buy one. The guy who refused to sell me the car is now my brother-in-law. Unbeknownst to either of us, I had just started seeing his partner's sister, who is now my wife.'

He started the play-off final against Gillingham, the rain-streaked afternoon where everything changed. Ten minutes before the end, Royle brought him off. He had also substituted Andy Morrison, another footballer whose commitment had driven Manchester City to Wembley. The score was 0-0.

Seven minutes after Brown came off, three minutes from the final whistle, Gillingham were two up. 'I looked at Joe and thought, "The grass isn't always greener, is it?"'

Random thoughts came to others. Shaun Goater, up front and leading City's attack, wanted the whistle to blow, craving the humiliation to end. Alongside him, Paul Dickov, who had just seen his shot blocked by Gillingham's keeper, Vince Bartram, who had been best man at his wedding, crouched down on all fours and could feel the tears welling up

Nicky Weaver wondered if City could repeat what Manchester United had done in Wednesday's Champions League final against Bayern Munich and score twice in stoppage time. In midfield, Jeff Whitley, who shared a house in Manchester with Brown, realised he was hungry. After Kevin Horlock and Dickov had equalised, the club had no Jaffa Cakes to offer the players as they waited for extra time to begin.

When he watched the team preparing for the shoot-out, Michael Brown knew City would win: 'Nicky Weaver was bouncing around. He looked so big, so confident.'

Jim Whitley, Jeff's older brother, who was watching from the bench, was less sure. When Richard Edghill ran up to take his penalty, Jim thought it was 'madness' he had been selected.

'Even in training, his penalties would end up in the trees. I don't think I can remember him scoring one. I couldn't watch.' In fact, Joe Royle had told Edghill before kick-off that, if he were still on the pitch if it came to penalties, he would take one. He scored.

For Brown the afterglow of victory did not linger. He was left out of the first game of the new season, which began with Royle claiming the play-offs to reach the Premier League were 'a feasible, reasonable target'. After Manchester City had lost their opening match, 1-0 at home to Wolverhampton Wanderers, it seemed an unrealistic ambition. In fact, they would win promotion automatically and in some style. Brown would not be part of it.

Royle offered him a loan spell at Hull, which in the bottom division and at a broken-down stadium at Boothferry Park was as much the edge of the world as Hartlepool had seemed to Brian Clough. Instead, Brown chose to rejoin Alan Ball at Portsmouth.

Ball is seen as a manager with too many failures, but keeping Portsmouth in the Championship in the season Manchester City collapsed into English football's third tier would count among his finest achievements.

When he returned to Fratton Park in January 1998, Ball found a club in financial chaos, losing £30,000 a week, seven points adrift at the foot of the Championship and whose supporters carried a coffin around town with 'Portsmouth FC Rest in Peace' written on the side.

His staff volunteered to take pay cuts if it meant keeping their jobs. For away games, hotels and coach companies would only accept cash. For home games the pre-match meal was egg on toast because it was all the club could afford. At Bradford, on the final day of the season, Portsmouth survived. At Stoke, on the same afternoon, a vastly-better resourced Manchester City did not.

By the time Michael Brown reached Fratton Park in November 1999, Portsmouth was under the control of Milan Mandaric, an owner who was driven to despair by defeats in pre-season friendlies and who would get through seven managers in his first six years. Ball would be the first and, after three matches, Brown was offered another loan deal, this time by Neil Warnock at Sheffield United.

A transfer fee of £425,000 made the deal permanent. His first match was against Manchester City. Sheffield United won 1-0 at Bramall Lane. Michael scored the goal. 'I was pleased, I was disappointed. I'd never wanted to leave. I'd made my point to the club. It was all very mixed,' he says.

'Ian Bishop came over to me in the middle of the park, put his arms around me, and said, "Well done son, you deserved that." It was a touch of class because Ian was passionate about City but he also knew football was more than about winning.'

For most footballers in Joe Royle's squad, the play-off final would be the most vivid experience of their lives. To come from two goals down with three minutes to go at Wembley was almost unrepeatable.

For Michael Brown the season in which Portsmouth, even more financially ruined than they had been under Alan Ball, reached the FA Cup final in 2010 eclipses that. 'The play-off final was amazing but that was all about bringing back Manchester City to where they belonged. Getting Portsmouth to the FA Cup final was taking a club that seemed finished, was about to close, to Wembley.'

Brown confesses he probably should have reached a cup final during his years at Tottenham. In January 2004, Spurs went to Manchester City, in their first season away from Maine Road, and drew 1-1 in the fourth round of the FA Cup. In the replay at White Hart Lane, Tottenham were leading 3-0 at the interval. Somehow, Manchester City, down to ten men, contrived to win 4-3.

'Joey Barton had been sent off for City which got them really wound up,' Brown recalls. 'We crumbled as soon as City scored. It's funny when you talk about fate in football but the moment they scored their first goal, you knew what was coming.

'By the time it was down to 3-2 both sides seemed to know. We were looking at each other, looking at them, and everyone on that pitch knew City were going to win. I am amazed we never got near a cup final during my time at Spurs because we had the team for it.'

Six years later, he was back at Portsmouth, a club nobody expected to go anywhere except under. They were bankrupt, in administration and, as captain, Michael Brown was expected to deal with the administrators. They reached the FA Cup final.

'Just before we played Birmingham in the quarter-finals, we were sitting in the team hotel and I got a call saying the club would be closing tomorrow,' he says. 'All the contracts, everything we had signed, were gone, void. The people who had jobs at Fratton Park would lose them.

'The Inland Revenue had been threatening us for some time but this was it. At one point the players weren't going to play because we had received no backing from the Premier League. We were being paid well in arrears and I had to take legal advice because they wouldn't let me play another game because, if I did, it would trigger another year in my contract.

'Portsmouth carried on but, in the semi-finals, we found ourselves playing Tottenham. Nobody gave us a chance. They had a team of superstars: Gareth Bale, Luka Modrić, Jermain Defoe, Peter Crouch, Niko Kranjčar. Harry Redknapp, who had won Portsmouth the FA Cup in 2008, was manager.

'They hit the bar, David James made a couple of great saves and we went in at half-time and I said, "Boys this is there for us." We won 2-0 in extra time. We lost the final to Chelsea, but I loved Portsmouth; there was something special about Fratton Park. It was old, it was atmospheric.

'Because Portsmouth's training ground was right next to Southampton Airport, I commuted from Manchester by plane. I would leave at eight o'clock, get in at quarter to nine. The Portsmouth Marriott looked after me. I had a car in Manchester, a car down there. I'd just had my little girl so I wanted to be back most nights. Avram Grant had been manager of Portsmouth for six months before he realised I lived in Manchester.'

The flight the Whitley brothers had taken was altogether longer than one from Manchester to Southampton. It began in Ndola, a city in the heart of Zambia's copper belt. Aside from copper processing, they built Land Rovers, manufactured Dunlop tyres and refined petrol here. Ndola, which lies on the border with the Democratic Republic of Congo, was a place where you made money.

Zambia had been an independent nation since 1964, but in many ways the British Empire lived on. Jim and Jeff Whitley attended a school where uniforms were pressed, where French and music were taught. There were trips to the golf course. At home there were servants, a swimming pool and guards.

Then, suddenly, things changed and the Whitley family found themselves in a council estate in Wrexham. Jim says he had never before seen houses 'so small, so squashed together'.

'I never got to the bottom of why we found ourselves in Wales,' he says. 'When I asked my father, he said it was for our education but I knew it wasn't for our education. There was something else.'

The answer may lie in Zambia's economy, which was heavily dependent on copper exports. In 1980, when Jim was five, the economy began to slide into a recession that would last twenty years. Ndola suffered dreadfully. By the time Jim was approaching his teenage years, Jack Whitley might have thought it was time to get his family out.

The Bryn Alyn school in Wrexham was to change his boys' lives. Given that their website advertises a school trip to the Real Madrid training ground at Valdebebas, complete with coaching sessions, it has always taken sport seriously.

'Robbie Savage was *the* kid at school,' says Jim. 'At eleven or twelve he was an amazing player. Everyone thinks he was a hacker, someone who just used to tackle, but then he was a striker who just walked past players.

'He was the reason I got into football. The one thing about him was that Robbie couldn't head the ball and then, suddenly, he started winning headers. He had done it by practising keepie-uppies on his head all the time.

'The school I was at in Zambia was predominantly black and, because my dad was white, I was always called white names. When we moved to Wrexham, I was called black names. Sav said he was not having that.

'He would walk past the school to my house and he would wait for me and we would walk back to the school together. He had no reason to do that. What I couldn't get used to was that in winter it was dark by four. Sav and I would find ourselves kicking balls underneath street lamps between two road signs.'

By way of compensation, Jim would allow Robbie to see his exam papers. In Bryn Alyn's examination room, where their desks were three feet apart, Robbie would cough and Jim would turn his paper to reveal the answers. 'Jim is the reason I have seven GCSEs to my name,' Savage said. 'I have cheated in my career and I cheated then.'

Jim's sister wrote to any number of clubs and Savage, who had joined

Manchester United, put a word in for him. Jim found himself at Manchester City. This would have been the 1991/92 season, the last for a generation that the two Manchester clubs would find themselves on equal terms.

'Peter Reid would stroll around like he was in the mafia,' says Jim. 'He was a daunting kind of guy. Sam Ellis, his assistant, would scare the hell out of you. You would say good morning to him and you wouldn't get anything back.

'I was fifteen or sixteen. I remember playing for the A team against the first team. I had just signed and I was playing up front. I scored a hat-trick and Peter Reid was watching from the top of Platt Lane and when he walked past, he just said, "Well done son." This was from Peter Reid. I was in heaven.

'One of my first coaches was Colin Bell. I had no idea how big an icon he had been at Manchester City, what he represented. He would tell me that he always used to meet players he had coached and they would tell him that they could have made it at football.

'He said that, if you gave 100 percent in everything you did and you didn't make it, that was fine. You weren't good enough. You wouldn't have any lingering doubt. Colin always encouraged you to run because he said no matter how good you were, even the great players could sometimes take a poor first touch. Then, even they would have to run and get the ball back.

'Francis Lee was another I have cause to be grateful to. City got through a lot of managers in my time at the club and they would always bring in their own players and sell those on the fringes of the team they thought weren't good enough.

'I was always kept on and I think that was down to Franny. When I was on my own, practising in the gym, he would sometimes watch and offer advice – and this was from a man who'd played in a World Cup. He'd shout, "Use the other wall" or "Why don't you try volleying it?"'

Jim Whitley's was not an ordinary apprenticeship. He did not clean boots or sweep the terraces. Instead, Manchester City allowed him to study A levels at Loreto College in Hulme. He achieved A grades in Sports Science and Art and Design.

Ricky Hatton, whose grandfather and father had both played for Rochdale, trained alongside the brothers, having been signed by City from Tameside Boys. Hatton's real talent lay in other directions, though his constant support for the club was reciprocated. Noel and Liam Gallagher would carry his belts to the ring in the MGM Grand in Las Vegas.

Jeff, who was four years younger, was first to break into the first team, in a 2-1 home defeat to Barnsley in September 1996. Jim's debut was also against Yorkshire opposition, a 2-0 victory over Bradford in the FA Cup. Their father was from Belfast and, six months later, the boys found themselves in Santander, playing for Northern Ireland against Spain, who were able to field Raúl and Fernando Morientes in attack. Spain won 4-1.

The game was played in the summer of 1998, the summer when everyone connected with Manchester City was gripped by the realisation they would be playing in what everyone still referred to as the Third Division.

'Someone sent me a tweet the other day and said they preferred those days,' Jim remarks. 'He said they felt more pure. I knew what he was saying. Then Manchester City was like a big family with loads of rows and loads of ups and downs. Now, the family has become richer. We're still a family but we don't talk much.

'In that season in the Third Division, every ground we went to seemed to be sold out,' he says. 'It was like having an FA Cup tie every week. One thing I did find was that the lower down you go, the ball is in the air much more. You had to be a good header of the ball. It was much more physical, much tougher to deal with.

'One part of our tactics under Joe Royle was to turn the opposition in the first fifteen minutes of games. The defenders would get it, play the ball long, get it into the corners and I and the rest of the midfield would pick up the second ball. After fifteen minutes we would start to play.'

As Manchester City climbed the divisions, repeated injuries wore his game down and he found himself on loan at Blackpool and then Norwich before being transferred to Wrexham in 2001. 'At Wrexham you knew you would get a game,' he says. 'You played even if you were on crutches.'

By this time, the art Jim had studied at Loreto College was becoming a source of income. 'The first picture I sold was of Tony Book. He was a wonderful man. I'd studied chiaroscuro at college, which is all about the dramatic effect of light. I saw Tony squinting into the sunlight which lit up the wrinkles and the crow's feet on his face.

'I did a portrait and showed it to him. He said he'd buy it off me. I hadn't a clue how to value a painting, I charged him £250. Then someone else asked me for a portrait so I phoned my old art teacher at Loreto to ask how much.'

His portrait of David Beckham hangs in the headquarters of the PFA in Manchester. Princess Diana's former butler, Paul Burrell, commissioned Jim for a picture of the woman to whom he had devoted his life. A study of Marilyn Monroe has been exhibited in New York and Los Angeles.

'It can be a lonely existence. My main material are pastels and the paper I use is almost like sandpaper so the pastel can stay within the grains of the paper. I've done loads for Robbie. I did an eight-foot by four-foot one of just his eyes and lips. When I showed it to him, I said, "Are you sure you want this?" He ordered another of his wife. They are on facing walls at his home.

'I use photographs to paint from, I never do anyone from life, particularly footballers. I know them too well. They wouldn't turn up and, if they did, they wouldn't sit still, they would keep telling me they had somewhere else to go.'

Jim now mixes art with acting, which he says is not so very far removed from playing football. Behind the scenes, there is the dressing room with its banter and its insecurities. Out in front is the crowd, the audience, the floodlights, the spotlights. A place where you must perform.

'You have to wear a mask as footballer and you put the mask on when you go on stage,' he says. 'On both, you have to act, you have to become a different person. You can see the nicest people in the dressing room but, once they are out on that pitch, they change.

'Robbie Savage and I grew up together and I couldn't believe it when he started shouting at me. Afterwards, he would come over to me and say, "I am on the football pitch to win. I do whatever I can to make it happen."'

When we met, Jim was touring with a musical comedy called *Crooners*, backed by a nine-piece band, featuring songs by Frank Sinatra, Dean Martin and Bobby Darin, among others. The schedule seems relentless. Sunderland, Crewe, Scarborough, Southport, Aylesbury, Buxton, Stoke and Porthcawl. That was just August.

'I was in the choir at school and played the flute, although that was something you kept very quiet about until you were well established in the dressing room at Manchester City,' he says. 'When I went to Wrexham, I started listening to a lot of Frank Sinatra, which sat very well with my voice. A girl came to the club who had written a song about Wrexham – I have no idea why – and asked the team to join her in the studio to sing the chorus line.

One of the guys in the studio approached me afterwards and asked if I wanted to do a guest spot at the theatre.

'These days I do a lot of Nat King Cole and Sammy Davis Junior. Nat King Cole was a very straightforward and conventional performer. He faced the audience front on. But Sammy lost the sight of an eye in a car crash and, as a result, he would often look down at the floor when he sang and that's what I do when I play him.

'The crash damaged his confidence for a while and Frank Sinatra got him back on stage, partly by taking the mickey out of him, saying, "You've taken your eye off it" or "You've got to get your eye back in." It was the sort of banter you would have in a football dressing room.

'There is another similarity between football and acting in that whatever is troubling you seems to disappear when you're on stage or on a football pitch. On stage you live in the moment. The spotlights go on and you can't be thinking about anything else. It's the same with football when you see the floodlights.

'Of all the members of the Rat Pack, Sammy Davis was the most talented. He sang, he danced, he acted, he told jokes, he did impressions. When I was asked to play him, I had to learn to tap dance. Tap is hard because when you strike a football your ankle needs to be solid, rigid. When you tap dance, your ankle has to be very loose because you almost have to flick your foot. You can just turn up and sing but you can't just turn up and tap dance.'

Resurrection Men

THERE WERE TWO MEN LEFT IN THE DRESSING ROOM; THE KIT man and the captain. Everyone else had gone. Manchester City had won the play-off final in the most extraordinary circumstances. Two down with a minute of normal time remaining, 2-2 at full time, winners on penalties.

Les Chapman was picking up the boots, preparing his kit bins. Andy Morrison was sat on one of the benches in the dressing room at Wembley trying to take it all in.

Morrison was not just Manchester City's captain, he was a recovering alcoholic. He has not touched alcohol since 2 February 1999. There had been booze everywhere in the dressing room. They would not be another meaningful match for two-and-a-half months. He had every reason to crack.

'There was no temptation,' he says. 'I think somebody who has been on my journey would understand why. While Chappy was getting the boots together, I was thinking about all the sacrifices I had made, the lengths I had gone through. I thought this was my reward.

'Then we walked out of the changing rooms together. It had been such a battle to put the drink down and yet even, here, in the changing rooms at Wembley, that need had been taken away from me. There was just a warm feeling inside as I got up to leave.'

It was the last day of an extraordinary season, Manchester City's first and you presume last taste of Third Division England. They had suffered defeats at York, at Lincoln. After they had lost 1-0 at Wycombe in November, Joe Royle, who was not one for screaming at his players, had stalked into the dressing-room at Adams Park determined to give the men inside a bollocking, slammed the door and heard it fall off its hinges behind him.

There were three minutes left when Robert Taylor scored Gillingham's second. Morrison had already been substituted and, from the bench, he looked across at the steps that led up to the Royal Box. 'I thought I am not going to be walking up them to pick the trophy up. It was a pity because, in my mind's eye before the game, I had visualised myself holding it up to the City fans.

'I could still hear Willie Donachie pushing us on from the touchline and things began to happen. Like some things in life I have no idea why. Once Paul Dickov got it back to 2-2 in the sixth minute of stoppage time or whatever it was, I knew we were going to win.

'Gillingham had gone, they were dead in the water. Once they went 2-0 up, they had taken off Carl Asaba, their main striker, to protect their lead. They seemed to have five centre-halves on the pitch.

'That it was Richard Edghill who scored the decisive penalty in the shootout, is to me poetic. He had been through the ranks, he was a City fan and the club was in his blood. He lived for it.

'The wonderful thing to me is that, twenty years on, Manchester City fans are being treated to the most incredible entertainment but they still have not forgotten that penalty shootout and what it represents. Magic can come from pain. I love what BB King said: "If you haven't lived the blues; you can't sing the blues."'

Andy Morrison was eight years old, growing up in Kinlochbervie, a fishing village on the north-western tip of Scotland, when his parents' car drew up outside his primary school. They told Andy to get in; they were moving to Plymouth, 750 miles away. It was as extraordinary a journey as the Whitley's flight from Zambia to Wrexham.

Plymouth was where Andy played football for Devon Schoolboys. It was where his father, who had been a Royal Marine, would take him out on his fishing boat, into Plymouth Sound, towards the Eddystone Lighthouse, to put the nets out for monkfish and skate. It was where he picked up his accent, a lovely West Country burr.

Plymouth was also where Andy experienced drink and violence in the bars behind the Fish Quay or on Union Street and encountered the kind of gang mentality that would have been recognisable in Moss Side. Until he gave up alcohol, he was a willing participant and it would wreck untold damage on his family.

In April 2002, there was a drunken brawl. His older brother Ian threw a punch, a lad called David Taylor struck his head on Union Street's hard pavement edge. The life support system was turned off and Ian served three years for manslaughter in Brixton Prison.

Four months later, Andy was on holiday in Tenerife with his family when his father phoned the hotel to tell him his beloved youngest brother, Cathel, had been found dead at a bus stop in the centre of Plymouth, killed by heroin. When Andy switched on his mobile phone, one of the voicemail messages was from Cathel, begging for help.

Andy had by then been sober for more than three years, but the pressure to blot out the pain with alcohol must have overwhelming. That he resisted it is a testament to an extraordinary will power.

By a very long way Andy Morrison was not the finest footballer to play for Manchester City. He was no Bell, no Silva, no Kinkladze. However, few possessed his fight, his drive, his determination to drag a result from a football field.

During their year in Third Division England, Manchester City needed Morrison like they needed no other footballer. They had employed the artistry of Georgi Kinkladze and they had been relegated twice. It was time to fight it out.

It is probably not a coincidence that the upswing at Maine Road coincided with Andy Morrison renouncing alcohol in February. His first game back was a 3-0 win over Millwall. Greater Manchester Police, who had helicopters clattering overhead, shadowing the trains taking Millwall's supporters north from London, had planned to intercept them at Piccadilly and escort them to Maine Road.

The Millwall fans outmanoeuvred the police by getting off at Stockport, where they fought with Manchester United supporters travelling to Nottingham, where they would see Ole Gunnar Solskjaer score five and United eight at Forest.

Once Paul Dickov had opened the scoring for City, seats in the North Stand were ripped up and Nicky Weaver was pelted with coins. Riot police moved in.

Of the last seventeen games of the 1998/99 season, ten were won and five were drawn. Had City maintained that kind of form throughout the season, they would have finished with 97 points and been promoted automatically with Fulham. There would have been no need for the Miracle of Wembley.

To this day, Andy Morrison wonders if Joe Royle really knows what part he played in transforming his life. In January 1999, two months after coming to Maine Road from Huddersfield, he found himself waking in a police cell in Inverness. There had been a long, savage drinking session that had ended in a familiar confrontation with a bouncer. Like so many alcoholics, his drinking disgusted him.

There were solutions. One lay in his uncle's garage, a .22 rifle used for shooting rabbits and foxes. It was a ten-minute drive away and Andy knew precisely where it was. He could take it out to the fields beyond his uncle's house and end this pain.

Happily, he carried on drinking and just as the bar was about to shut, he ordered a half-bottle of vodka and eight cans of lager. When the barmaid, a family friend, asked if he was sure he wanted this, Andy replied, 'No, you're right. I'd better have twelve cans.'

He took them to Drummond's Pier. The sound was of the sea, of the rain and wind beating down on his car, the music from the CD on the dashboard and the fizz of each can being opened one by one.

'When I got back to Manchester, I was called to a meeting. I thought the directors would be there. I thought I was going to get fined, get hammered. But when I walked in it was just Joe in the room. He said, "Sit down."

'I was waiting for the speech that would include a big, wagging finger, the fine of two weeks' wages, the phrase that I had let the club down. I knew that speech because I'd had it all my career.

Joe just said, "What were you thinking?"

'I said, "I am so sorry. I have let you down, I have let the club down. It won't happen again."

"I am not interested in that," said Joe. "I am interested in you. What about you, what about your quality of life, what about what you've not achieved? What about you selling yourself short?

"What you're doing is killing yourself. This football club will move on. My life will move on but what about you?"

'It was the first time someone had talked to me like that. That was on the

Tuesday morning. I had missed training on the Monday. I went to an AA meeting on the Wednesday night and I have not picked a drink up for twenty years.'

As a recovering alcoholic, Andy would have been well placed to judge the charge that was laid against Joe Royle, when the time came to fire him. That there had been a drinking culture at Manchester City which played a part in the club's relegation in 2001.

'The game has moved on,' he says. 'Then, the culture was all "work hard, play hard". When they were going up two divisions, they were perceived as young men having fun. When, suddenly, they were bottom of the Premier League, they were accused of being unprofessional. Nothing had changed, except the perception. It was an absolute nonsense for that to be thrown at him.'

When in May 2001, immediately after the club's relegation, the six directors of Manchester City met at the Midland Hotel to discuss Royle's future, the minutes record 'specific attention was drawn to hotel bills that have been the subject of previous analysis'.

This was the bar bill from the Forest of Arden Hotel where Manchester City had been staying before their fixture with Coventry on New Year's Day. It had been more than £1,000 plus £150 in tips. The bill had been batted back and forth between hotel and club.

In March, the accounts department at Maine Road had sent a memo to Royle's secretary, Julia McCrindle: 'Finally, I have got a breakdown on the bar bill from the Forest of Arden Hotel for New Year's Eve. I think you'd better have a world with Joe. Did they really drink that much?'

The board seemed to think they did. However, if Royle's squad whose captain was a teetotal recovering alcoholic and whose assistant, Willie Donachie, was virtually a non-drinker, really did down £1,000 worth of booze, including 52 vodkas and 27 gins, and played Coventry the next day, the 1-1 draw they earned at Highfield Road must count as one of the finest results in Manchester City's history. Royle thought the suggestion ludicrous and so did his captain.

'The charge against him was completely unfair,' says Morrison. 'I don't know how much Joe realises what an impact he had on me, but now I am a manager I just hope I can have something of the impact he had on me on just one young man.'

The men on whom Andy Morrison is having an impact play for Connah's Quay Nomads in the Welsh Premier League. Morrison is a manager now and a successful one.

In May 2018, Connah's Quay had beaten Aberystwyth 4-1 to win the Welsh FA Cup and qualify for the Europa League. Though they lost to Shakhtyor Soligorsk, from a mining town in Belarus, just qualifying earned them €240,000, enough to keep Connah's Quay going for six months.

When we met, Connah's Quay had just beaten New Saints, the only full-time club in the Welsh Premier League, a team who have won seven league titles on the bounce.

New Saints were fresh from playing Midtjylland, the Danish club who in February 2016 in their neat stadium on the frozen plains of Jutland had inflicted the most humiliating defeat in Manchester United's European history.

Connah's Quay's 1-0 win had been quite a triumph, though Andy had been forced to watch it from the stands, having been sent off at the end of last season. As a manager he is as passionate as he was a player.

Curiously, on the day of the game, two of his former clubs, Manchester City and Huddersfield, had been playing. City had won 6-1.

In November 1997 Morrison had been part of a Huddersfield side that had gone to Maine Road and won 1-0. He had been shocked by the low quality of some of the players in Frank Clark's team.

'Rob Edwards scored the winner for us and he was a massive City fan,' he says. 'Rob had come to Huddersfield from Crewe and used to come in wearing a City shirt. He was obsessed with the club. His goal finished off a move that had sixteen or seventeen passes that ended with him smashing in the volley at the far corner. Rob said his first instincts had been to run to the Kippax to celebrate. That had been his dream as a kid; scoring a goal at Maine Road.

'Afterwards, we were locked in the changing rooms for an hour and a half because of a protest from the Manchester City fans against Francis Lee meant we couldn't leave. It was a poisonous atmosphere. The players were being intimidated before they even kicked off.

'It was still going on when I went to City. Willie Donachie would warm us up at the school over the road and then take us to the ground rather than warm up surrounded by all this negativity.'

Both as a player and a coach, Donachie is one of Manchester City's most underrated men. Donachie had grown up in Castlemilk, a 1950s housing estate to the south of Glasgow that had been built to take the overspill from the Gorbals tenements but which had quickly grown rancid.vHe had joined Glasgow Amateurs, a feeder club for Celtic, but in 1968, the year when Manchester was the centre of European football, he came south to join City. By 1971 he had replaced Glyn Pardoe as Manchester City's first-choice left-back. Three years later, when Tony Book brought him from Goodison Park, he met Joe Royle, whom as a coach he would follow to Oldham, Everton and Manchester City.

Asked to describe their relationship, Brian Clough said he was 'the shop window' while Peter Taylor was 'the goods at the back'. There was something of that in the way Royle and Donachie worked. Royle was the front man, Donachie the one who fine-tuned the footballers behind the scenes.

When they were transforming Oldham from a stagnant backwater to a club that played Nottingham Forest in League Cup finals and Manchester United in FA Cup semi-finals, Donachie employed sprint and fitness coaches when football still looked on them as very optional extras. Malcolm Allison, who had coached him at Manchester City, used sports psychologists, Donachie persuaded Oldham to do the same.

'Football's a masculine game so you don't use the word 'love' very easily but I loved him,' says Andy Morrison. 'Willie Donachie is the finest coach I have ever worked with anywhere. His standards were immense.

'He made me realise I was more than just a footballer, I was a human being. He took me to study practical philosophy for eighteen months in Manchester. It was a huge time in my life. I had just stopped drinking and I needed an anchor in my life. The things I learned in that institute are things I still use in management today.

'What they taught me was to pay attention to the moment – to give it your full and complete attention. Otherwise, you can't master something. When I talk to the players at Connah's Quay, I tell them to leave your life behind when you come and train.

'If you were depressed or lonely or your marriage wasn't going well, Willie would tell us to take a moment, put it to one side and then start training. We'd laugh about it sometimes when Willie wasn't there but, if you ask

Shaun Goater or Paul Dickov or Kevin Horlock what they learned from him, it would be an awful lot.'

Morrison had gone to Huddersfield from Blackpool in the summer of 1996. Blackpool had missed out on automatic promotion to what would now be the Championship by a point. Having beaten Bradford, 2-0 at Valley Parade, they lost the second leg of the play-off semi-final 3-0 at home. The matchday programme at Bloomfield Road had featured directions to Wembley and ticket information for the final.

To compound matters, seven days later, the club's owner, Owen Oyston, was sentenced to six years imprisonment for rape and indecent assault which did not prevent him from firing his manager, Sam Allardyce.

Morrison moved to Huddersfield to be managed by Brian Horton. 'He had these intense eyes and was a ferocious competitor,' he remembers. 'Brian saw very quickly that I was someone who couldn't enter a changing room without expressing an opinion, so he made me captain.'

When Horton's successor, Peter Jackson, took the captaincy from him, it led to a disagreement in the manager's office. The disagreement climaxed with Jackson and the table he was sitting at being hurled into a wall.

'That's how I came to go to City,' Morrison says with a smile. 'When I first came through the door at Maine Road we had 38 players and three dressing rooms. One was for the first team, one was for players who would train with the first team and one was for lads who weren't even involved and who, because they had been signed when the club was in the Premier League, were on three times the money the first team were on.'

Nigel Clough was one of those in dressing room three. He had been signed by Alan Ball from Liverpool in January 1996 for £1.5m. However, once City had been relegated and Ball had been sacked, Clough had fallen completely from favour.

There had been loan spells, one back at Nottingham Forest, another at Sheffield Wednesday which had led nowhere. He was still nominally an employee of Manchester City, earning £6,000 a week. In October 1998 his contract was cancelled and Clough was paid £250,000 in compensation. Two months later, he was appointed player-manager of Burton Albion, where Clough was to become as loved as he had been loveless at Manchester City.

Very soon, Royle, like Horton, summed Andy Morrison up as captaincy material. He was a damaged and passionate man but Manchester City were a damaged and passionate club. They needed one another.

The month before Morrison signed, the club had held its AGM at the Bridgewater Hall, Manchester's great venue for classical music. The team had just been booed off after a 1-0 home defeat to Preston. 'I hate this division, it drives me mad,' Royle had said at the meeting. Andy Morrison was to prove his best route out of it.

He scored on his debut, a 2-1 win at home to Colchester. He scored in the next game, a 3-0 win at Oldham. For a centre-half that was quite an impact.

'I often wonder why the crowd at Manchester City took to me,' he says. 'I suppose it was because I didn't give a shit about anything except winning games of football. Nothing matters to me except what goes on inside this arena. I have to win. A ferocity overtakes me.

'It's not about banging the badge and kissing it because people see through that. I think the City fans saw someone who would head and kick anything.

'We were going to some horrible places, Colchester for example, and, if I brought anything to the club, it was that I wasn't going to be fazed by any of that. Because of where I'd been and what I'd seen in my life, none of that pressure was going to get to me.'

Much of the pressure came from the stands. When City were being relegated at Stoke, Alan Parry remarked in his commentary that 'the finance directors of Division Two (what League One was then called) will be rubbing their hands with glee'.

The level of support was genuinely astonishing. In their season of third-tier football, Manchester City attracted an average home attendance of 28,261. This was slightly more than had watched them during their last season in the Premier League. Virtually all the away fixtures were sold out.

Sunderland drew average crowds of 17,425 in their season in the old Third Division in 1987/88, although that was in a season in which no club, not even Manchester United or Liverpool, averaged 40,000.

Nottingham Forest's crowds in their three seasons in League One between 2005-2008 ranged from 19,000-20,000. Sheffield Wednesday's two seasons in the third flight would draw crowds of between 22-23,000. The attendances at Roker Park, Hillsborough and the City Ground were impressive, but nowhere did the support shine as brightly through the gloom as at Maine Road.

'What those fans went through made their strength of character,' says Morrison. 'They lived through something that was embarrassing, that was catastrophic. Manchester City had always been a big club but they had never had to live with ridicule and embarrassment.

'United were in a different stratosphere to us. You couldn't relate to them in any way. They won the European Cup in the year that we got promoted and that emphasises just how catastrophic it was being 2-0 down to Gillingham in the play-off final.'

The play-offs are a lottery but they had been loaded in Manchester City's favour. They had finished third, they were in better form than any of their rivals and possessed a deeper squad.

The team few of City's players wanted to face was Preston, who under the management of the 36-year-old David Moyes had taken four points from them. Preston were beaten by Gillingham in the other semi-final. City beat Wigan, whose manager, Ray Mathias, was sacked immediately afterwards.

Gillingham were a small, fast-rising club. When Tony Pulis was invited by the club's new owner, Paul Scally, to join him in the summer of 1995, Gillingham had finished nineteenth in English football's bottom division.

While Scally, a Millwall fan who had sold his photocopier business in south London to buy Gillingham, put money into the redevelopment of Priestfield, his manager employed the tactics that were to become well known at Stoke and West Bromwich Albion.

Tony Pulis liked big centre-forwards, plenty of tackling, set pieces and clean sheets. In his first season at Priestfield, Gillingham were promoted to the third tier alongside Preston and Bury.

They had kept 29 clean sheets and conceded a total of just twenty goals. In the same season, Arsenal, with their famous defence of Adams, Bould, Keown and Winterburn, conceded 32 in eight fewer games. That is why Gillingham's collapse in the last few minutes at Wembley was so remarkable. It was a totally un-Pulis thing to do.

However, a few days before the play-off final, the relationship between Pulis and Scally broke down completely and irretrievably, although the full details would have to wait until Pulis took the club to the High Court two years later for wrongful dismissal.

On Wednesday, 26 May, the day of Manchester United's Champions League final against Bayern Munich, Pulis had asked Scally to meet him in one of the stands at Priestfield. When the chairman arrived, Pulis pulled a nine-page document from the front of his shorts. It alleged details of misappropriation of club funds. In a statement to the court, Scally said Pulis told him he had 'a suitcase full of stuff'.

Pulis was alleged to have told Scally that if he did not pay him £62,000, which he believed had been wrongly taken from his pension fund, plus £140,000, which was his share of the sale of three players – Ade Akinbiyi, Jimmy Corbett and Iffy Onuora – he would take the documents to the police and the Inland Revenue. The case was settled out of court with Gillingham paying £75,000 to their former manager.

For Pulis to have then held everything together and engineered what was, until the last minute of normal time, a near-perfect performance demonstrated a remarkable ability to compartmentalise. Pulis was sacked after the final but, even had Gillingham won, it is hard to imagine how he could have remained.

Manchester City went to Wembley without their club chaplain, Tony Porter, who objected to the fact the game was on a Sunday. 'I hope the supporters have a good day out,' he told journalists. 'But Sunday is the day we celebrate the resurrection and I would rather keep it that way.'

To most of their supporters, Sunday, 30 May 1999 is the date of Manchester City's resurrection, the great turning point in the club's history.

There are some like the former fanzine editor Noel Bayley who disagree, pointing out that if the club had not been promoted at Wembley, it would have gone up next season. It was too big, too powerful for Third Division England.

The turning point, he argued, was another game at another Wembley, against another team managed by Tony Pulis, the 2011 FA Cup final against Stoke and the semi-final against Manchester United that preceded it.

'We took United on and beat them on a big stage,' he says. 'The United fans had a banner on the Stretford End which looked like a mileage counter that detailed how many years City had been without a trophy. Every season the number would go up by one.

'It was put up with the connivance of the authorities at Old Trafford and when he was manager Roberto Mancini said he would force them to take that banner down. When we won the FA Cup they did. If you compare our record to any other club in the Premier League since then, Manchester City

MANCHESTER CITY IN THE 1990s

have been dominant. That was the turning point.'

Less than twelve months later, Manchester City had returned to the Premier League; their final match was at Blackburn. The only way they could not be promoted was if they lost at Ewood Park and Ipswich beat Walsall. Ipswich won at Portman Road while, at Ewood Park, Matt Jansen opened the scoring for Blackburn who then struck the frame of Nicky Weaver's goal four times. This, however, was a different Manchester City. The tide was running with them. They won, 4-1.

For Andy Morrison, it felt different to Wembley. He was still club captain, but his knee had gone again and he watched the game in a suit. 'There was a feeling of emptiness,' he recalls. 'It was not as if I had played all the games leading up to Ewood Park and just missed out. I'd been injured after sixteen games. I felt 'they' had done it, rather than 'we' had done it.

'Considering we had only really brought in Mark Kennedy we did astonishingly well. Mark brought a different dimension to the team and he had the season of his life. It was not just the goals he scored, it was the goals he made. They would be called assists now but then we just called them crosses.

'The team we had in the Third Division was composed of Championship and Premier League quality players – Kevin Horlock, Gerard Wiekens, Ian Bishop, Shaun Goater and Paul Dickov. They were just in a bad place and then, suddenly, they found themselves on the right stage.

'I got back, played a few more games and then I was sent on loan, to Blackpool, Sheffield United and Crystal Palace, but the knee couldn't stand it and it was all over for me.

'It is a closed book the football world. So much depends on who you know and when it happens. All I know is that when I have left Connah's Quay I will have left an impression. When I left Manchester City, I left an impression. If you go to Blackpool or Plymouth, they will remember me.

'When I went to Southampton as a thirteen-year-old, my father said to me, "Make sure you leave an impression." They didn't take me on but years later I was signed by Blackburn and the first player I met when I walked through the door was Alan Shearer. He looked at me and said, "You were at Southampton weren't you?" I'd left an impression.'

Commonwealth

'IT WAS LIKE AN OUT-OF-BODY EXPERIENCE,' SAYS CHRIS BIRD, recalling his first encounter with Manchester City.

'My brother took me to my first game, a reserve game against Bury. I must have been about six. We stood on the Kippax and, because I was small, I sat on the wall. Tony Book, who was playing right-back, made a clearance down the line, shanked it and knocked me clean off the wall. They all ran over to see if I were all right.

'At the end of the game, when they were all walking off, a copper came over and said that Tony Book wanted to see me in the tunnel. As I walked down the tunnel, I saw Rodney Marsh and Colin Bell playing head tennis. That was my first experience of Manchester City.'

Bird came to run the club, first as Manchester City's head of press and then as their chief operating officer. He took over as the club prepared for the oblivion of third-division football and left just before the bulldozers and the wrecking balls came to tear down the Kippax.

He grew up in Hattersley, where the family's local doctor was Harold Shipman, who practised at the Donnybrook Medical Centre in Hyde. In 1993, his mother, Violet, had phoned Chris to say she wasn't 'feeling very well' and had called Dr Shipman. Later he received another call from Violet Bird's doctor saying she had 'died of a massive heart-attack'.

'I found out six years later that she hadn't died of natural causes, she had been murdered by Harold Shipman. The police came to our door to tell us. We had watched him on telly being arrested and we were going, "Why have they arrested our doctor?" He had saved my dad's life three years before. It was incredible.'

By this time, Bird was Manchester City's chief operating officer. The realisation that Violet had been murdered triggered guilt and depression. When she had phoned to say she wasn't well, Chris had turned to his work colleagues and said, "My mum's ill, what can I do?" Meanwhile, Shipman was on his way over. The phrase, "What can I do?" stayed with him.

We meet at the Sharp Project in Manchester, which is full of open steel girders, young designers with shorts and big beards. It is young and optimistic, based in what was once a warehouse that housed the video recorders and televisions made by Sharp, whose name appeared across every Manchester United shirt as they steamrollered their way towards world domination.

Bird runs a sports travel business and a PR consultancy that advises, among many others, Fred Done, who with his brother opened his first bookies in Salford in 1967. The one shop became Betfred. The story they tell is that the first shop was financed by a bet on England to win the World Cup. The business is now worth upwards of £1 billion.

There have been more controversial clients such as Ched Evans, who will not be remembered for being part of the Manchester City side that played Liverpool in the 2006 FA Youth Cup final. Bird became involved in Evans' campaign to have his conviction overturned for raping a teenager in a hotel room in Rhyl. The campaign was successful. The conviction was quashed.

Bird's advice to Evans was the same as he gave to Manchester City. 'When I first met Ched Evans, I told him that his reputation was now so low there is nowhere else to go. It was the same with City. They were rock bottom.

'My involvement started when I was working at Granada Studios, hosting a lunch where Alan Hansen was the guest speaker. I had been working as an advisor for JD Sports since about 1989 and that afternoon I was talking to Dennis Tueart, who was then representing John Wardle and David Makin on the City board. It was during Francis Lee's last days as chairman.

'I said to Dennis, "Your PR is all over the place. I can find out what's happening at the club before you do. You leak like a sieve and, if you want me to change it, I will work for free." I knew the 'work for free' bit would appeal to someone like Dennis.

'John Wardle then rang me and said Frank Clark would be going and

Joe Royle would be coming in. I handled that and some of the early transfers like Jamie Pollock and Shaun Goater. Then, they told me they were changing chairman.

'Franny was going, David Bernstein was coming in and that would need careful handling. Without that moment in time, I don't think there would have been a Manchester City.

'Something had to change; we were plummeting and plummeting and plummeting. We were the biggest worst story in football. People were working on the medical side who were unqualified. They had employed some good managers in the past – Howard Kendall, Frank Clark, Peter Reid – but they were one-man bands. There was no infrastructure to support them. David Makin was a Manchester City fan with the cash and the shares in the club to make things happen.

'We were professional in a way I don't think Manchester City had been. I did the media, Dennis did the football, Alistair Mackintosh did the finance, John was all about merchandising and keeping the ship calm. Bernstein brought gravitas. We didn't have drink in the boardroom, the working lunches were not sit-down meals. Everything was under the microscope.'

When he travelled down to Stoke for the afternoon that would damn Manchester City with third-division football, Bird had two prepared statements in his pocket. 'One was to be used if we stayed up. The theme was that the game had been a turning point in Manchester City's history and now we should go forward together.

'The other was for if we went down. It was about the need for stability. Obviously, I delivered the one about stability. I'd originally told Bernstein I would give him six months but after relegation I went over to him and said, "We are right in the shit, I'm all in."'

In 1998, the summer of Michael Owen scoring in Saint-Étienne and effigies of David Beckham being hanged from lampposts in east London after his red card against Argentina, the club was approached by *The Times* who wanted to run a weekly column about how Manchester City coped with life in the lower leagues.

'The board were not impressed with the idea. I told them, "We are in the old Third Division, the only people who are going to write about us are the *Manchester Evening News*. Unless we do something completely dreadful, or completely brilliant, the national press will not touch us. If we can be in *The Times* every week, then great." We gave the journalist, Mark Hodgkinson, total access. I told him it was hard round here to trust a journalist but I will trust you.'

The columns, like the season, climaxed at Wembley and the play-off final against Gillingham. It was this game, not the one against Stoke, that was the turning point in Manchester City's history.

'Wembley was a pilgrimage but some of us had gone there to pray, because if it didn't work out Manchester City were in big trouble. We were negotiating an investment with Sky and a move to the new stadium. If we had not gone up, all that would have fallen away, the investment along with the stadium. Manchester City moving to a new stadium while in the Third Division would, shall we say, have been a difficult financial model.

'I started in the Royal Box but was asked to leave because I was swearing too much. I went downstairs and a steward, examining my credentials, said the best place for you to be is downstairs. Go and ask your manager if you can sit on the bench.

'I sat down on the subs bench next to Michael Brown. When the equaliser went in, I turned to Tony Pulis and shouted, "Fuck Off!"

'A steward approached me and said, "You are not staying here." So, they put me on my own in a room with a telly. I watched the penalties from there. I was close to Richard Edghill because he had a dog's life – as most Manchester City right backs did – but when he scored that penalty and held his badge like a proper Mancunian, I was in ecstasy.

'I went home with the trophy and invited all the kids off the street to come into my front room and have their photos taken with it. I was living in Newton, in Hyde, right in the middle of Cityland. It was as if we had won the Champions League.'

Manchester United had won the Champions League, they had won the FA Cup and the Premier League. It was English football's first Treble of any kind since Liverpool in 1984. Manchester City did not consider parading the cup awarded for the play-off winners. The reality was they had finished third in the old Third Division. 'But, if we had,' Chris Bird remarks, 'we'd have got more people on the streets than United did.'

He enjoyed working with Joe Royle, who was open, honest, funny. He was also thin-skinned. If he was criticised, he did not brush it off as he would have brushed off an elbow from a defender while leading the forward line for Everton and Manchester City. Inside, he bruised easily.

'The momentum after the play-off final was incredible,' Bird recalls. 'We played some really good, strong football. Joe was always going to be the person to drive it forward. He was a dream to work with. He told me, "Always remember your local sheriff." By that he meant, "Don't screw the local press. The caravan moves on but they stay." He also taught me that footballers can never be your best mates. They will just make you think they are, just to curry favour with you.'

Much of Bird's time was spent selling the move to the City of Manchester Stadium in the wake of the Commonwealth Games in 2002. Only Bernard Halford, the club secretary, tried to explore ways of staying at Maine Road. However, the vast majority of the supporters had had enough of Moss Side. There were too many memories of failure.

In this they were driven forward by Howard Bernstein and Richard Leese, the chief executive and leader of Manchester City Council, both supporters of the club. Bernstein had been a consistent advocate of using sporting events to underpin regeneration.

Manchester had long yearned for the Olympics. In the race to stage the 1992 Games, where a stadium in Salford was proposed, they had fallen at the first. Birmingham was chosen by the British Olympic Association to do what proved a very unequal battle with Barcelona.

For the next Games, an 80,000-seater arena was proposed at what would become the site of the Etihad Stadium. In the bidding process, Manchester finished fifth out of six, although any one of the competing cities might have done a better job than the surprise winner, Atlanta.

They tried again, this time with £70m of backing from John Major's government. A stadium was designed and for the first time it was suggested Manchester City would move into it after the Manchester Olympics were done.

There would be a velodrome, which was built and opened in 1994 and which was to become the heart of British cycling. Work began on the Manchester Aquatics Centre on Oxford Road which was finished by 1997.

What was to become the Manchester Arena would stage boxing and gymnastics. Manchester Airport would get a second terminal, Hulme would be regenerated, the metro system would be extended. More than 11,500 jobs would be created and £574m of business would be created for the city.

In September 1993, the IOC would vote on the destination of the Millennial Games. It might have been better had the promotional video for the Manchester Olympics not featured Buckingham Palace and Tower Bridge but, otherwise, the bid team had committed very few errors and some sensed victory. Their chief rivals, Beijing, had been the subject of a sustained, American-led campaign to highlight China's abuses of human rights.

On the night a crowd of 50,000 gathered in Castlefield to watch the vote from Monaco on a big screen. Manchester were second favourites.

When Sydney was named as the hosts for the 2000 Olympics, the crowd in Castlefield broke into the Monty Python song, 'Always Look on the Bright Side of Life'. They took it better than the crowds in Beijing who promptly marched on the American embassy. Five months later, Manchester was awarded the 2002 Commonwealth Games.

There was little opposition to leaving Maine Road. There was only a scattering of nostalgia for what was about to be left behind. 'We held open days at Platt Lane to get feedback from the fans,' says Chris Bird. 'Everyone seemed to say, yes, we know we have to leave.

'We were already moving forward. I had negotiated with Manchester University to buy the training ground at Carrington for half a million quid, which was probably the best half a million the club ever spent. We had built a medical centre. Juan Carlos Osorio, who was manager of Mexico in the World Cup in Russia, was our first-ever fitness coach.'

Things were moving too quickly. Within twelve months of escaping the Third Division, Manchester City were back in the Premier League. They were not remotely ready for it.

'It was too fast. We did not expect to be in the Premier League in 2000,' Bird says. 'There was nothing in the business plan that allowed for us going straight back up. In the first game of the season we were heavily beaten by Charlton and you could see we were off the pace.

'Nicky Weaver didn't know what day it was. He told me after the first few games that the ball was coming at him quicker and harder than he had ever seen, and the signings did not work terribly well.'

The signings included the former World Footballer of the Year and the future President of Liberia, George Weah. His goals had won the Scudetto for AC Milan in 1996 and a loan spell at Chelsea had climaxed with an FA Cup final win. He would bring glamour and 34-year-old legs which had started to go.

Weah was the second Manchester City footballer of that generation to go into politics. Mikheil Kavelashvili, who joined Georgi Kinkladze at Maine Road and scored in the Manchester derby on his debut, later won a seat in the Georgian parliament for the left-of-centre, Georgian Dream party. He did not, however, become head of state.

'George Weah certainly had a presence about him,' says Bird. 'He was having his inaugural press conference in the Blue Room at Maine Road and I asked how he wanted to do it. He said, "Give me a chair, put me in the middle of the journalists and we will have a chat." He held court.

'I remember after one game something had kicked off back in Liberia, something political. He told me: "I need to do something." I put him in the boot room at Maine Road with Pete Spencer, the sports editor of the *Manchester Evening News,* so they could write a statement together.

'Joe didn't like George. Dennis Tueart and I worked hard to save that relationship but Joe wasn't having any of it. Paulo Wanchope was another who Joe didn't get on with.'

Weah's London agent, Ian Anderson, had driven up to Manchester in his Rolls-Royce and negotiated a one-year contract with City, on wages of £25,000 a week that would make him the highest-paid player at Maine Road. Anderson's fee was £100,000.

It was Alan Hansen's rule of thumb when captain of Liverpool that nothing divides a dressing room like money. The men whom Royle had brought to Maine Road – Weah, Wanchope and Alfie Haaland – were on more than the men who had brought them back to the Premier League. Wanchope, who cost £3.6m from West Ham, was on international duty with Costa Rica the week before the season opened with a 4-0 defeat at Charlton.

Royle saw Weah as an impact player who could be brought on from the bench, Weah saw himself as an integral member of the side. After a 1-0 defeat at home to Newcastle in September, Royle was attempting to debrief the side when he noticed Wanchope and Weah talking to each other at the back of the dressing room. There was a row, the row got out of hand.

There were meetings between Tueart and Bird with Anderson and Weah. It was decided Weah's contract would be terminated, the player would be paid a severance fee of £500,000. If you include Anderson's fee, the deal had cost Manchester City £850,000. For this their return was a single league goal, in a 3-2 defeat at Anfield.

George Weah promptly pitched up at Marseilles. He did not go gently into the Provencal night but issued a lengthy, damning statement, very different to the one he had written with Pete Spencer.

'I was made to feel like the worst player who ever existed,' he said. 'I am not willing to subject myself to feeling small in front of the younger players that I hope to be an example and inspiration to. I didn't come for the money. I could have stayed at AC Milan but instead I sacrificed $2m from them in order to come here. I didn't leave Milan for somebody to tell me to shut up and fuck off. I was made to feel old and of no real use to the club. I felt I was being used for publicity to attract other players.'

Royle's relationship with Wanchope disintegrated and by December it was over in a flurry of fists and recriminations in the dressing room at Stamford Bridge. Manchester City had lost their fifth successive league game, which included the first Manchester derby in four years, which had been settled in two minutes by David Beckham's free kick. Sir Alex Ferguson was not at Maine Road, having flown to South Africa for his son's wedding.

Wanchope, whom Royle found 'a self-confident and self-opinionated boy', was substituted before the interval against Chelsea and took it badly, gesturing to the bench. At half time, he turned on Royle and tried to punch him. The players intervened, Wanchope was dragged away.

Royle was 51, not old by managerial standards but he was feeling weary. His father, who was dying of emphysema, would not give up smoking, his wife, Janet, had been diagnosed with cancer. His knees hurt terribly.

'In his deeper moments, I wonder if Joe thought he should have walked away after he had won us promotion back to the Premier League and told us that he had done his bit,' says Bird. 'He was knackered, he was so tired, he was riddled with arthritis in his knees. It took a lot for him to get going. Willie was disillusioned with everything, training methods, the medical side.

'Willie rang me and asked me to meet him at the ground on Saturday morning for a cup of tea. He told me everything he felt was wrong and what needed to change. That was a cry for help almost.'

On 11 April 2001, Arsenal came to Moss Side and were four up by half time. Then, as they so often did under Arsène Wenger, they slid down the gears and turned the match into a training exercise. 'They were awesome,' Royle said in the press room. 'They were too bloody good for us. They were on a different planet.'

It meant Manchester City could be relegated at Old Trafford by the team that had won the Premier League with a month to spare. It would be payback for 1974. The film of Denis Law back-heeling the ball past Alex Stepney, who was now City's goalkeeping coach, would be shown again with the narrative that the wheel had turned full circle.

Manchester City were not relegated at Old Trafford. They did not even lose in a match recalled for the Roy Keane's deliberate, knee-high tackle on Alfie Haaland, which seen through the narrow focus of the Manchester United captain was perfectly acceptable revenge for Haaland's mocking of his cruciate ligament injury four years before.

In September 1997, Manchester United were playing Leeds at Elland Road. Keane was more wound up than usual. On the Wednesday before, Manchester United had drawn 2-2 at home to Chelsea. They had only grabbed a point through a late goal from Ole Gunnar Solskjaer. There had been a fight in the tunnel at Old Trafford.

Keane should have gone home. Instead, fuelled by the news that his brother, Johnson, was now the father of a baby girl, he joined some friends who had come over from Cork for the game at the Chester Court, a modest hotel near Old Trafford. Some fans from Dublin were also drinking at the hotel bar. Soon, a Cork-Dublin fight broke it out. Naturally, Keane was involved, naturally someone phoned the tabloids.

By his own admission Keane was in no shape to captain Manchester United at Elland Road – 'bloody awful would be a fair description of my performance'. Haaland had needled him, suffocated his play and five minutes from time, Keane tried to pay him back with a tackle that went so wrong that it snapped his cruciate ligament. He heard the ligament go and then he heard Haaland telling to 'get up and stop faking it'.

Keane nursed those words for four years during which time, he played against Haaland several times without incident. There had been nothing in the first derby at Maine Road in November but by April 2001, the title had been sealed, any suspension would be meaningless and everyone in the Manchester City dressing room knew this would be the day.

'We knew it was coming,' said Steve Howey. 'There was talk about it. It was just boiling up and boiling up. Everyone knew he was going to do it, it was just a case of when. I thought he had broken his leg. Alfie did quite well, rode the tackle a little bit. If his foot had been planted, it would have been game over.'

Haaland's career had only a few games to run; he played only six more games before retiring in 2003. His career was finished by a knee injury – but not the knee Keane had attempted to wreck. He played for Norway against Bulgaria the week after the incident but his left knee required surgery and it was surgery he did not properly recover from.

Keane was fined £5,000 and given a three-game ban for making the tackle. For writing about it he was fined £150,000 and banned for five matches. Keane tried to claim that the offending sentences were entirely the responsibility of his ghost-writer, Eamon Dunphy, which suggested that someone as meticulous as Roy Keane would not have bothered to read the manuscript of his own life story.

When at an FA disciplinary hearing, convened at Bolton, Dunphy was asked whether he thought Keane had attempted to deliberately injure Haaland. 'Without a doubt,' came the reply. For his second volume of memoirs, Keane employed Roddy Doyle.

Haaland became involved in the property market in Norway. His son, Ering, played for Solskjaer at Molde and in July 2018 scored four times in 21 minutes against the league leaders, SK Brann. Manchester United were reported to be interested in a deal.

The draw at Old Trafford only delayed Manchester City's relegation, which triggered the brutal, messy removal of Joe Royle, the man who had salvaged the club.

It was not automatic for a Manchester City manager to be fired immediately after relegation. John Benson had been sacked in 1983 but he had been a stopgap appointment who doubted his own ability to do the job. Jimmy Frizzell was kept on and moved to the post of general manager in 1987, while Alan Ball had been given three games of the new season until Francis

Lee realised the hopelessness of his situation.

Royle was on a salary of £750,000, the most he had ever been paid to manage a football club. However, if his contract was terminated, the compensation depended on whether Manchester City were in the Premier League at the time.

City attempted to argue they were now a Championship club and rushed through their notice of relegation which was delivered to the Premier League at 8.28 on the Monday morning. Royle thought this shabby and unforgiveable and sued the club. In his autobiography, Royle headed the chapter on his dismissal 'Betrayal'.

The 'betrayal' had begun with dinner with David Bernstein on Rusholme's Curry Mile after Manchester City had been relegated, but before the final game of the season against Chelsea.

Bernstein was critical of many of Royle's backroom staff: the chief scout, John Hurst, the goalkeeping coach, Alex Stepney, and the physio, Roy Bailey. While conceding that Nicky Weaver had performed poorly and put on weight, Royle defended his men, all of whom would be dismissed following Royle's departure. Bailey, who had worked for fourteen different managers at Maine Road, said he was not officially told the reasons for his dismissal.

Like Frank Clark, Royle was suspicious of Dennis Tueart and asked Bernstein to stop him coming to the training ground at Carrington and giving his opinions to the squad. Royle also said he disapproved of the fitness coach, Juan Carlo Osorio, a Colombian who had been conditioning the New York Metrostars and would later take charge of the Mexican national team. Royle thought they should not have had to go to the United States to have found a fitness coach.

Royle thought the meeting had gone well but attacking Tueart, the appointee of the club's majority shareholders and refusing to budge on his backroom staff, would almost certainly have sealed his fate. Like Peter Reid in 1993, Royle was being offered the chance to make a sacrifice of one of his assistants. Like Reid he refused and he paid the same price.

'Getting rid of Joe was horrible,' says Chris Bird. 'After the last home game of the season – a 2-1 defeat to Chelsea – I met him in the Chairman's Lounge. We met there after every game at Maine Road. We would always have a can of cider together. Joe had developed a taste for cider when he was at Norwich.

'He said, "Are you having one?"'

"No thanks, Joe I have to go home."

'I shut the door and I felt such a shit because I knew what was coming. What I should have done was sat him down and prepared him for the news that he was going tomorrow. I just couldn't. I was the chief operating officer, I had a loyalty to my chairman.

'When he found out he rang me: "You cunt, you knew."

'Nobody could have done what he did for Manchester City in the lower divisions. He became the heartbeat of the club. He had a story for every occasion. He allowed me to take players to supporters' clubs all over the country every time I asked. He was a joy to work with.

'When we talked about a replacement, I suggested David Moyes, who was then at Preston. I told the board that, if they were thinking of appointing a manager who would leave a legacy, then he was the man.

'He would have been there for ten years and he would have been our Fergie. He was young, strong, tough. He had taken Preston to the play-off finals; he was on the way up. But David Bernstein knew Kevin from England and he wanted him in.

'Kevin Keegan gave me some of the best and worst times I have ever had in football. He was full on. There could be no shades of grey with Kevin. One day he rang me, asked me where I was.

'I said, "I'm in the office," and he said, "Can you come to the ground and we'll have a chat." I went to Maine Road, looked for him; couldn't find him and then my phone went. "I'm up here."

'I looked up and he was with Arthur Cox, his assistant, at the top of one of the open stands, we called the Gene Kelly Stand because everyone was forced to sing in the rain.

'He told me to get up top with him. I was muttering to myself whether Kevin knew that I was, *de facto*, his boss. At the top of the stand, Keegan turned to me and said, "This is crap. How do you expect the fans to enjoy the view from here?"'

'He took me all around the ground. He pointed out what needed painting, showed me where the tiles had come off in the toilets. There were loos that didn't flush. We went into the changing rooms and he told me what he didn't like about them. He said, "Unless the work I've pointed out has been done by the time I come back I will not be playing a game of football in this stadium."'

Arthur Cox, who had been Keegan's assistant at Newcastle and with England, turned to Bird and said, 'What you have to remember is that Kevin is like the Queen. On the first day of the season he likes to smell fresh paint.'

In this Keegan was repeating exactly what he had done when taking over at Newcastle in 1992. Then, he had demanded the club repaint and repair the dilapidated training ground at Maiden Castle – which was considerably less grandiose than it sounds. He and his assistant, Terry McDermott, had even done some of the work themselves.

'He told me later that he did it for a reason,' says Bird. 'He didn't want players coming to him with excuses for defeat. If there was something he could do to fix it, he would. Then he said, "I can look them in the eye and tell them that it's about their game." They cannot blame the surroundings.

'When we signed Nicolas Anelka, he told me that we had better facilities than Real Madrid. Kevin had signed him on the spur of the moment. He was driving through some vineyards in France in the summer of 2002 and rang Nicolas and said, "I would like you to play for me."

'He never negotiated with his brothers, who acted as Nicolas' agents. Louis Fernandes, who was Anelka's lawyer, came over from Paris, we signed the contracts. It was the easiest deal I have ever done. It was done so quickly that we drove over to House of Fraser on Deansgate because he wanted to buy some Molton Brown shampoo.

'It was that easy. Stuart Pearce was the same, Peter Schmeichel was the same. They got phone calls from Kevin and they came.

'Schmeichel was such an influence. In 2002 we beat Manchester United in the derby and afterwards Schmeichel stood up in the dressing room and said, "Tonight you wear your club tie and go out for dinner in your club suit." Pearce was a huge influence. When he agreed to join he said, "I want to play, I want to coach and I want to attend some board meetings. Everything was an education for him."'

Chris Bird resigned from Manchester City in 2003, the summer they abandoned Maine Road for the future. There was a part of him that would have wanted to see his club in their new stadium but the divisions between Bird and Alistair Mackintosh, the club's finance director, were deep and personal. Bird resigned as chief operating officer and says that in the intervening years he has rarely felt welcome at Manchester City.

'I was surprised by the Abu Dhabi takeover,' he says. 'I got a call from Fred Done and he said this was the best thing that could happen to Manchester City. I said, "Why? Because of the money?"

'He said no, it was because of the culture. He said their culture when it came to horseracing was transformative. They invested in talent, they built stables and they brought kids through. Fred said they wanted to create something, they wanted a legacy.

'In that, they were different from the Americans who were really only interested in the bottom line and that extends to football. Randy Lerner built the mosaic on the Holte End when he came to Aston Villa but, pretty soon, he reverted to type.

'I believe there is a real desire at the club to create a legacy for Manchester. I don't think Manchester City's CEO, Ferran Soriano, gets it. All he is focused on is world domination, conquering America and Australia, but you look at the level of management below that and they still represent the heart and soul of Manchester.'

What Becomes
of You My Love?

BUILDINGS, LIKE SHIPS, ARE OFTEN THOUGHT OF AS FEMALE AND in the bleak November of 2003 as Manchester City, now installed in a sleek new arena, stumbled out of the UEFA Cup in a little stadium in Poland, whose crowd the Kippax could have accommodated twice over, she waited for the end.

Maine Road had already been stripped of her gladrags. Anything saleable had been auctioned off. The front door to the manager's office had gone for £70, the doors to the main reception had fetched nearly ten times that. Some 4,000 seats had been sold for £12 apiece.

Then came the bulldozers, including the largest demolition caterpillar in the country, which could be raised 134 feet. It would be needed to take down the Kippax, which had been redeveloped less than a decade ago at a cost of £16m.

As Francis Lee pointed out, this was more than four times Manchester City's turnover in 1994 and that, coupled with relegation from the Premier League two years later, had left the club a financial cripple.

The contractors, Connell Brothers, had spent the summer reducing Filbert Street in Leicester to rubble and now they turned their attention to Maine Road. First was the North Stand, where Helen Turner, the lady with the Bet Lynch beehive, had rung her bell throughout every game, stood.

Before kick-off, Helen, who ran a flower stall outside Manchester's Royal Infirmary, would present City's goalkeeper with a sprig of heather for luck. Joe Corrigan was her favourite.

Next they came for the Kippax, and then the Main Stand – the roof of which had once cost £1m – was removed, before the great cantilever girders were cut away. The DJ Mark Radcliffe, who from the top of the Kippax could recall being able to see the distant lights of Old Trafford 'where they were playing some European game while we were losing 1-0 to Bury', drove down to see the demolition. He found himself presented with a sky-blue brick from the Main Stand.

Because it contained all the radio and broadcasting equipment, the Platt Lane Stand had been the last to go. Then, it was over. She was gone.

The last season at Maine Road was documented by Kevin Cummins, perhaps Britain's best-known music photographer, who had been passionate about Manchester City from the moment he first set eyes on the ground aged eight. The book was called *We're Not Really Here.*

To gauge Kevin's devotion to Manchester City, you need to know he was one of fourteen fans who accompanied the club on a pre-season tour to China after their relegation under Alan Ball.

'I started going to away games on my own when I was ten. We had a corner shop in Salford and my mum would put me on the coach and just tell them to "look after him, please". In 1996 we went to Tianjin, which is about 250 miles north of Beijing.

'Gerry Creaney, who was still at the club, saw the fourteen of us at the airport and genuinely could not believe why we were there. When Alan Ball saw our group at the hotel, he came over to us and said, "While you are here, you will pay for nothing. Make sure everything goes on the tab for my room."'

Alan Ball famously liked a sing-song. One of his fondest memories of Francis Lee was the chairman sat at a piano in the boardroom after they had beaten Coventry in an FA Cup replay singing the Stanley Holloway monologue 'Albert and the Lion'.

Now, in the hotel's karaoke bar, he invited Cummins to sing, 'Tie a Yellow Ribbon Round the Old Oak Tree'.

'There was only one player in the bar because everyone else had bought slabs of lager from the local supermarket because it was so cheap and taken them up to their rooms,' he says. 'There was just Uwe Rösler and he had fallen out with the manager. Ball whispered to me, "Watch this," and began a rendition of 'And I Love You So' looking straight at Rösler who got up, gave the manager the finger, and walked up to his room.'

In Manchester, as nowhere else, music and football were bound together. Rod Stewart supported Arsenal and once had a trial at Brentford. Robert Plant had a passion for Wolverhampton Wanderers and Elton John bought Watford. But they were rarities and by the 1980s they were seen as dinosaurs.

However, as Cummins acknowledges, football itself was by the mid-1980s deeply unfashionable.

'I moved down to London in 1987 and I would go back to see City each weekend and the record companies would say, "Don't you want to go to Paris to see this or that gig?" and I would reply, "No, I'm going to see City," and they would say "Football?" as if it were the worst thing in the world. They regarded it as something from the gutter.

'We put Liverpool on the cover of *NME* when John Barnes and Craig Johnston did 'The Anfield Rap' before the 1988 FA Cup final with Wimbledon. When we went to Anfield for the shoot, they were amazed a music paper wanted to do anything on them.

'It was the World Cup in 1990 that changed their perception and, for the music industry it wasn't just Gazza's tears in Turin, it was New Order recording 'World in Motion'. Suddenly, it was fashionable.'

In Manchester, it had always been. As a teenager, Johnny Marr attended every City home game and went away with a blue-and-white scarf wrapped around his wrists. When he recalled Dennis Tueart's overhead kick to win the 1976 League Cup final against Newcastle, he said, 'The only way he could have been any cooler was if he were playing a Gibson Les Paul while he was doing it.'

One of Cummins' most famous photographs is of Ian Curtis, the doomed lead singer of Joy Division, taken on a bridge in Hulme, holding a cigarette to his lips in the bleak January of 1979. He points out that the shoot only happened because City's FA Cup tie against Rotherham had been postponed. He would certainly have been at Maine Road otherwise and Curtis probably would have joined him.

'Ian was really into Manchester City,' he says. 'They lived in Macclesfield but his wife, Deborah, has told me that he was looking to buy a house near Maine Road because it would be more convenient to live near the club.

'Billy Duffy from The Cult was living in Malibu in a giant house with two tennis courts and then had them ripped out so he could install five-a-side football pitches. Three of the Stone Roses were United fans but, when I had an assignment to photograph them covered in paint, I made sure the paint was blue and white.

'I wanted the final season at Maine Road to be documented and Chris Bird and Manchester City backed it, but I learned as the start of the season approached that nobody had mentioned it to Kevin Keegan. Without his approval, none of this would happen because I didn't want to shoot from the perimeter, I wanted be in the crowd and behind the scenes with the team.

'When I met him, he was fabulous. He said, "The only thing I don't want you to do is come into the dressing rooms before the game and go on the team coach to away matches. Other than that, you can go where you please and I will never tell you to get out of my face."

'I said, "So, if they have lost, and you are standing on the training pitch on a Monday morning giving them a bollocking, I can stand there?"

"Yes, I will never tell you to go."

'He was true to his word. He would be ripping them apart and I would be taking pictures of the players responding to all this. Not once did he say, "Haven't you taken enough?" What I really liked about Keegan was his honesty. He was a genuine bloke.

'I saw him turn Shaun Wright-Phillips into a better player. Shaun's crossing and corner-taking were quite wayward and Keegan would keep him out there on the training pitch and tell him what he had to do.

'Once training had finished he would keep Shaun out there, call up a goalkeeper, and Keegan would take three absolutely perfect corners. Eventually, he got Shaun to do the same by constant repetition.

'Training would usually finish with a penalty competition and the last three remaining would invariably be Nicolas Anelka, Kevin Keegan and Kevin Horlock. Once it went to 35 penalties until there was just Anelka and Keegan left.

'Keegan tried to be too clever, hit the inside of the post and it came out. As they walked off, Keegan said, "I'd have beaten you twenty years ago," before adding, "but you would have only been eight" (actually he would have been three).'

'He did the right thing in buying Anelka because, if we were to stay up, we needed a great player and, until a few years ago, I considered Nicolas Anelka to be the best footballer who had ever played for City.

'I was doing a shoot for *FourFourTwo* magazine with Anelka and Robert Pirès out in Monaco, because they were both sponsored by Puma, and after the shoot I was just chatting to him and asked why he had signed for Manchester City? He would surely have had other offers.

'He said, "Because Kevin Keegan was a great striker and I thought I could learn from him." I found Keegan far too self-deprecating. Whenever he was asked about his ability, he would say, "I was a lucky player," or add something about being in the right place at the right time. He had been European Footballer of the Year twice.'

While most photographers, especially sports photographers, now shot digitally, Kevin Cummins was more old school, employing roll after roll of Fuji film. 'I wanted very saturated colours. My first memory of going to City was in August 1961. We had just signed Bobby Kennedy and we were playing Leicester.

'I walked into that ground as an eight-year-old through one of those wide tunnels in the old Scoreboard End, the sky was vivid blue and, for an inner-city kid, I had never seen such an expanse of green. When City came out, their shirts were ice-blue and they mirrored the sky. It was the most magical thing and I wanted the book to give you the feeling of going to your first football match.

'Stewards would come up to me and say, "There's a bloke in Row C, he's white but he's got dreadlocks and piercings, you ought to take a picture of him." So, I went over and this lad said to me, "Do you want the pie in or out of the shot?"

'There were some absolute villains in the corner of the Kippax, who would stand next to the away fans and would spend their whole time just goading and baiting them. One of them said to me, "We'll look after your gear, mate."

'I said, "Really?"

"We will and, if anyone touches your cameras, we'll fucking lay them out."

'So, I left my bags and then when I came back for the next game, one of the lads came over and said, "You left this behind" – and handed me my lens cap.

'It's a different crowd now at the Etihad Stadium. I'm guessing but I'd reckon there are 12,000 people who had season tickets at Maine Road and who have them at the Etihad. By the time the last game came around against Southampton, I was ready to move. The stadium was looking weary; the players' gym looked like something you would find in someone's loft.

'I remember being with Keegan as he walked with us into the photographers' room and, as usual, there had been a spread laid on for us. Keegan said to Rosie, the woman behind the counter, "This is nice. How much do the club give you each week for food and drink?"

Rosie said, "Nothing. I pay for it myself." The photographers would sub her a pound each for the food. Keegan told her that was ridiculous and ordered the club to pay for the food and drink.

'Rosie was embarrassed and said she didn't like to make a fuss. She was working for a club in the Premier League. That was typical of the people who worked at Maine Road. When Francis Lee took over, he said there were "people working in cupboards for the same money they were on in 1960".'

Inside the dressing room the club was changing fast. The money had improved since 1990, let alone 1960. In the summer of 1997, Gerard Wiekens arrived from Veendam in northern Holland.

The club had, like Manchester City, been founded in 1894, but there were few other similarities. Its stadium, De Langeleegte, which translates as 'The Long Stretch of Nothing', held 6,000 and was rarely full. The club was declared bankrupt in 2013.

Then, Veendam's manager, Henk Nienhuis, had been able to offer Wiekens £40,000 a year for ten years if he rejected Manchester City, but the opportunity to play in England proved too strong. When he arrived at Maine Road he was introduced to Nigel Clough, whom he thought was the goalkeeper. He had never heard of his father.

Gerard, his wife Angelique and their dog, Joey, moved to Woodford in Cheshire, where George Best and Cristiano Ronaldo also made their home. Wiekens' house was considerably more modest than the half-timbered mansion where Ronaldo lived.

In an interview with the Dutch magazine, *Voetbal International*, Wiekens vividly described how money was beginning to change Manchester City.

'Angelique had to find her way among the WAGS – blond hair, fake nails; you know what I mean. We had bought her a car, a Nissan Micra, a perfect fun car. When she told the other WAGS, they could not believe it. A Nissan

Micra was totally unacceptable.

'Cars are really important in England. In some rough areas you can see the most beautiful cars. I had a Volkswagen Golf. I thought it was a good car but my teammates asked me, "Is it your wife's?"

'The atmosphere at Maine Road was such a contrast with the surrounding area. Moss Side was a really poor place with drugs and crime. They told me that, if I left the stadium at night, to have my car doors locked and not stop for anything.

'The stadium itself was beautiful; narrow corridors, pretty stands, great pitch, genuinely beautiful. The dressing rooms were very old and the players' lounge was small, but it breathed football all over.

'When Kevin Keegan promoted us to the Premier League was the time things changed for Manchester City. Suddenly, there was money. We got Robbie Fowler, Steve McManaman, Marc-Vivien Foé, Sylvain Distin, Nicolas Anelka, Peter Schmeichel and then, after that, David Seaman.

'The amount the top players earned was enormous. Even then they got £20-30,000 a week. We were on a coach to an away game and heard Steve McManaman on the phone: "Put £10,000 on that horse and £10,000 on the other one." He had been transferred from Real Madrid so he didn't have to worry about money. Robbie Fowler owns more than 100 houses. More than 100. Whole blocks.'

Wiekens' finest hour came in November 2002, the final derby at Maine Road and the first Manchester City had won since the September day in 1989 when Alex Ferguson had taken to his bed, put a pillow over his head and tried to blot the world out.

Wiekens was a man affected by nerves before big games, but it might have helped that he had not expected to play. However, the first-choice centre-backs, Distin and Steve Howey, were injured and Wiekens' partner was Lucien Mettomo, who had been signed from Saint-Étienne and would never quite make the grade at City. It was Mettomo's third game of the season and Wiekens' first.

Wiekens had known Ruud van Nistelrooy, the cutting edge of United's attack, when he was playing for Den Bosch, where he had been converted from a central midfielder to a striker. Now, he marked him out of the game completely.

The crux of the game came at 1-1. Gary Neville, who seemed to be attempting to shield the ball out of play, made a late, fatal decision to pass it back to Fabien Barthez. Shaun Goater anticipated it and scored his 99th goal for Manchester City.

It was the season when Maine Road implored their team to 'Feed the Goat' and now Eyal Berkovic fed him with a through ball. Goater knew that Barthez's strength in one-on-ones was saving low shots. The keeper anticipated Goater would indeed shoot low but the ball bounced and Goater shot high. Goater did not know the goal had brought up his century.

When he had last lost a Manchester derby, thirteen years before, Ferguson had been so shocked that he had barely been able to speak when he entered the dressing room. This time, when he spoke to the Sky Television cameras, he said he wished he could open the dressing-room doors, let in the United fans so they could tell his team exactly what they thought of the performance.

When he did enter the dressing room, Neville saw Ferguson glancing around, looking for a target. Then he spotted Van Nistelrooy walking in, a swapped City shirt over his shoulder. 'You don't give those shirts away. Ever,' he shouted.

'They are Manchester United's shirts, not yours. You treasure those shirts. If I see anyone give a shirt away, they won't be playing for me again.'

It was probably not the right time for Goater to wander in to Kevin Keegan's office and ask Ferguson, who was having a drink with the Manchester City manager, if he could have Paul Scholes' shirt. Ferguson turned around and gave Goater a mouthful.

It would have been fitting, poetic if this had been Manchester City's final game at Maine Road. The season demanded a Wagnerian climax. The final seasons at Roker Park and Filbert Street had seen Sunderland and Leicester relegated. There might have been a certain appropriateness in that had Manchester City joined them.

Instead, it all fizzled out with a 1-0 defeat by Southampton that saw City finish ninth, their best finish since 1993, the year when the landslide properly began.

For Noel Bayley this was a double farewell. It would be the last time he would be selling his fanzine, *Bert Trautmann's Helmet*. 'Things come and things go,' he says. 'But you don't expect your football ground to go.

'On the big nights, under the lights, it was never better. What do I remember when I think of Maine Road? The 10-1 against Huddersfield on horrible, grey November afternoon. The Charlton game in 1985 when we won promotion with people literally watching from halfway up poles and hanging from girders.

'It was such a different place to the Etihad, where they run probably the most professional club in the country. Maine Road was all dark wood and narrow corridors and people would just wander in. You'd see Denis Law sat in Ken Barnes' office or in the kitchens making toast. When Mike Summerbee and Tony Book went to the Etihad, they were asked for their passes.'

In time, Maine Road will be seen as an aberration. It opened in the same year as Wembley, 1923, and took the club from its old heartland in Hyde, to south Manchester. The Etihad, more or less, took the club back to its geographical beginnings.

When Kerry Packer launched his cricket circus with coloured clothing, white balls and matches under sodium floodlights, the England captain, Mike Brearley, who was nowhere near good enough to be asked to join, said he preferred 'the chugging tramp steamer with its cargo of pig iron to the monstrous super-tanker, hurriedly constructed'.

By the end, there was something of the tramp steamer about Maine Road. Frank Clark remarked that the best kind of club is a 'benevolent dictatorship' and the Abu Dhabi-funded regime that has taken Manchester City to its greatest heights is an autocracy.

The old Manchester City, the Manchester City of Maine Road, was a republic and republics are messier things, more democratic, harder to control. Peter Swales and Francis Lee, among the last of the Saturday Caesars, found they could not rule without the approval of the crowd or what the Romans called the mob.

As the Etihad Stadium celebrated championships won with 100 points and a constant flow of European football, there is just Maine Road's preserved centre circle, set among housing, to mark the heart of Manchester's lost republic.

Ta-ra.

Acknowledgements

SPECIAL THANKS TO: Jimmy Ball, Noel Bayley, Chris Bird, Andrew Bridge, Michael Brown, Frank Clark, Angie Clarke, Kevin Cummins, Neil Custis, Karen Gabay, Bernard Halford, Simon Heggie, Brian Horton, Dave Horwich, James Fletcher, Andy King, Andy Morrison, Peter Reid, Bill Rice, Uwe Rösler, Phil Shaw, David White, Jim Whitely.

Bibliography

Ball, Alan, **Playing Extra Time** [Pan Macmillan, 2004]

Barnes, Ken, **This Simple Game** [Empire Publications, 2000]

Buckley, Andy & Burgess, Richard, **Blue Moon Rising** [Milo Books, 2000]

Clark, Frank, **Kicking with Both Feet** [Headline, 1999]

Clay, Catrine, **Trautmann's Journey** [Yellow Jersey Press, 2010]

Clayton, David, **Kinkladze The Perfect Ten?** [Parrs Wood Press, 2005]

Conn, David, **Richer than God** [Quercus, 2013]

Coton, Tony, **There to be Shot at** [deCoubertin, 2017]

Crick, Michel, **The Boss: The Many Sides of Alex Ferguson**
    [Simon & Schuster, 2002]

Edehill, Richard, **Once a Blue** [Pitch Publishing, 2014]

Ferguson, Alex, **A Year in the Life** [Virgin Publishing, 1995]

Friend, Dante, **My Blue Heaven** [Empire Publications, 2004]

Gatenby, Phil & Waldon, Andrew, **Teenage Kicks** [Empire, 2013]

Hodkinson, Mark, **Blue Moon** [Mainstream Publishing, 1999]

Howey, Lee, **Massively Violent and Decidedly Average**
    [Biteback Publishing, 2018]

James, Gary **Manchester, The City Years** [James Ward Publishing, 2012]

Kanchelskis, Andrei, **Russian Winters** [deCoubertin, 2017]

Keane, Roy, **Keane, The Autobiography** [Penguin, 2002]

Kendall, Howard, **Love Affairs and Marriage** [deCoubertin, 2013]

Lake, Paul, **I'm Not Really Here** [Arrow, 2011]

Lawton, James, **Forever Boys** [Wisden, 2015]

Leighton, James, **Rocky: The tears and Triumphs of David Rocastle** [Simon & Schuster, 2016]

Morrison, Andy, **The Good, The Mad and The Ugly** [Fort Publishing, 2011]

Quinn, Niall, **Niall Quinn, The Autobiography** [Headline, 2002]

Read, Jim, **Justin Fashanu, the Biography** [DB Publishing, 2012]

Reid, Peter, **Cheer Up Peter Reid** [Sport Media, 2017]

Rösler, Uwe, **Knocking Down Walls** [Sport Media, 2014]

Roach, Stuart, **On a Wing and a Prayer: Searching for the real Steve Coppell** [Know The Score Books 2009]

Rollin, Jack, **The Rothmans Book of Football Records** [Headline, 1998]

Royle, Joe, **Joe Royle, The Autobiography** [BBC Books, 2005]

Shindler, Colin, **Fathers, Sons and Football** [Headline, 2001]

Tossell, David, **Big Mal** [Mainstream, 2009]

Tossell, David, **The Man in White Boots** [Hodder & Stoughton, 2017]

Tueart, Dennis, **My Football Journey** [Vision Sport Publishing, 2011]

Walsh, Paul, **Wouldn't It Be Good** [Sport Media, 2015]

Ward, Mark **Hammered** [John Blake Publishing, 2010]

White, David, **Shades of Blue** [Michael O'Mara, 2017]

Newspapers and magazines

Manchester Evening News
The Guardian
Sport Bild
Voetbal International
The Independent

www.decoubertin.co.uk